SUBHUMAN

SUBHUMAN

The Moral Psychology of Human Attitudes to Animals

T. J. Kasperbauer

OXFORD
UNIVERSITY PRESS

OXFORD
UNIVERSITY PRESS

Oxford University Press is a department of the University of Oxford. It furthers
the University's objective of excellence in research, scholarship, and education
by publishing worldwide. Oxford is a registered trade mark of Oxford University
Press in the UK and certain other countries.

Published in the United States of America by Oxford University Press
198 Madison Avenue, New York, NY 10016, United States of America.

Library of Congress Cataloging-in-Publication Data
Names: Kasperbauer, T. J., author.
Title: Subhuman : the moral psychology of human attitudes to animals /
T. J. Kasperbauer.
Description: New York : Oxford University Press, 2018. |
Includes bibliographical references and index.
Identifiers: LCCN 2017021975 (print) | LCCN 2017047676 (ebook) |
ISBN 9780190695842 (online course) | ISBN 9780190695828 (updf) |
ISBN 9780190695835 (epub) | ISBN 9780190695811 (cloth : alk. paper)
Subjects: LCSH: Animals (Philosophy) | Human-animal relationships. |
Animal welfare—Moral and ethical aspects. | Animal welfare—Philosophy.
Classification: LCC B105.A55 (ebook) | LCC B105.A55 K37 2018 (print) |
DDC 179/.3—dc23
LC record available at https://lccn.loc.gov/2017021975

1 3 5 7 9 8 6 4 2
Printed by Sheridan Books, Inc., United States of America

*For the bonobos of Iowa, who first made me
wonder what it means to be human.*

CONTENTS

SUBHUMAN

Introduction

1.1 COMPARING HUMANS AND NON-HUMANS

Our identity as human beings is in many ways dependent on our conception of ourselves as different from animals. Some have even claimed that, across cultures and languages, we have arrived on the same meaning of "animal": not human (Russell, 2011, p. 4). Our attitudes toward animals have been formed by a history in which 1) we hunted them; 2) they hunted us; 3) we kept them for food, labor, and other useful products; and 4) we kept them for companionship. But we didn't just establish criteria for what made something an animal to help make our terminology or practices around animals clearer. We designated certain creatures as animals because doing so helped us think about ourselves and our place in the world.

This book is about the moral psychology that arises out of our comparative relationship with animals. Across the cognitive sciences, there are many accounts of the behavior and psychology of animals themselves. One can also find well-developed ethical theories for how we ought to think about our treatment of animals. But there is strikingly little about how we actually think about animals and specifically what determines our moral evaluations of them.

The basic thesis I advance is that our attitudes to animals, both positive and negative, are largely a result of their role as a contrast class to human beings. To make my case, I draw from research on what is known as "dehumanization." Much of the literature on dehumanization focuses on the negative effects for humans when they are compared to other animals (for reviews, see Bain, Vaes, & Leyens, 2014; Haslam et al., 2012;

Haslam & Loughnan, 2014). For instance, to justify cruel treatment the Nazis compared Jews to rats, and black slaves in America were compared to apes. However, many of the processes used on human beings to make them seem unworthy of dignity and respect are also used on animals. The processes at work when we demean other human beings by comparing them to animals are also at work in our everyday evaluations of animals.

Understanding the influence of dehumanization on our attitudes toward animals is important for making sense of apparent contradictions in human–animal relationships. Many of the animals we love become targets of abuse, and many that we fear are nonetheless revered and hold great cultural importance. We also spend significant resources in caring for animals just to eat them. Why is this? Are we just confused? Or cruel? Dehumanization research offers an explanation that is not rooted in inherent kindness or cruelty, nor stupidity or confusion. Rather, dehumanization suggests that we are fundamentally motivated to compare ourselves to animals and find a way to view ourselves as superior.

By "animal" in this book I am referring broadly to any member of the kingdom Animalia. Many different types of animals possess properties capable of triggering a dehumanization response. Some animals, however, are more relevant than others to the psychological processes I aim to illuminate. Understanding moral attitudes toward animals is strongly dependent on people's concepts about animals, and concepts are notoriously varied and resistant to definitions (Prinz, 2002; Machery, 2009). For instance, in chapter 2, I discuss animals that pose threats as predators and as sources of disease, but some animals are seen as more threatening in these respects than others. So although I aim to capture any member of Animalia in my account, some animals better characterize dehumanization attitudes than others. As we go along, I will make it clear which animals I have in mind and how I envision their role in human moral psychology.

The idea that we use non-humans for comparative purposes is not new. Within anthropology, for instance, this comparative relationship is the standard way of conceptualizing human attitudes toward animals. Many draw from Lévi-Strauss' (1963) observation that animals are "good to think with." This idea is also not new to philosophy. Dennis Des Chene (2006), for instance, characterizes the concept "animal" in the history of philosophy as "charged not only with designating a class of creatures, real and imagined, but also with supplying a contrast case to the human" (p. 216). This aptly describes the phenomenon explored throughout this book.

My primary source, however, is recent research in social psychology, where interest in human–animal relations has been steadily increasing (Amiot & Bastian, 2015; Herzog, 2010). Though psychologists have begun investigating the theoretical foundations of dehumanization in greater detail (Bain, Vaes, & Leyens, 2014), relatively little attention has been paid to the role of animals. And no philosophers have contributed to theoretical work in this area. My aim is to fill this gap in the psychological and philosophical literature on dehumanization and help make sense of our occasionally puzzling attitudes toward animals.

1.1.1 Dehumanization and Infrahumanization

Dehumanization research tends to focus on the psychology of ingroup/ outgroup relations. People who are seen as members of an outgroup are often dehumanized, and conversely, the act of dehumanizing others typically consists of attributing outgroup characteristics to them. One of the main proposals of this book, developed in chapter 3, is that a particular type of ingroup/outgroup psychology characterizes how dehumanization processes are applied to animals.

Dehumanization consists of two closely related processes. The first explicitly identifies other people (or other groups of people) as nonhuman, while the other identifies other people (or groups of people) as *inferior* human beings. This second process is known as "infrahumanization." In chapter 3 I suggest that infrahumanization provides the key to understanding human attitudes to animals. Though this proposal may at first appear counterintuitive, it is well supported by the empirical evidence.

Infrahumanization consists of both negative and positive evaluations of animals. First, the negative. Central to our comparative relationship with animals is a negative judgment that animals are members of an outgroup (or multiple outgroups) and should be avoided. The strength of this aversion varies by species and is influenced by a number of factors, but the evidence indicates that this is a categorical response in human psychology. Any animal elicits this response to some degree. As we will see in chapter 2, this response is partly an adaptation to evolutionary pressures. As both predators and prey, animals elicited antagonistic responses in our evolutionary ancestors. This response has been co-opted by other aversive responses to animals, such that animals are seen as presenting a broader *psychological* threat to humanity, as we will see in chapter 3.

It is not all aversion and hostility, however. Also central to this comparative relationship is a positive judgment that animals deserve care and concern. Some animals possess features that counteract the negative response. This too is part of our evolutionary history. For instance, our history with domesticated animals, particularly those kept as companions, led us to develop positive approach-related responses to animals. We instinctively want to offer comfort to a puppy, for example.

These positive responses also help us cope with the presence of psychologically threatening animals. Animals present a categorical threat, according to dehumanization research. This means that even animals many of us are disposed to show great concern for, like dogs and cats, pose some degree of psychological threat. Domestic animals can in fact exacerbate this psychological threat by sharing human spaces. A dog living inside of one's home, for example, is not appropriate for an allegedly inferior creature. It violates the human–animal boundary. If animals are intuitively seen as members of an outgroup, treating them as ingroup members causes some psychological discomfort to us. This could be expressed, for example, by feeling disgust at the thought of letting a dog sleep in your bed or paying for expensive food because it's "just a dog." Part of the positive responses we have developed toward animals is a result of needing to cope with this discomfort. We can't always avoid animals, and in many cases we benefit from keeping them around. Caring attitudes toward animals help us overcome underlying aversion and resist feeling threatened by their presence.

Because animals do not conform to the picture of ingroup/outgroup psychology that treats an entity as thoroughly degraded, we need some other way to account for the comparative relationship between humans and animals. This is where the concept of infrahumanization is instructive. In short, infrahumanization leads people to treat an entity as inferior to human beings without thoroughly treating the entity as worthless. While people generally dehumanize other people by comparing them to the most universally reviled animals possible (e.g., rats and cockroaches), the standard model for animals is a more modest comparison. We think of animals as inferior to humans while still attributing to them various positive qualities. This allows us to cope with the presence of animals and the psychological threat they pose.

1.1.2 Case Studies in Human–Animal Comparison

The idea that animals are judged negatively, to any degree, may seem implausible to some. Concern for animals seems to be at an all-time high. And not just for animals kept in our homes. Animals of all types are arguably treated better than ever before. It may thus seem that any comparison we make to animals primarily results in positive, not negative, judgments. Although tempting, this generalization fails to capture a wide range of attitudes about animals; care and concern do not tell the whole story. Chapters 2 and 3 discuss the relevant empirical evidence on this issue. Before entering into a fuller discussion, however, let's briefly consider some examples of how animals have been and continue to be evaluated negatively.

(1) *The Great Chain of Being.* Arthur Lovejoy's (1936) classic *The Great Chain of Being* provides some historical background for human–animal comparisons. The book lays out the history of the idea that there is a hierarchical scale in nature and humans' place within that scale. One common conception of humans' place in the natural scale, according to Lovejoy, is inherently paradoxical. Humans are "constitutionally discontented" with their relatively low rank in the scale, compared to angels and gods, but they also see this as "appropriate to [their] place in the scale" (p. 205). Humans constantly strive to ascend the scale of nature while knowing that they will inevitably fail. This conception of human beings would seem to have implications for conceptions of non-humans. One way of ascending the scale is to be less like animals, which are invariably beneath humans. But animals, like humans, are only filling their role in the natural order of things. So we would expect animals to be denigrated if they threaten human superiority but not in order to help humans ascend the scale; pushing animals down does not lift humans up. Lovejoy's scale of nature suggests that animals will be viewed as mostly benign but threatening when they seem to be too close to humans on the natural scale.

(2) *Proximity Threats.* Ascending the chain of being presents a symbolic, or psychological, threat to humanness. There are different ways that this threat can come about. In his classic analysis of animal metaphors, Edmund Leach (1964) proposed that denigration of certain animals was a result of their *physical* closeness to humans. It is well known that animal terms are used to insult and demean others (Haslam, Loughnan, & Sun, 2011; Loughnan et al., 2014). Leach suggested that the most common animal insults involved animals that encroached on human lives. Pigs, for instance, are commonly used in animal insults in many cultures (e.g., "filthy pig," "fat as a pig") and have historically been raised near or sometimes even inside of human homes, even when intended for slaughter. This physical breach of the human–animal boundary, Leach proposed, would have caused psychological discomfort. Pigs have also participated in other characteristically human activities, such as receiving human food, and are often seen as being social and having a family life, which would exacerbate the psychological threat. To deal with the threat, we put an extra stigma on pigs in order to reaffirm, with language and taboos, that they are separate from us. We alleviate our concerns with physical closeness by insisting on a fundamental metaphysical difference.

(3) *Mortality Salience.* The line of research that has explored the psychological threat of animals in greatest detail is known as "terror management theory." The basic assumption behind terror management theory, as it applies to animals, is that animals remind us of aspects of our humanity that cause existential anxiety, particularly our mortality. This is often referred to as "animal reminder" or "mortality salience." Being reminded of one's mortality presents a psychological threat and disrupts normal psychological functions, so we have developed various strategies to suppress these feelings when they arise. For instance, Rozin and Fallon (1987) argue that, as a result of this threat, human beings "wish to avoid any ambiguity about their status by accentuating the human–animal boundary" (p. 28). More will be said about the theoretical foundations of mortality salience in chapter 3.

An excellent illustration of how animals elicit mortality salience comes from Beatson and Halloran (2007). They presented participants with a prompt that made them think about death. They also presented an animal stimulus, which was a video of bonobos having sex. In one condition the researchers emphasized to participants how similar bonobo sex is to human sex. In another condition, the *differences* between the species' sex habits were emphasized. They also measured participants' self-esteem because increasing self-esteem is a well-confirmed method for reducing the effects of mortality salience (Gailliot et al., 2008; Schmeichel et al., 2009; Schmeichel & Martens, 2005). In the condition where bonobo sex was seen as similar to human sex, those with low self-esteem evaluated animals more negatively, while those high in self-esteem evaluated animals more positively. These results indicate that bonobo sex elicits mortality salience, which presents a psychological threat. Reminding people of their animal nature caused negative evaluations, unless the level of self-esteem was sufficient to fend off the attendant existential anxiety.

These examples illustrate different ways animals present psychological threats to humanness. Further examples will be discussed throughout the book, primarily in chapter 3 as well as in chapter 4, which focuses on how animals' mental states are used to assign moral status. Chapter 5 contextualizes research on moral attitudes to animals within research on broader psychological obstacles to moral progress. Chapters 2–5, as a whole, are aimed at presenting a new picture of the moral psychology behind our attitudes to animals, looking through the lens of infrahumanization.

1.2 ETHICAL IMPLICATIONS OF HUMAN–ANIMAL PSYCHOLOGY

Most of this book will be focused on uncovering how people think about animals, but I will also explain how we *should* think about and treat animals. These two matters are not entirely independent of one another because the psychology of human attitudes to animals has implications for our treatment of them. Chapters 6–8 lay out how we should think about ethical issues concerning animals, given the psychological details provided in chapters 2–5.

Using empirical moral psychology to inform ethical issues is an increasingly popular approach in philosophy. It is less common among those who focus specifically on animal ethics, however. Recent advances in empirical moral psychology are mostly absent from prominent discussions of, for example, the moral status of non-humans, intensive animal agriculture, species rights, and a variety of other issues but not because there is nothing interesting about what moral psychology has to tell us about animals. Chapters 6–8 show how we can use studies from the cognitive sciences, primarily psychology, to improve and inform the development of theories in animal ethics. I seek to develop moral prescriptions about animals that are morally defensible *and* psychologically plausible.

1.2.1 Using Psychology to Inform Ethics

Cognitive scientists generally explore statistical regularities, usually as observed in controlled experimental conditions. Many of the experiments described throughout the book show a statistically significant difference in the responses of an experimental group when compared to a control group. There is, of course, variation within each group, but the experimentally manipulated variable—whatever it is—has enough of an effect to allow researchers to conclude that a pattern exists within the variation. The effect is due to a specific factor that cannot be attributed to chance. This is one of the main tools of scientific discovery.

Ethics, we might think, looks nothing like this. The target of inquiry is entirely different. Normative ethics, for instance, is about what we *ought* to think and do—it is prescriptive (providing advice like "intelligent animals shouldn't be treated cruelly"). But normative ethics is also, according to many philosophers, distinctly first person–oriented. It asks, What ought *I* do? The statistical approach of cognitive science, by contrast, is descriptive and third person–oriented. It asks questions like, What do cognitive agents do? and How do cognitive processes operate? A common view among ethicists is that these targets reflect a fundamental difference between science and ethics. A classic expression of this idea can be found in the work of Christine Korsgaard (1996). She argues that normative ethics is distinctly unlike science in that it aims to provide individuals with reasons for action. The bare descriptive facts of science, she thinks, cannot provide this.

Moreover, many ethicists seem to think that being mistaken about human moral psychology is only trivially bad. If I have the *right* moral theory, then what relevance is moral psychology? If I have *correctly* identified a moral duty, why does it matter what I say about human beings' capacity to realize that duty? For instance, suppose I claim that our highest moral duty is to increase the amount of pleasure and decrease the amount of pain in the world. And suppose I derive from this that our current treatment of non-human animals must change dramatically. Assuming these claims are right and the reasoning sound, what relevance is whatever moral psychology that follows? For instance, why should it matter if people are unmoved by the pain felt by animals?

Of course it is true that descriptive facts do not directly translate into normative prescriptions. But they do have implications for normative prescriptions, as we will see. Normative ethics should take more seriously the third-person perspective. It should ask, What ought *people* do, in general? Numerous criticisms have been put forth in recent years suggesting that many mainstream ethical theories are working with an inaccurate conception of human psychology (e.g., Doris, 2002; Prinz, 2007). These criticisms have, as a consequence, called into question the utility of the first-person approach, as well as empirically uninformed third-person perspectives. First-person ethics appears to serve as a guide only by assuming a significantly uniform, and substantially inaccurate, human psychological profile. Similar problems arise when third-person ethics takes psychological facts for granted. The answers ethicists provide fail to sufficiently generalize to other human beings.

Rather than ask what individuals should do, ethics should ask what psychologically similar groups of human beings should do. Statistical regularities uncovered by cognitive scientists illuminate commonalities in thinking styles, personality traits, and other aspects of our psychological profiles. Understanding these statistical regularities helps ensure that ethical prescriptions generalize beyond one's own perspective while also making sure they don't overgeneralize, to psychological profiles that are very different from one's own. An empirically informed third-person ethics can provide recommendations that take into account what people are capable of and what actions their psychological profiles are best suited for, while still providing substantial advice about what they ought to do. This may ultimately culminate in an individual (or individuals) asking the first-person question, What ought I do? But the general framework for ethical decision-making is done in accordance with broader patterns existing among groups of human beings. This is not to say that these broader psychological patterns *settle* any ethical issues but that ethicists must understand these patterns in order for their theories to have "psychological grip" on a variety of psychological profiles. To do this, ethicists must look more closely at empirical research in moral psychology.

Those who are accustomed to first-person accounts in ethics may be suspicious about this approach. All I can do is invite the skeptically minded reader to give this book a chance to see how this sort of third-person perspective on ethics looks. The reader will not receive direct advice on how he or she should personally treat animals. My account does aim, though, at helping the reader to better engage with moral discourse about animals. This shift toward a third-person ethics is, as I hope to show, hugely important for moral thinking about animals. For the most part, animal ethicists have not engaged with recent findings in contemporary moral psychology, and animal ethics remains heavily first person–oriented. The results of my account will provide new tools for anyone who wishes to provide more psychologically realistic prescriptions for the treatment of animals.

For example, many people have the moral goal of changing how we treat animals (e.g., by ending factory farming). These people often admit that this may be tough for people psychologically but maintain that because it is the *right* thing to do, these moral goals must be pursued anyway. Others, however, take a different approach. Many routes to changing our treatment of animals are too psychologically difficult; whatever their moral rightness, our goals are often painful to pursue and frequently seem unachievable, despite our best efforts. So instead some people have begun pursuing more psychologically realistic moral goals. Adam Shriver (2009), for instance, has proposed that in lieu of improved standards of care for livestock, animals reared for consumption could instead be genetically engineered so as not to feel pain and other forms of suffering. Insofar as the technology is available and the animals can otherwise function normally, Shriver argues that this is likely a more feasible moral goal than abolishing intensive production systems.

My approach, which I develop in chapters 6–8, similarly aims to take psychological constraints seriously when formulating moral prescriptions. Whatever one's moral goals, they have to be constrained by our moral psychological profiles, by the actual processes employed when we judge what is right and wrong. Chapter 6 takes on the importance of psychological constraints by exploring the role of *ideals* in moral thinking. For instance, when constructing theories about what people ought to do and what society ought to be like, ethicists and political theorists often make certain false assumptions about human beings and the social and political conditions they live in. Doing so is meant to help identify important moral factors that would otherwise be difficult to disentangle from our complicated social reality.

There are numerous cases of ideal theorizing about animals. For instance, it's widely acknowledged that we possess various biases toward animals: we like those that resemble humans or are cute, dislike those that are disgusting, and are partial toward dogs, cats, and other animals we take into our homes as companions. But ethicists tend to ignore these biases when constructing prescriptions for how we ought to treat animals. Moral prescriptions about experimenting on animals, eating them, and keeping them for our entertainment are generally put forth without taking into account these biases. Of course there are constraints in meeting a prescription like "we ought not eat meat" (including psychological biases and much else), but these are frequently put aside in order to more directly assess the merits of a moral goal.

Though this can indeed be helpful in certain cases, idealizations about our moral psychologies often fail to provide any concrete guidance for ordinary human agents. We will evaluate common claims made by animal ethicists to show how, given certain empirical facts, these claims will likely fail to have any psychological impact. The only remedy is to look more closely at empirical research on how our moral psychologies operate, including many of the factors discussed in chapters 2–5.

1.2.2 The Psychology of Moral Change

A common objection to the idea that human psychology should be taken into account when constructing moral goals for animals is that our attitudes toward them are easily modified. It is often claimed that our treatment of animals has steadily improved, particularly in the last 30 years. Improved standards for laboratory animals, livestock, and animals kept as companions might seem to provide a particularly compelling illustration that psychological obstacles are easy to change and thus should not factor into ethical theorizing.

Chapter 7 counters this objection by considering the hypothesis that our "moral circle" is expanding. Historical and cross-cultural variation in attitudes to animals suggests that despite significant variation and significant changes in attitudes to animals, we can nonetheless identify strong psychological constraints in thinking about animals. Many historical changes in attitudes toward animals can be explained on psychological grounds. Current intractability in those attitudes can also be explained by human psychology, particularly the dehumanization processes outlined in chapters 2–4. So while certain animals are receiving improved treatment and in some ways we show greater moral concern to animals than ever before, there remain important reasons to take psychology into account when identifying long-term moral goals.

Chapter 8 supplements the discussion in chapters 5–7 by proposing ways to alter human moral psychology in order to meet moral goals concerning animals. The constraints on human behavior identified throughout the rest of the book are explored in a more practical way in this chapter. The goal is to help ethicists diagnose obstacles to moral change in order to develop methods for changing human psychology and creating laws and policies that would limit the impact of morally objectionable biases.

This approach to ethics explicitly aims to use moral psychology to serve normative ends. As Mark Alfano (2013) describes it in his book *Character as Moral Fiction*, this approach "attempts to bridge the gap between moral psychology and normative theory by proposing ways in which we, as moral psychology describes us, can become more as we should be, as normative theory prescribes for us" (p. 9). In chapter 8, I address common claims in animal ethics that meet a minimal standard for psychological plausibility but are nonetheless psychologically difficult. My suggestions are meant to make certain classic prescriptions in animal ethics easier to achieve.

Chapter 2

Evolved Attitudes to Animals

Our attitudes to animals have been shaped by various roles animals played in our evolutionary history. There is significant variation in how humans view animals, but there is also much that is shared by all humans; and interestingly, both positive and negative attitudes toward animals can be traced back to adaptive pressures faced by our evolutionary ancestors.

Research on knowledge about animals in early childhood reveals many ways in which we may have evolved to hold the attitudes that we do as adults. Certain assumptions about animals appear early in development and seem to be shared across cultures, which suggests that these ways of thinking about animals are largely inherited, rather than learned. This research illustrates how we may have inherited specific knowledge about non-human animals as a result of their role in our evolutionary history.

There are three main relationships our evolutionary ancestors had with animals that have shaped current attitudes toward animals. The first two are predatory–prey relationships and transmission of diseases from animals. Both entail negative or antagonistic judgments of animals. The third relationship is caring for animals, which entails positive attitudes. All three relationships persist in human psychology, but the negative relationships predominate, resulting in an overall negative bias toward animals. This is not to say that people dislike animals or lack positive feelings for them; the popularity of cute and cuddly animal videos is sufficient to refute that idea. The research presented in chapter 3, however, shows how certain positive attitudes should be understood as reactions to threats posed by animals. But first we need a broader evolutionary framework to make sense of these reactions as well as other attitudes toward animals discussed throughout the rest of the book.

Some have criticized the sort of picture of human psychology presented here on the grounds that certain groups of indigenous people have harmonious and non-antagonistic relations with animals. The existence of these groups appears inconsistent with an evolutionary account. While there is indeed variation in attitudes toward animals, a closer look at the empirical evidence supports the negative bias toward animals I identify in our evolutionary psychology.

2.1 EVOLVED BIOLOGICAL KNOWLEDGE

Over the last 30 years, an interesting line of research has developed on "folkbiological" knowledge, or the assumptions and intuitions people have about biological entities, prior to formal education about biology or science generally (for an important collection of essays summarizing research in the field, see Medin & Atran, 1999). This research combines studies of child development with anthropology and cultural psychology, providing crucial data on what assumptions might be shared across diverse belief systems and experiences with biological entities.

2.1.1 Animacy and Animal Motion

One of the most robust lines of research on child development is on young infants' understanding of "agency" and "animacy." Agents seem to be identified by being *self-propelled* and *goal-oriented*. Infants as young as 3 months will treat entities that are self-propelled and goal-oriented differently from other objects, particularly in assuming they have traits that will be consistently expressed across different contexts. For instance, if basic shapes are made to appear as if they are moving according to their own power, 3-month-olds will assume that their actions will persist across situations (Luo, 2011). Infants generally assume that action tendencies will remain consistent across situations, but particularly so if an entity is seen as acting by its own power and in order to achieve a certain end state.

This research suggests that anything that appears self-propelled and goal-orientation will be treated as agential. Although animals possess these features, so do many other entities. There is a great deal of evidence showing that entities that look nothing like animals will be treated as animal-like if they possess agential features. For example, animated shapes made to look like they are chasing each other will elicit heightened attention from infants as young as 4 months (Frankenhuis et al., 2013). Early sensitivity to chasing is thought to be a result of predator–prey relationships in evolution.

This sensitivity to agential properties has been found with older children as well. Opfer (2002), for example, found that 4-, 5-, 7-, and 10-year-olds were more likely to ascribe biological properties, like eating, growing, reproduction, and sustenance needs, to an animated blob that acted in goal-oriented ways than to a blob that moved aimlessly. Agential cues, like moving when a target was present, changing directions in response to a moving target, and ceasing movement when the target was reached, led children to attribute basic biological properties to something that otherwise had no physical resemblance to animals.

Clearly infants and young children will treat a wide range of entities as agential if they have these properties. But there seems to be a bias toward attributing agency specifically to animals. For instance, 3-year-olds are more likely to think that an animal is self-controlled than is a wind-up car (Gelman & Gottfried, 1996). One proposed explanation for this is that animals display prototypical agency-indicating features and that they display these in a particularly salient way. Sometimes this is described in reference to a broader capacity for "biological motion." Children from a very young age seem to be attuned to motion patterns characteristic of biological entities (for a recent review of research on biological motion, see Poulin-Dubois, Crivello, & Wright, 2015). For instance, 2-day-old infants will look longer at a pattern of lights that mimics a chicken walking than at a random pattern of lights or a pattern that matches a chicken walking upside down (Simion, Regolin, & Bulf, 2008). The pattern of movement expressed by an upright walking chicken is attention-grabbing, even for newborns.

Developmental psychologists have also investigated how animals' morphology, or outward physical appearance, factors into attributions of agency. From a very young age, children seem to assume that animal-like physical features can be used to predict agential behaviors. Because self-propulsion and goal orientation are characteristic of animals, children learn to associate animal-like physical features with certain types of behaviors. For example, in an experiment conducted by Pauen and Träuble (2009; also Träuble & Pauen, 2011), furriness appeared to be an important agency cue for 7-month-olds. When a furry toy animal and a ball were clearly being moved by a human experimenter, 7-month-olds would look longer at the experimenter's hand. However, when the furry animal and the ball moved seemingly on their own, without any contact from the experimenter's hand, infants looked longer at the furry animal, suggesting that they thought the source of motion had to be the animal and not the ball.

So from a very young age, children seem attuned to both the morphology and the motion cues of animals. A recent experiment by Setoh, Baillargeon, and Gelman (2013) nicely illustrates their combined effect. They showed 8-month-olds an object that was made to appear either animal-like or like an ordinary object. For example, a can would be shown hopping, would be furry, and would make a "quacking" sound; or instead it would be quiet, furless, and still. Then infants were provided a way of determining what was on the inside of the object, either by it being shaken or by showing what its underside was made of. Sometimes the object appeared empty (by rattling when shaken or by having a hollow inside), or it would seem to be solid (by making no noise when shaken or having a solid bottom). Across multiple experiments, with many variations, infants would look longer when an animal-like object indicated that it did not have anything inside, suggesting that the infants were surprised. There were no differences in looking time, by contrast, when an ordinary object was shown to have no insides. Infants thus had expectations about specific properties an animal-like entity should have, based only on relatively crude morphological and agential features.

2.1.2 Essentialism About Animals

The expectations infants expressed about animal insides in the Setoh et al. experiment illustrate *essentialist* reasoning about animals. Once something has been classified as an animal, it is seen as having certain properties that are inherent to all members of the category "animal." A number of experiments have been conducted on essentialist reasoning about animals, indicating that young children from very diverse cultural contexts appear to engage in relatively rigid ways of thinking about animal identity and development (for reviews, see Gelman & Legare, 2011; Solomon & Zaitchik, 2012).

One prominent form of essentialist reasoning in childhood is assumptions about inheritance among animals. A line of research originally inspired by Carey (1985) and Gelman and Wellman (1991) has found that children assume that an animal inherits the properties of its parents, even if raised by animals of another species (so-called adoption studies). For example, children predict that if a baby turtle is raised by toads, it will still have a hard shell and walk slowly when it grows up, just like its birth parents. Even if the animal is attributed generic qualities true of many species (e.g., turtles open their eyes when afraid, while toads close their eyes), children expect offspring to inherit the attributes of their parents. This "birth parent bias" has been observed among adults and children as young as 4 years (persisting throughout the teenage years) and across a wide array of cultures and socioeconomic backgrounds, including Americans (Johnson & Solomon, 1997), the Yukatek Maya (Atran et al., 2001), Brazilians (Sousa, Atran, & Medin, 2002), the Vezo of Madagascar (Astuti, Solomon, & Carey, 2004), and the Menominee, a Native American tribe in Wisconsin (Waxman, Medin, & Ross, 2007).

Young children also seem to assume that inheritance is strongest for internal properties. Sousa et al. (2002) and Waxman et al. (2007), for instance, found that Brazilian and Native American children considered a hypothetical blood transfusion from an animal's adopted parents to be capable of altering the qualities otherwise inherited from their biological parents. Waxman et al. argue that this is a result of explicit discussion among Brazilians and Native Americans about the transformative power of blood. Inheritance is still treated by young children in these communities as an internal biological property, but it is not limited solely to the parent–offspring relationship.

Another nice illustration of essentialist reasoning about inheritance comes from Diesendruck's (2001) study of animal classification among 4-year-old children from lower- and middle-class families in Brazil. The children were shown pictures of two animals that were from the same species but looked very different (e.g., a relaxed snake and a snake about to strike). One of these pictures was designed to provide an atypical representation of the animal and thus have ambiguous identity for young children. The children were then told that the animals shared either an internal property (bones, blood, muscles, and brain) or an external property (same size, lived in the same zoo with a similar cage). They were also told that the animal either was or was not a "zava," which was a novel word the children presumably had never applied to animals before.

When the animals were described as sharing an *external* property, children were less likely to apply familiar species labels (e.g., snake) to the atypical photo and less likely to apply the term "zava" to the more typical picture. However, this was flipped when the animals were described as sharing *internal* properties. Here children were more willing to say that a familiar species name could be applied to the atypical picture and that the unfamiliar name "zava" could be applied to the typical picture. An animal's internal properties were seen by the children as providing clues to an animal's category membership, thus verifying for them that information about the animal could be generalized to other members of that category. Furthermore, there were no significant differences between social classes in Brazil, nor did either social class differ significantly from previous studies conducted with 4-year-old children in the United States. This suggests that this form of essentialism might be innate.

2.1.3 Classification of Animals

Research into children's classification of animals was also inspired by Carey (1985). Carey argues that only with formal education do children learn that humans are animals, which raises the broader question of how children generally categorize the animal world. A great deal of research now indicates that infants and young children reason in essentialist ways about animal classification. In particular, they seem to endorse a form of *classification realism*, in that they treat the category of "animals" as something that reflects reality and not something that can be altered by human conventions. By the age of 5, regardless of culture, socioeconomic status, or experience with animals, children seem to view animals as natural kinds, whose category membership cannot be changed. This contrasts with children's understanding of ordinary objects, which they assume are more easily changed by external factors and whose function and identity are determined by human conventions (Rhodes & Gelman, 2009; Springer & Keil, 1991).

Classification realism seems to have its origins in distinctions formed in early infancy. Infants as young as 7 months will respond differently to animals than to other categories of objects. When given an array of randomly assembled toys, 7- and 9-month-olds will play with toys in categorical clusters—for example, playing with a bird after playing with a dog (animal cluster) and playing with a plane after playing with a car (machine cluster) (Mandler & McDonough, 1993; also see LoBue et al., 2013). The categories of animals and machines also elicit unique neural patterns in infants. For instance, viewing photos of animals (e.g., lizards, cockroaches, dogs) and photos of furniture (e.g., beds, chairs, lamps) produces distinct neural signatures in 7- and 8-month-olds (Elsner, Jeschonek, & Pauen, 2013; Jeschonek et al., 2010). This distinct neural representation of animal photos at 7 months also appears to be similar to that of adults (though it does not seem to be present in 4-month-olds; Marinovic, Hoehl, & Pauen, 2014).

This early classification of animals remains salient throughout early childhood. Jean Mandler and colleagues have found that throughout the second and third years of life children are able to distinguish animals from other entities, despite not having a stable ability to classify animals in more precise ways (e.g., by species or by phyla; see Mandler, 2000, for a review). There is also some evidence that infants classify animals at the level of "animal," rather than at the level of species or phyla. This contrasts with how classification works as an adult, where many psychologists have thought that the default form of classification is at the species level. This is known as "basic" or "entry" level classification and lies in between subordinate (a specific breed within a species) and superordinate classification (e.g., "mammal"). Infants appear to start by classifying animals at the highest superordinate level of "animal," suggesting that attunement to animals is psychologically more fundamental than classification by species. There is also some evidence to indicate that this superordinate level bias persists into adulthood. When presented with different entities embedded within a visual scene, people are faster to identify whether something is an animal than whether it belongs to a certain species (Macé et al., 2009; Poncet & Fabre-Thorpe, 2014).

The place of *humans* in children's conceptualizations of animals remains a contentious topic without a definitive conclusion. However, a number of recent experiments have provided persuasive evidence that young children are reluctant to view humans as animals. For example, Herrmann, Medin, and Waxman (2012) assessed the conditions in which 3- and 5-year-olds would extend the concept of animal to humans. In one experiment, they told children that a dog and a bird could each be called a "blicket." They then presented pictures of other animals as well as humans and asked if they could also be called blickets. Neither 3- nor 5-year-olds were willing to classify humans as blickets, though they were for other animals (bees and ants). In a second experiment, humans were used as a model, such that children learned that humans and either a bird or a dog (depending on the condition) could be called blickets. Here, an age difference appeared: 5-year-olds extended the term "blicket" to both humans and other animals (e.g., squirrel and deer), but 3-year-olds limited the term "blicket" only to non-humans. This suggests that 5-year-olds have a concept of shared animal nature between humans and non-humans but 3-year-olds do not, which is consistent with Carey's (1985) suggestion that seeing humans as animals requires significant directed instruction.

Further cross-cultural evidence for Carey's thesis comes from Leddon et al. (2012). They argue that children do not spontaneously classify humans as animals and are reluctant even with formal education instructing them to do so. From a review of previous studies, they concluded that children aged 6–9 categorized human beings as animals about 30% of the time. To test this further, they conducted a study with three different groups of 5- and 9-year-old children: an urban sample from Chicago; a rural sample from Shawano, Wisconsin; and a sample from the Menominee, a group of Native Americans living in rural Wisconsin. Menominee children provide an interesting test case because they are taught from a young age that humans originated from five different animals (bear, eagle, crane, wolf, and moose). Previous research also had found that Menominee 5-year-olds would infer that properties possessed by animals would generalize to humans (Medin & Atran, 2004). However, in this study, 9-year-olds were willing to categorize humans as mammals but not as animals, and 5-year-olds would not categorize humans as either animals or mammals. Crucially, there were *no* statistically significant differences across the different communities, despite significant differences in education and experiences with animals. So despite significant differences in conceptions of humans' animal nature, young children from very different cultures may nonetheless share in the belief that humans should not be classified as animals.

The three types of knowledge about animals identified here do not exhaust the full range of assumptions made about animals in early childhood. They are meant to show what types of knowledge about animals are plausibly inherited rather than learned, thus illustrating how evolution may have prepared our species to come into the world thinking about animals in specific ways.

2.2 RELATIONSHIPS WITH ANIMALS IN HUMAN EVOLUTION

When members of biological species possess a trait that provides a fitness advantage (typically by improving the chance of successful reproduction), we say that the trait has been "selected for." An adaptive pressure is anything that would make it more likely that some traits will be selected over others. For example, global warming provides an adaptive pressure on thermoregulation in animals. Individual animals with thermoregulatory traits equipped for rapidly increasing temperatures will have a fitness advantage over less equipped individuals, thus making it more likely that those traits will persist.

Different relationships we had with animals would have led to the selection of some traits over others in our evolutionary history. In many cases (e.g., predator–prey relationships), much of the underlying psychology was in place long before ancient hominids (our immediate ancestors) existed. Human–animal relationships continued to develop in directions that increased selection of these traits, which likely had an effect on more recent attitudes toward animals (in the last several thousand years).

It should be noted that there might be alternative non-adaptive explanations for the psychological processes discussed here. Unfortunately, little research exists to draw from in order to provide reasonably detailed non-adaptive proposals. Why, then, focus on adaptive pressures? Because, in the words of philosopher of science Peter Godfrey-Smith, adaptation provides "a good 'organizing concept' for evolutionary research" (2001, p. 337). I am not committed to exclusively adaptive explanations for attitudes toward animals but think it the best way to begin an investigation.

2.2.1 Hunting and Being Hunted

Arguably the oldest human–animal relationship is that of predator and prey. Our most immediate evolutionary ancestors played both roles for millions of years (Stiner, 2002). This made a lasting impression on human minds. Barrett (2005) argues that predator–prey relationships posed particularly strong adaptive pressures because the underlying goal remained invariant across situations. Unlike human social interactions, for instance, in which goals change frequently, interactions with animals for much of our evolutionary history would have involved one very specific goal: to kill or be killed.

The most general consequence of this relationship is increased sensitivity to animal information. This comes in different forms, but one of the most important in evolutionary history is *visual* sensitivity to animals. For a long time, human–animal relations took place primarily over large distances, whether in the forest or on the savannah. We should thus expect people to display extra sensitivity to animals in their visual field.

One source of evidence for this comes from research on New, Cosmides, and Tooby's (2007) "animate monitoring hypothesis." This hypothesis holds that humans evolved a specialized system to detect animacy in their surroundings, or movement indicative of the presence of animals. Cosmides and Tooby (2013) characterize this system as "category driven, that is, it is automatically activated by any target the visual recognition system has categorized as an animal" (p. 206).

For example, in one experiment, New et al. (2007) showed participants scenes depicting animate entities, like animals and humans, and inanimate entities, like trees and houses. They also included scenes with cars since cars possess features indicative of both animacy and inanimacy. The scenes were then surreptitiously altered to remove certain items from the scene, and participants were asked to report when they noted any changes. The results showed that people were faster to detect changes in animals and humans and much more accurate at detecting those changes as well. This would seem to provide support for the animacy hypothesis and the primacy of animals in the human visual system.

This general finding has been widely replicated and does not seem attributable to a generalized sensitivity for all non-human life. People more quickly and more accurately detect the presence or absence of animals in a visual scene than they detect vehicles or trees (Crouzet et al., 2012). Even when presented subconsciously, animals are detected in scenes faster and more accurately than plants (Balas & Momsen, 2014).

Visual sensitivity to animals also seems to arise independently of visual experience with animals, suggesting an innate disposition for thinking about animals. Mahon et al. (2009), for instance, found that thinking about the size of animals, compared to thinking about the size of tools, activated the same part of the ventral visual system in both sighted and blind individuals. Innate thinking about animals is also supported by research on "adaptive memory," or enhanced memory for information that would have been important for our evolutionary ancestors (Nairne, 2010; Nairne & Pandeirada, 2008). Schussler and Olzak (2014) argue that remembering information about animals would have been more important than remembering information about plants in our evolutionary history because animals were more deadly and more beneficial. To test this hypothesis, they conducted an experiment in which American undergrads were asked to memorize information (including photos) about a series of plants and animals (e.g., "apple tree" and "snail"). They were then asked to identify as many of those plants and animals as possible based solely on their photos. On average, students successfully recalled 92% of the animals and 65% of the plants. Similar results were found even with students who had completed a botany class, further indicating that people are naturally better at remembering information about animals than plants.

Visual sensitivity to animals entails neither a positive nor a negative relationship with animals. We are alerted by their presence. However, visual sensitivity to animals arose out of antagonistic predator–prey relations, and thus we should expect the animate monitoring system to include various negative biases toward animals.

One feature of our animate monitoring system is a bias toward *threatening* animals. This is not limited to predators but includes poisonous animals as well. There is a long tradition of research on our evolved "preparedness" in responding to animal threats (Öhman & Mineka, 2001; Seligman, 1970). For example, pictures of threatening animals (e.g., a scorpion with a raised tail) cause an increase in galvanic skin response, even when the pictures are shown subconsciously (Tan et al., 2013). Some studies have also suggested that animal threats (e.g., showing bared teeth) generate a unique neural response in the amygdala, a part of the brain generally responsible for processing emotions (Cao et al., 2014; Yang, Bellgowan, & Martin, 2012). The emotional salience of threatening animals typically generates an approach/avoidance response (what is often called "fight or flight"). We are strongly motivated to deal with threatening animals either by attacking to neutralize the threat (approach) or by fleeing from the situation until the threat has dissipated (avoidance).

This sensitivity to threatening animals has made us particularly sensitive to *subtle* indicators of threat. We are predisposed to view animals as threatening even if they pose very slight threats to us or pose no threat at all. For example, even animals that are typically classified as nonthreatening (e.g., rabbits) can trigger the unique neural response in the amygdala (Mormann et al., 2011). The main evolutionary reason for this disposition is that we have evolved a tendency to be proactive and precautionary toward animal threats. Our threat detection system has evolved to act quickly. It prioritizes responses to animal threats over their accurate identification. Killing an innocent rabbit, for instance, would have been much less costly in our evolutionary history than hesitating a bit too long before striking a legitimate predator. Nonthreatening animals also share certain features with threatening animals (e.g., being four-legged), so it is relatively easy for our evolved sensitivity to animal life forms to quickly identify these threats.

In summary, the history of predator–prey relationships has made human beings 1) alert to the presence of animals, which entails vigilance but not antagonism toward animals; 2) sensitive to animal threats, including strong motivation to neutralize animal threats by approach or avoidance; and 3) precautionary toward animal threats, leading us to treat animals as threatening even when they present no actual threat. In short, our evolved response to animals as predators or prey is inherently antagonistic. Though this can be modified and counteracted by other evolved responses to animals, as we will see, it is important to remember that this is at the core of our oldest relationship with animals.

2.2.2 Vectors of Disease

Disease transmission is an underappreciated factor in human–animal relations. An estimated 58% of all pathogens currently affecting human beings are "zoonotic," or can be transmitted between humans and animals (Woolhouse & Gowtage-Sequeria, 2005). A significant number of these were originally transmitted from animals thousands of years ago. Though disease researchers generally acknowledge the pathogenic role of animals both now and in our evolutionary history, rarely are the moral-psychological implications of this pathogenesis discussed (additional evolutionary considerations are discussed in Kasperbauer, 2015a).

Diseases are typically transmitted from animals passively. Accidental exposure to an infected animal can be sufficient. This is hypothesized to be the main method of transmission for many of the oldest zoonotic diseases. During the migration out of Africa (roughly 50,000–70,000 years ago), humans and animals increasingly came into close contact, allowing for passive transmission. Some diseases, like tuberculosis and Epstein-Barr virus, are suspected to have been transmitted from animals that opportunistically scavenged off these transient human settlements (like birds, rodents, and some primate species; Comas et al., 2013; Harper & Armelagos, 2013).

Aside from the move out of Africa, the most significant disease transmission event in our evolutionary history was the development of agriculture, around 10,000 years ago. During this time, increases in the size and density of human populations coincided with closer contact between animals and permanent human settlements. A number of recent analyses have found that the rise of agriculture brought about sharp increases in zoonotic disease transmission (see Table 2.1; Barreiro & Quintana-Murci, 2010; Karlsson, Kwiatkowski, & Sabeti, 2014; Morand, McIntyre, & Baylis, 2014; Wolfe, Dunavan, & Diamond, 2007). Not only did older diseases (like malaria and tuberculosis) become more severe and more lethal, but new zoonotic diseases arose as well, including measles, rotavirus, and many others. Domesticated livestock are thought to have served as carriers

Table 2.1 ILLUSTRATION OF THE NUMBER OF PARASITES AND DISEASES SHARED BETWEEN HUMANS AND DOMESTICATED ANIMALS

Animal	Time since domestication (years)	Origin	Nature of relationship	Parasites shared with humans	Diseases shared with humans
Dog	17,000	E Asia	Work, meat, pet	71	29
Cat	9,700	Fertile Crescent	Pest control, meat, pet	54	10
Cattle	11,000	SE Anatolia	Work, milk, meat, leather	34	25
Swine	10,500	SE Anatolia, E Asia, SE Asia	Meat, leather, pet	34	18
Sheep	12,000	SE Anatolia	Meat, milk, wool, leather	84	15
Horse	5,000	Central Asia	Work, milk, meat	9	6
Camel	5,000	Arabia	Work, milk, meat	2	
Rabbit	2,000	Europe	Meat, fur, leather, pet	6	7
Rat	12,000	S Asia	Meat, commensal	27	23

Adapted from Morand et al. (2014), who found a positive correlation between the number of shared diseases and parasites and the time since domestication.

for these diseases, though people did not recognize the animals' disease-carrying potential at the time (Harper & Armelagos, 2013; Weiss, 2001; York & Mancus, 2013). This prevented adequate treatment as the infected animals remained in close contact with humans, allowing for reoccurring outbreaks of disease.

Other prominent sources of disease in our evolutionary history are animal carcasses. The archaeological record suggests that our ancestors were scavengers as well as hunters. While scavenging avoided the risks of hunting, it presented new risks associated with diseased meat. Both handling and consuming diseased meat are thought to be key methods of disease transmission. Tapeworms, for example, were likely transmitted from consuming tainted meat (Harper & Armelagos, 2013).

So it's quite clear that animals posed serious pathogenic risks to our evolutionary ancestors. The pathogen avoidance system that developed and that we have inherited, as a result of these risks, has many of the same features as the threat detection system described above. Most prominently, we possess a tendency toward false positives and an exaggerated response in avoiding potential pathogens (Curtis, 2014; Hart, 2011). The evolutionary reasons are also quite similar. It is more costly, in evolutionary terms, to approach an infected animal than it is to avoid an animal one has misidentified as infected. Of the 25 most deadly diseases in human history, 9 are due primarily to animal vectors (Curtis & Biran, 2001). It thus makes sense that we would possess an exaggerated aversion to animals.

We can see numerous behavioral effects from this history of disease transmission. Fessler and Navarrete (2003), for instance, found that meat is the most highly regulated food item across 78 different cultures. This makes sense, given the possibility of infection from eating meat. People are also more likely to rate unfamiliar foods as disgusting and to avoid them if they originate from animals (Martins & Pliner, 2006). This would seem to be the result of a pathogen avoidance system that motivates precautionary behaviors toward animal-based food.

This disposition toward precautionary behaviors has other effects with significant implications for moral psychology. Mark Schaller (2011) attributes our precautionary pathogen avoidance to an evolved "behavioral immune system." He reasons that it would have been far too costly in evolutionary history to rely on one's immune system to neutralize infections. Even a very strong immune response has physiological effects, for instance, that require increased energy consumption. There would thus be adaptive benefits in being proactive and avoiding infections entirely, rather than being reactive and relying on the strength of one's immune system post-infection.

Part of this proactive response, Schaller argues, is aversion toward a "very broad category of superficial cues connoting non-normative physical appearance" (2011, p. 3421). Throughout our history, human communities have identified members of their community by various physical markers, from brute physical features like their height or race to social features like the gods they believe in or the foods they consider taboo. Those who are identified as strangers, according to these features, are more likely to be treated as potential vectors of disease. There are numerous reasons for this in evolutionary history. Schaller points to two: 1) strangers are more likely to carry novel diseases that our immune system is not prepared to handle and 2) strangers are less likely to follow local norms pertaining to hygiene and other behaviors that prevent disease transmission (also see Kelly, 2011, ch. 4; 2013; Oaten, Stevenson, & Case, 2011).

Animals are important here because they clearly possess a number of features that would signify that they are not members of the local community and should thus trigger the behavioral immune system. For evidence that they do, consider an experiment by Prokop, Fančovičová, and Fedor (2010), which found that sensitivity to pathogens was positively correlated with general avoidance of animals. They presented people with pictures of insects that are known to transmit diseases to humans (e.g., lice) and others that do not (e.g., wasps) and asked them to rate the extent to which they were disgusted by and afraid of each insect. They also measured the degree to which people engaged in pathogen avoidance behaviors, some of which were relevant to animals. For instance, one question asked, Do you pet wandering cats or dogs? The results showed that people who were more disgusted and afraid of disease-relevant insects also engaged in more pathogen avoidance. Though the animal-related questions did not receive their own analysis, these results suggest that people with aversive reactions to disease-relevant insects are also likely to engage in animal avoidance more broadly. This sort of response is likely the result of a proactive behavioral immune system.

The two evolved responses to animals described thus far indicate that animals primarily elicit aversive behaviors. The threat detection system and the behavioral immune system both dictate that we will be extra sensitive to animal threats and precautionary in neutralizing those threats. These two responses primarily entail negative attitudes and antagonism toward animals. However, our ancestors also faced adaptive pressures for showing care and concern toward animals. Understanding these relationships is important for understanding how positive attitudes toward animals developed.

2.2.3 Caring for Animals

Pet-keeping became common around the same time as the development of agriculture, about 10,000 years ago (Serpell & Paul, 2011). Both pet-keeping and agriculture entailed caretaking for animals. This was an important milestone in our relationships with animals as it required us to attend to their well-being for the first time.

It is much disputed, however, whether these relationships with animals produced overall positive or negative attitudes toward animals. Keeping animals as pets and for food required caretaking but also historically involved significant amounts of domination and exploitation (see Russell, 2011, chs. 6–7). Certain species engaged in cooperative mutually beneficial relationships with human beings (e.g., dogs) or were in commensal relationships (e.g., rats), with little direct impact on human activities (Larson & Fuller, 2014; Russell, 2011). Animals that were captured for consumption or transport (e.g., sheep and donkeys) were not initially put under direct breeding pressure. However, nearly every animal species cohabitating with human beings from roughly 11,000 to 7,000 years ago was eventually subject to intense human control of their behavior and breeding (Larson & Fuller, 2014). So although these relationships clearly benefited our evolutionary ancestors, it is difficult to conclude that they featured active concern for animals, in a way that would indicate positive attitudes toward them. Here we will focus mainly on how pet-keeping likely evolved since that has clearest implications for positive attitudes toward animals, as I will explain.

A long-standing puzzle is *why* we started keeping animals as pets. One leading theory is that they possess physical features that remind us of other human beings, particularly offspring. Neotenous features, which indicate infancy, motivate us to treat certain animals with care, as if they were our children (the so-called cuteness response). These neotonous features, as described by Horowitz and Bekoff (2007), include "large round eyes (especially with distinct irises); a discernable mouth, ears, and nose; the ability to raise the mouth at its edges, approximating a smile; alterable, non-rigid facial features; reactive posturing of the head (enabling the expressive use of the face or head); and the use of limbs on one's face (such as to cover or scratch it)" (p. 29). The possession of these features, it is hypothesized, would have led our evolutionary ancestors to care for animals and allow them to live within permanent human settlements, even if they served no other purpose. There is some evidence to indicate that observing neotenous physical cues can increase care-related behaviors. For instance, Sherman, Haidt, and Coan (2009) found that viewing pictures of puppies and kittens improved performance in the game "Operation," which requires focus and carefulness.

Another view, suggested by James Serpell (1996, 2003; Serpell & Paul, 2011), is that pet-keeping was a result of anthropomorphism, or attributing characteristically human qualities to animals (or attributing human qualities beyond what there was reason to think animals possessed). Serpell argues that this feature is necessary to explain why *adult* animals were cared for and not just offspring with enhanced neotenous features. Anthropomorphism first developed out of predatory–prey relations, but Serpell suggests that this could have been extended to social relationships. Anthropomorphism in predator–prey relations would have consisted of overattribution of goals and desires in order to aid in predicting an animal's behavior. For instance, a hunter might speculate that an animal will follow a river in order to stay close to water. This type of overattribution could have spread to other domains. For instance, in the social domain, humans might speculate that an animal desires to be comforted or to spend time with its family. This could have kickstarted the inclusion of animals in human communities.

A third possible adaptive reason to keep animals as pets is that they provided various health benefits. For instance, there's some evidence that pets can reduce stress, anxiety, and blood pressure; increase recovery time after illness; and improve overall well-being (for a review of the psychological and health benefits of pets, see Amiot & Bastian, 2015). Animals could have provided similar benefits to our evolutionary ancestors, thus increasing survival rates of those who took animals as companions.

Each of these proposals offers some insight into why we would have formed positive attitudes toward animals. Whether for neoteny, exaggerated anthropomorphism, or health benefits, we developed the disposition to show caretaking attitudes toward animals. As mentioned above, we can make a distinction between approach and avoidance emotions. "Nurturing attachment," the term used to describe the care and concern we show toward infants (both human and non-human), is categorized as an approach emotion (Campos et al., 2013). This likely motivates us to approach certain animals and attend to their well-being. This stands in contrast to the influence of predatory–prey relations and pathogenesis, which primarily predict antagonism toward animals.

However, it would seem that the evolutionary pressures placed on us by animals produced, on balance, negative attitudes toward animals. Not only do animals require additional food and other resources, but they also pose a pathogenic threat, as we have seen. As John Archer (1997) first put this challenge, "in evolutionary terms, humans are manipulated by pets: they are cuckoos in our nests" (p. 253). So selection for caring attitudes toward animals would likely have arisen alongside other pressures to avoid animals.

We also have to keep in mind that the adaptive benefits of caring for animals were likely a result of psychological processes that entailed a range of attitudes toward animals, some of which would have been negative. We can see this by looking at the role of anthropomorphism in human evolution. Anthropomorphism likely developed because it improved prediction of animal behavior, thus enhancing survival both as prey and as predator (Barrett, 2005). Thinking about animal behavior in terms of more familiar human beliefs and desires would have made animals' behavior more comprehensible. A number of studies have shown that we anthropomorphize in order to better make sense of an entity's actions. For instance, dogs that are rated as unpredictable are also more likely to be described as having a personality and a conscious will and as being aware of their emotions (Epley et al., 2008). Similarly, a study by Waytz et al. (2010) found that unpredictable gadgets (e.g., a clock that might jump on top of you or run away when the snooze button is hit) were more likely to be ascribed intentions, free will, and consciousness and increased activation in parts of the brain that are normally used when ascribing mental states to other human beings (primarily the medial prefrontal cortex and anterior cingulate cortex).

So if we did begin caring for animals because of exaggerated anthropomorphism, as Serpell suggests, the caring function likely co-opted the more general process that helped to make sense of the behaviors of animals. This is important because this general function first arose out of antagonistic predator–prey relations. Making sense of animals helped to control them. The first steps toward pet-keeping may thus have had a dual purpose, with caring for animals secondary to controlling them. Importantly, people need not have conceived of pet-keeping in this way for there to be adaptive effects. Selection for the type of exaggerated anthropomorphism that, by hypothesis, led people to care for animals and bring them into human settlements would also have impacted the type of anthropomorphism that entailed controlling attitudes toward animals.

2.3 HARMONIOUS RELATIONSHIPS WITH ANIMALS

When we look at human attitudes toward animals through the lens of evolutionary research, it may seem as though the moral psychology we have inherited was primarily shaped by antagonistic relationships with animals. This might not be the full picture, however. Some have objected that this conception of past relationships with animals is a projection of current treatment of animals in Western societies back into evolutionary history. Various communities of indigenous people, it has been argued, have very different conceptions of human–animal relations, according to which animals and humans are equals and must be treated accordingly. The existence of these communities might be taken as evidence that either the evolutionary explanation is wrong, and I am guilty of projecting back, or the evolutionary account is irrelevant to understanding current moral psychology because indigenous communities indicate the prevalence of non-antagonistic relations with animals.

So does the evolutionary explanation hold water? Is it possible to know? Thankfully, there is evidence that might help navigate these questions. In short, harmonious relationships with animals are not as straightforward as they might seem, and many indigenous groups have a significant amount of antagonism in their relationships with animals, even when animals are viewed as equals. Ultimately, these relationships are compatible with the evolutionary factors already identified.

2.3.1 Human–Animal Equality and Hunting-as-Sharing

A core belief in human–animal equality has been identified across a wide variety of indigenous groups in different regions of the world. Details about specific indigenous groups will be provided as we go along, but speaking generally, a significant number of indigenous groups believe that animals are equal to humans in some important sense, and thus deserve to be treated as similar to other human beings. These views about equality typically derive from spiritual beliefs about animals. Animals are often seen as representatives of the spiritual world or as connected to individual spirits that communicate through animals. Nurit Bird-David (1999) argues that human–animal equality and the spiritual world that is intertwined with animals are not mere metaphors for many indigenous communities. Groups who hold this belief in equality see animals as agents that can be known just like other human beings and, because of this, treat animals as important subjects with which they can interact and do not use them solely for meeting their own, human, ends.

Many different indigenous groups are said to have reciprocal relationships with animals, where each side is expected to benefit the other in some way. This too is typically driven by spiritual beliefs about animals. For example, people as diverse as the Chewong of Malaysia, the Siberian Yukaghirs, various Amazonian communities, and the Rock and Waswanipi Cree of Canada all believe that animals give themselves up to hunters who treat animal spirits appropriately (Brightman, 1993; Feit, 1973). This spans a wide range of hunting-related behaviors: the Chewong believe that animals will refuse to present themselves if certain practices are not followed to honor animals after they have been hunted and killed (Howell,

1996), the Yukaghirs believe that the hunter must mimic the behavior of an elk in order for elk to present themselves because animals and human lives are "locked in a pattern of mutual replication" (Willerslev, 2007, p. 11), and certain Amazonian communities think that how they treat pets is viewed by the pets' wild counterparts as an indicator of whether they should give themselves up to humans in a hunt (Erikson, 2000).

Interestingly, if you put yourself in this mindset of reciprocal relationships with animals, hunting is non-violent. Knight (2012, p. 334) calls this the "hunting-as-sharing thesis" because animals are seen as willful participants who supposedly gain as much from the hunt as the hunters. In other words, as Nadasday (2007) argues, hunting represents a "long-term relationship of reciprocal exchange between animals and the humans who hunt them" (p. 25). Similarly, in describing the hunting behavior of the Rock Cree in Canada, who are expected to mimic animal behavior to achieve a successful hunt, Brightman (1993) says, "The event of killing an animal is not represented as an accident or a contest but as the result of a deliberate decision of the animal or another being to permit the killing to occur" (p. 187). Hunting is non-violent in reciprocal relationships because animals must always present themselves by their own volition and must not be tricked by the hunter. As Tim Ingold (1994) puts it, "coercion, the attempt to extract by force, represents a betrayal of the trust that underwrites the willingness to give. Animals thus maltreated will desert the hunter, or even cause him ill fortune" (p. 15).

The more we examine the attitudes behind indigenous peoples' relationships with animals, even, or perhaps especially, the animals they hunt, the more it might seem that these relationships are non-antagonistic. Although it may come as a surprise, even hunting—which I suggested is a key evolutionary driver behind aversion toward animals—is supposed to be fundamentally a relationship built on trust and respect. If these claims have merit, then we have some reason to be suspicious of the evolutionary account. On the one hand, indigenous communities' relationships with animals might be taken to show that the evolutionary account is simply mistaken. For instance, perhaps in some cases the enhanced visual salience of animals is driven by the role of animals not as predator and prey but as social and spiritual entities. On the other hand, indigenous communities' relationships with animals might be taken to show that the evolutionary factors identified no longer have much influence on human beings. That indigenous people do not have antagonistic relations with animals might be seen as evidence that human moral psychology is extremely flexible and that the evolutionary role of animals is easily modified. If this is true, then why care about the picture of human–animal relationships coming from evolutionary psychology?

For reasons that will soon become clear, we don't have to accept any of these claims. There is more antagonism in indigenous attitudes toward animals than anthropologists have generally acknowledged. Rather than refuting the evolutionary account, indigenous relationships with animals can be understood to support the hypothesis that our evolutionary heritage primarily entails negative attitudes toward animals.

2.3.2 A Critical Assessment of Indigenous Relationships with Animals

Before going any further, it is worth clarifying that there is significant dispute about how widespread beliefs about reciprocity and human–animal equality are among indigenous people. For instance, Hayden (2013) reports that none of the indigenous communities in Australia believe that animals offer themselves to hunters (neither as part of the spiritual world nor for any other reason). It is also clear from the ethnographical literature that there is significant variation in how indigenous people conceive of their moral duties to animals (e.g., in terms of improved treatment). However, for the sake of argument let us assume that beliefs about animals among indigenous communities pose an obstacle to the evolutionary account.

Knight's (2012) critique of the hunting-as-sharing thesis provides compelling reasons to reject the idea that indigenous communities have truly reciprocal relationships with animals. He argues that hunted animals are never in a position to have an actual relationship with indigenous people and so cannot truly enter into a reciprocal exchange with hunters. Instead, he suggests, indigenous people view themselves as interacting with the spiritual world, with individual animals acting only as intermediaries. The animals themselves are not part of the relationship. Accounts of relationships with individual animals are just surface descriptions; they are actually referring to animals' role as temporary intermediaries.

The evidence supports this challenge to the very premise that the human–animal relationship in indigenous communities is a reciprocal one. Actually, beliefs about hunting-as-sharing are often used to justify wastefulness. The Siberian Yukaghir, for example, reportedly view the world of living animals as capable of being replenished by dead animals; as a result, prey are seen as an inexhaustible resource (Willerslev, 2007, pp. 30–35). Since they also view prey as animals that have chosen to offer themselves to the hunters, they kill every animal that presents itself so as not to disrespect the animal spirits. This results in significant waste. For instance, when Yukaghir slaughter elk they only take selected parts, leaving most of the carcass to rot. Willerslev (2007) suggests that this is the case for many indigenous groups because "if a hunter is offered much, he must take much. Failure to kill all the animals available is to put one's future hunting luck at risk" (p. 35). Similar accounts have been described of other indigenous groups appearing unconcerned by unnecessary killing of animals that they claim are important parts of the spiritual world (see Harrod, 2000, p. 115; Kelly, 2013, p. 110; Russell, 2011, p. 54).

Another source of support for Knight is that many indigenous communities do not seem concerned about animals' welfare. For example, Brightman (1993) describes the Rock Cree as concerned about animals stuck in snares only because it makes the meat taste bad. The animals' pain and suffering did not seem to matter. They also seem to acknowledge that animals are taken against their will, despite the behaviors Cree must perform to convince animals to offer themselves to hunters. Moreover, many indigenous communities do not show high levels of concern for *all* animals. It is primarily prey animals that are viewed as engaging in reciprocal relationships with human beings. The Yukaghir, for example, reportedly view dogs as extremely helpful but still dirty and unworthy of respectful treatment, unlike elk, bears, and other animals that they hunt (Willerslev, 2007, p. 76).

In short, it's not clear what benefits animals actually receive from these relationships. They seem not reciprocal but thoroughly asymmetrical. Animals are treated well primarily to ensure future hunting success; much of the affection shown toward prey seems designed to assist in attracting and killing them. And respectful treatment is often applied only to the animals *after* they have died, in the form of rituals and tributes to the spirit world. As Brightman (1993, p. 201) characterizes this phenomenon amongst the Rock Cree, "Rituals of control occur before the hunt, while those emphasizing reciprocity and respect occur after" (p. 201).

A more cynical interpretation of the ethnographic literature is that these beliefs are merely used to justify killing animals. Humans and animals may indeed be seen as fundamentally the same, which may lead certain indigenous groups to treat animals differently, particularly in thinking of them as having value beyond their usefulness in a hunt. But these beliefs also lead to excusing behaviors: animals can be killed so long as sacrifices are made, animal suffering is unimportant because it is part of a broader spiritual process, and so on. At the very least, we should be suspicious that these behaviors result from caring attitudes toward animals. Animals are still seen as both predators and prey, they are still seen as threats, and even if certain indigenous groups do genuinely intend for animals to benefit from the relationship, the animals receive these benefits only by paying with their life.

If these criticisms have been convincing, then the beliefs of certain indigenous people would seem to be consistent with the evolutionary account of our relationships with animals. They do in fact possess antagonistic relationships with animals, despite (and perhaps because of) other beliefs about the spiritual importance of animals. This provides a rebuttal to the objection that focusing on predator–prey relationships in human evolutionary history merely reflects a Western bias. If this analysis is correct, indigenous people have clearly been influenced by the evolutionary role of animals as predators and prey.

To drive the point home, it should also be mentioned that the threat responses described earlier in this chapter—both for predators and for pathogens—appear to be widely shared across human cultures and to develop very early in life. For example, when taught about novel animals, young children (4- to 8-year-olds) from Los Angeles, Fiji, and the Shuar of the Ecuadorian Amazon had a significantly better memory for whether the animal was safe or dangerous (e.g., whether it was a predator or poisonous) than whether it was a herbivore or carnivore or what its name was (Barrett & Broesch, 2012; Broesch, Barrett, & Henrich, 2014). Threat information took priority despite very different experiences with animals and instruction in identifying animal threats.

To be clear, the point is not that indigenous people treat animals poorly or that their conception of animals is identical to that of technologically advanced, Western societies. My aim is only to demonstrate that the relationships between animals and indigenous people are compatible with the evolutionary account. Cross-cultural variation in how animals are treated will be discussed again in chapter 7.

2.4 CONCLUSION

This chapter has discussed the adaptive pressures on human–animal relationships in our evolutionary history. The evidence indicates that our ancestors would have faced adaptive pressures to both like and dislike animals, to both approach and avoid them, and to show both concern and aggression. Overall, however, it seems that the picture emerging from evolutionary psychology would predict antagonistic relationships with animals.

To some, this might seem implausible. Our current relationships with animals may not seem inherently antagonistic. So how, more precisely, have these evolutionary pressures impacted current psychology? As we will see in the next chapter, an answer to this question lies in the core psychological processes that determine our attitudes to animals.

Chapter 3

Dehumanizing Animals

Dehumanization research has primarily focused on human beings, not animals. When dehumanizing someone, we might compare him or her to an animal, like a rat or pig, with the intention of demeaning the other person. But this does not obviously have any impact on animals themselves. Animals are members of a preset contrast class that the dehumanized target is put into. But we use this same process on animals, as we will see in this chapter. When we evaluate animals, we are strongly influenced by the psychology of dehumanization, even when we are not performing direct comparisons between humans and animals.

3.1 DEHUMANIZATION AND INGROUP/OUTGROUP PSYCHOLOGY

3.1.1 Dehumanization and Infrahumanization

Although it may seem from the word itself that to dehumanize something is merely to take away from it qualities that are human, really dehumanization is best defined as the process of attributing what one takes to be non-human qualities to an entity. This definition allows for a wide range of entities to be the target of dehumanization. Anything that is seen as sharing attributes with humans can have those attributes removed and others attributed to them.

Dehumanization typically occurs by comparison to two different types of non-humans: machines and animals (Haslam, 2006). The first, mechanistic dehumanization, compares an entity to machines, like robots, particularly in being unemotional. Animalistic dehumanization, by contrast, compares an entity to animals, particularly in being unintelligent. Just as we could humanize any entity by attributing it emotions and intellectual capacities seen as characteristically human, we can dehumanize any entity by attributing those qualities in ways that are characteristic of machines or animals (for reviews of dehumanization, see Bain, Vaes, & Leyens, 2014; Haslam et al., 2012; Haslam & Loughnan, 2014).

The animal dimension of dehumanization can be used to get a better understanding of the psychology of human attitudes toward animals. To gain this sort of insight, we must look at how animal comparisons are used to demean other human beings. Many discussions of dehumanization draw from a classic paper by Leyens et al. (2001), which argued that dehumanization researchers often overlook subtle ways in which we demean others. One way to dehumanize is to explicitly identify certain people (or certain groups of people) as non-human. A more subtle way, however, is to identify certain people (or groups of people) as *inferior* human beings. Leyens et al. call this second process *infrahumanization*. Infrahumanized others are still attributed various key human qualities but are treated as inferior to some other group by comparison.

For example, Leyens et al. (2001) found that when demeaning other human groups, people tended to deny them emotions that are often considered uniquely human, like remorse, pride, and compassion. They would still, however, attribute emotions that are considered widely shared with animals, like surprise, fear, and pleasure. One key insight here is that denying that someone possesses uniquely human emotions involves a very subtle negative evaluation and in some cases may not include a negative evaluation at all. Being incapable of pride, for instance, could be considered a virtue. What is thus surprising about infrahumanization is that it is not intended to thoroughly demean others, only to do so enough to make it clear who is superior (for reviews of infrahumanization, see Leyens, 2009; Leyens et al., 2007; Vaes et al., 2012).

A similar phenomenon has been found with dehumanized animals. Haslam et al. (2008) conducted a study with participants from Australia, China, and Italy, in which they were asked to rate the "humanness" of 37 mental states. They also rated the extent to which those mental states were possessed by animals, robots, and supernatural entities. Animals were consistently believed to have lower levels of emotions thought to be uniquely human, including love, shame, resentment, admiration, hope, and pride. However, biologically basic emotions, like anger, disgust, fear, and pleasure, were seen as being shared equally between humans and animals. And mental states pertaining to sensations, like hearing, seeing, and smelling, were attributed in a greater degree to animals than to humans.

This study did not assess negative evaluations of animals, but the results show a similar pattern as dehumanized people in Leyens et al.'s study. Animals were denied uniquely human emotions even in the absence of overt negative evaluations. Some of these denials might even be taken as implying positive evaluations. Thinking that someone is incapable of feeling resentment, for instance, might in fact be praising his or her character. Perhaps we make similar positive evaluations about animals when denying that they possess certain uniquely human qualities. Animals are also attributed other emotional abilities that imply a level of positive evaluation. Heightened perceptual abilities, for instance, are often seen as one of the virtues of animals.

Based on these results, it seems reasonable to believe that infrahumanization, whereby we attribute characteristics that establish our superiority, is central to our evaluations of animals. This is a subtle form of dehumanization. We attribute qualities that we think are appropriate for the category "animal" but without explicitly demeaning animals.

This proposal stands in contrast to arguably the dominant conception of how mistreatment of human beings might apply to animals, which focuses primarily on derogatory attitudes that are explicit and absolute. Scott Plous' (1993, 2003) account, for instance, treats negative attitudes and harmful behavior toward animals as a form of prejudice, like racism. This views human attitudes of superiority over all other animals as a uniformly negative response. Though animals can and are dehumanized in overtly negative ways, this is not the whole picture.

Research by Leyens and his colleagues, as well as parallel lines of research, indicates that absolute dehumanization occurs in special cases, typically when there is overt conflict or hostility, and does not adequately characterize the standard way we dehumanize others. To some, this might seem like a revisionist take on dehumanization; typically dehumanization is understood to have derogatory implications. It need not though.

For instance, being "saintly" is a non-human quality, but saintliness is usually an attribute of praise. If someone is unswayed by characteristically human temptations, like power or money, we might call them saintly; but this would seem to imply that the person is better than ordinary human beings. As the studies I will go on to discuss indicate, dehumanizing animals often includes attributing various positive qualities to them.

To get a better understanding of both the absolute and the subtle forms of dehumanizing animals, more needs to be said about what motivates people to engage in dehumanization. The standard model for this is ingroup/outgroup psychology.

3.1.2 Animals as an Outgroup

The usual targets of dehumanization are those we see as belonging to an outgroup, or a group we do not identify with. Typically we use various external features, like skin color, clothing, and other forms of body modification, to determine group membership (Boyd & Richerson, 2005; Gil-White, 2001). Although the exact physical markers used in this process vary, human beings generally use *some* physical markers to identify group membership. In experimental conditions, when one physical marker of ingroup membership becomes unreliable, people will switch to another physical marker. If race, for instance, no longer usefully tracks one's affiliations, gender or even shirt color will be used instead (Kurzban, Tooby, & Cosmides, 2001).

Animals uniformly possess outward physical features signifying that they are not members of human ingroups. They are not the same size as human beings, move at different speeds, typically don't walk bipedally, and don't wear clothing. Their outgroup status is also indicated by a range of other behaviors. As discussed in chapter 2, in the context of the behavioral immune system, a common way to indicate one's group membership is to follow certain behavioral norms. People generally assign outgroup membership to those who fail to follow local customs. Animals occasionally follow rules dictated to them by humans (e.g., dogs can be taught not to sit on the couch) but do not generally conform to behavioral norms that are followed by other human beings.

Research by Susan Fiske and her colleagues has found that, besides external physical features, another way we assign group membership is by assessing people's warmth and competence (Fiske et al., 2002; Fiske, Cuddy, & Glick, 2007). Warmth is determined by traits like friendliness, helpfulness, and trustworthiness, while competence is determined by a person's intelligence, skill, and efficacy. In the one existing study of animal warmth and competence (Sevillano & Fiske, 2016), dogs, cats, and horses were ranked highly on both variables, while fish, reptiles, and rodents scored low (see Figure 3.1). Some animals were seen as warm but relatively incompetent (e.g., rabbits), while others were seen as cold but competent (e.g., lions). This could explain why dogs and cats are viewed essentially as honorary members of human ingroups. They do not look or act like us but possess other features that lead us to judge that they are warm and competent (e.g., perhaps their cuteness or their obedience). Much of the rest of the animal kingdom, however, are likely to be judged members of an outgroup.

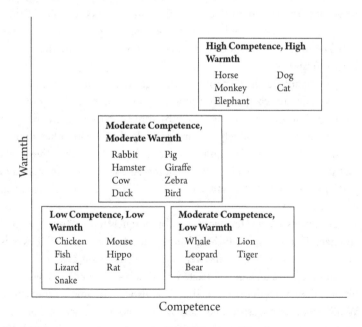

Figure 3.1. Ratings of animals on the dimensions of warmth and competence. Based on research from Sevillano and Fiske (2016).

That animals are indeed perceived as members of an outgroup has been supported by a number of recent studies. Most of this research illustrates this indirectly, however, by showing how human outgroups are compared to animals. Demonstrating that these studies in fact indicate the outgroup status of animals thus requires more detailed discussion, to bring out the relevant pieces of information. Three experiments shed light on the different ways in which animals are treated as outgroups.

First, let's consider an experiment by Saminaden, Loughnan, and Haslam (2010). They used what is called the "go–no go task," which requires people to make quick judgments about category membership. Participants push a button if they think a stimulus (like a word or a picture) does fit into a category (a "go" response) or elect not to push the button if it does not fit into the category (a "no go" response). A quick judgment is used in order to prevent participants from reflecting on their responses. With time to reflect, social expectations and concerns about how their attitudes might be perceived can lead people to change their responses. The go–no go task, and other similar tasks described below, avoids this by forcing people to follow their immediate reaction. This technique allows researchers to assess the content of implicit attitudes that are harder to control.

Participants in this experiment were given 700 milliseconds to categorize different words as belonging to either "traditional" or "modern" societies. The words were first rated by other participants according to whether they were uniquely human or widely shared with other animals (similar to Leyens et al.'s stimuli discussed already). The hypothesis was that people's choices would reflect that modern societies were treated as part of an ingroup (a "society like mine") and traditional societies as an outgroup.

The results showed that words rated as uniquely human (e.g., "person," "human," "family") were attributed more to modern societies, while words like "cat," "animals," and "cattle" were attributed more to traditional societies. This indicates that animal-related words are associated more with traditional than modern societies. There was also an infrahumanizing effect. While animals were associated more with traditional societies, there was no difference in the *positivity or negativity* of the words associated with traditional societies. Negative words like "hatred," "assault," and "death" were no more likely to be attributed to traditional societies than positive words like "peace," "freedom," and "health." Animals and traditional societies were treated as inferior to modern societies, but this was apparently not driven by explicitly negative attitudes toward traditional societies.

This experiment appears to show that both animals and traditional societies are treated as outgroups. However, it shows the outgroup status of animals indirectly. A more direct demonstration of this comes from two experiments conducted by Boccato et al. (2008). In the first experiment, they presented participants with pictures of either humans or gorillas, which the participants were asked to classify as "human" or "animal." Names were rapidly flashed on the screen immediately prior to presentation of the pictures, which were intended to prime participants with either ingroup or outgroup stereotypes. Since the participants were from northern Italy, names that are typically found in northern Italy were included as ingroup names, while names typically found in southern Italy were included as outgroup names. Their most significant finding was that humans were identified faster when preceded by names from northern Italy. The proposed explanation for this is that northern names primed ingroup concepts, making other ingroup content (like humans) more accessible.

In a second experiment, the presentation of stimuli was flipped. A picture of either a human or a chimpanzee served as a prime this time, while the Italian names were presented more overtly, along with other words. The main task for participants was to identify if the words were names. The results were consistent with the first experiment and further demonstrate the outgroup status of animals. Northern names were identified faster when preceded by human faces, while southern names were identified faster when preceded by chimpanzee faces. This provides more direct evidence that animals are seen as an outgroup. Even chimpanzees, which share many features with human beings, prime outgroup concepts.

A third demonstration of the outgroup status of animals comes from Viki et al. (2006). They too used an implicit measure, known as the "implicit association task." The participants, who were all British, were shown characteristically British and German names (e.g., "Charles" and "Klaus"), which they simply had to identify as British or German. They were also shown characteristically human- and animal-related words (e.g., "citizen" and "critter"), which they had to identify as human or animal. These two tasks were then combined, with all four categories of words shown. In one presentation of the stimuli, the same button was used to identify both German names and animal words, while another button was shared between British names and human words. This combination was then switched, such that German names and human words were identified with one button and British names and animal words with another. This technique is used in the implicit association task in order to test which combination is easiest for participants. Participants are expected to be faster and more accurate in their responses for the pairing that they find most intuitive.

The results of this experiment showed that people were faster to identify words when German names were paired with animals and British names were paired with humans. This provides yet another indication that animals, as a category, are viewed as an outgroup. They also conducted related experiments aimed at determining if these implicit attitudes influenced more overt attitudes toward outgroups. In one, participants were more likely to connect animal-related words (like "critter," "creature," "pet," "feral") to French and German names and human words ("person," "wife," "husband," "civilian") to British names. In another, participants were asked to choose from a number of words that they thought characterized British, German, and Italian people. Even on this more explicit task, where people could reflect on their responses, animal words were used more to characterize outgroups while human words were used more to characterize the ingroup.

These experiments provide good evidence that animals are seen as members of an outgroup. Much of this evidence is admittedly indirect: outgroup human beings are seen as more animal-like. But a plausible explanation for these results is that animals are members of an outgroup and, as a result, are readily associated with outgroup human beings. There is also direct evidence, though. Chimpanzees in Boccatto et al.'s experiment, for instance, led people to think about outgroup human beings. And participants in the Viki et al. study associated animal words with outgroup humans.

These results further illustrate that outgroup dehumanization exists even in the absence of explicit antagonism or hostility. Each of these experiments thus portrays the phenomenon of infrahumanization. None of the human groups being compared to animals in these experiments were explicit enemies or seen as serious threats to anyone. Yet they were still attributed derogatory terms as outgroups.

As suggested above, animals are seen as outgroups largely because of their lack of ingroup signifiers, in terms of both gross physical features and their behavior (including their perceived warmth and competence). This might still seem odd, however, since animals do not obviously present any threat to human ingroups, unlike other groups of human beings. Animals cannot enter into intergroup conflicts and so do not seem like candidates for ingroup/outgroup demarcation. Chairs and trees, for instance, also do not possess ingroup signifiers for human beings, but they are not typically considered outgroup members or targets for dehumanization. So what makes animals special? Chapter 2 presented some of the evolutionary reasons for this—primarily that animals posed unique threats to our ancestors. But to answer this question we also must look to additional forms of animal threats, as they are currently perceived and represented in human psychology.

3.2 THE PSYCHOLOGY OF ANIMAL THREATS

3.2.1 Animals as Physical Threats

Underlying the assignment of animals as members of an outgroup is a subtle negative evaluation. Chapter 2 argued that we have inherited an aversion to animals as threats, both as sources of disease and as predators. We return to the psychology of aversion here as it helps explain the subtle negative evaluations we make of animals.

The most pertinent research on aversion to animals comes from studies of how animals elicit disgust and fear. Disgust is an emotion that primarily functions to protect us from infection and the consumption of pathogenic substances (Chapman & Anderson, 2012; Oaten, Stevenson, & Case, 2009; Tybur et al., 2013), while fear functions to protect us from danger (Öhman & Mineka, 2001). Fear and disgust are functionally unified in that they tend to motivate avoidance and inhibition behaviors (Olatunji et al., 2008). Both emotions can be triggered by animals.

A taxonomy widely used by researchers distinguishes between predators, which primarily elicit fear; rodents and slimy invertebrates, which primarily elicit disgust; and other animals that elicit both fear and disgust. Tigers and sharks, for example, elicit fear, while snails and maggots elicit disgust; and rats, cockroaches, and spiders elicit both fear and disgust (Matchett & Davey, 1991; Ware et al., 1994; Webb & Davey, 1992).

What is particularly interesting is how disgust and fear are often combined in aversive reactions to a wide range of animals. Both emotional systems seem to be recruited when responding to animal threats. For instance, fear of animals, including both predators and slimy invertebrates, seems to be positively correlated with disgust toward those animals (Arrindell et al., 1999; though see Davey, Forster, & Mayhew, 1993). Similarly, Prokop and Fancovicová (2013) found that people who perceived themselves as more vulnerable to diseases (a disgust-related function) also rated predators (e.g., sharks and bears) as more dangerous. Some studies have also found that inducing disgust can increase fear of certain animals. For instance, Webb and Davey (1992) found that watching a disgusting video clip from a surgery increased ratings of fear for animals normally considered "fear-relevant" but mostly harmless, including rats, snakes, jellyfish, cockroaches, and beetles. This research seems to indicate that while fear and disgust are attuned to specific types of animals, they work together to motivate aversion to animal threats from either category of emotional response.

When fear and disgust toward animals are combined in excess it is known as animal *phobia* (Davey & Marzillier, 2009). In the United States, animal phobias are the most common type of clinical diagnosis for specific phobias (compared to, for instance, fear of heights and flying), with an estimated lifetime prevalence of 3.3–7% in the general population (LeBeau et al., 2010). Phobias involve fear and anxiety far beyond what is called for by an object or situation, but they are also indicators of general tendencies. For instance, a study of over 8,000 people in the United States found that 22.2% reported fear of animals, 5.7% of whom had fear strong enough to be considered phobic (Curtis et al., 1998). These numbers further illustrate that animals are indeed seen as threatening to a large segment of the population and likely elicit aversive reactions as a result.

We can describe such fear and disgust as responses to a *physical* threat posed by animals. They trigger aversion because they pose threats to our bodily health and integrity. However, animals also pose a *psychological* threat. Some examples of the psychological threats animals present were mentioned in chapter 1. The area of research that has studied these in the most depth is known as terror management theory (TMT). To get a better understanding of psychological threats posed by animals, we must thus look at the empirical and theoretical foundations of TMT.

3.2.2 TMT and Animals as Psychological Threats

Within psychology, TMT was first developed by Sheldon Solomon, Jeff Greenberg, Thomas Pyszczynski, and colleagues (Greenberg, Pyszczynski, & Solomon, 1986; Greenberg et al., 1994; Rosenblatt et al., 1989; Solomon, Greenberg, & Pyszczynski, 1991). This research drew from Ernest Becker's work in anthropology, particularly his Pulitzer Prize–winning book *The Denial of Death* (1973). Central to TMT is the idea that human beings are emotionally averse to reminders of their own mortality. This psychological threat is known as *mortality salience*. In experiments, mortality is typically made salient by asking people to describe the emotions they feel when they think about their own death and what they think will happen, physically, when they die. Other common and more implicit death primes include reading articles about death as well as word searches and sentence completion tasks that include death-related words.

According to TMT, animals pose a unique threat to our mortality, for two main reasons. The first stems from their role as threats to our physical well-being. Things that are pathogen-related, like feces, decaying bodies, open wounds, and of course animals, all have been shown to elicit mortality salience. As discussed in the last chapter, we avoid certain animals to an exaggerated extent because, in our evolutionary history, they presented a threat to us. Mortality salience is likely part of this exaggerated response. Second, in addition to being connected to pathogens, animals threaten the uniqueness and superiority of human beings in the natural order of things. One major finding from research on mortality salience is that being reminded of one's worldview and important ideals helps resist the negative consequences of thinking about death. Many believe, and consider it among their core beliefs, that humans are special and superior to animals. As one would thus expect, many experiments have found that highlighting the differences between humans and animals is an effective way of reducing the psychological threat posed by mortality salience. So animals play a dual role in mortality salience: their mere existence causes thoughts of death, and thinking of them as significantly different from humans is an effective way of suppressing these thoughts.

Let's take a look at the evidence that animals indeed play these two roles in the phenomenon of mortality salience. First, let's consider the threat they pose to human superiority. As just mentioned, a well-confirmed method for repelling mortality salience is to affirm one's core values and beliefs or the values and beliefs of one's culture (Gailliot et al., 2008; Greenberg et al., 2000). For example, a number of experiments have found that, for Americans, reading an essay that praises the United States reduces the negative effects of thinking about the experience of death (Schmeichel & Martens, 2005). This also applies to beliefs about animals. Affirming the belief that humans are superior to other animals helps defend against mortality salience. As Rozin and Fallon (1987) explain, human beings "wish to avoid any ambiguity about their status by accentuating the human–animal boundary" (p. 28).

An excellent illustration of how mortality salience and the human–animal boundary influence thoughts about animals comes from a study of pet owners conducted by Beatson, Loughnan, and Halloran (2009). They used the typical method for eliciting mortality salience, where participants are asked to describe the experience of dying. In a control condition, participants were asked to describe the experience of giving a public speech. Participants then read a passage emphasizing either the similarities or differences between humans and animals. The Similarity passage read as follows:

> the boundary between humans and animals is not as great as most people think . . . what appears to be the result of complex thought and free will is really just the result of our biological programming and simple learning experiences.

The Difference passage, by contrast, stated the following:

> although we humans have some things in common with other animals, human beings are truly unique . . . we are not simple selfish

creatures driven by hunger and lust, but complex individuals with a will of our own, capable of making choices, and creating our own destinies.

Additionally, the experimenters assessed participants' attitudes toward pets. One measure asked people to rate how much they thought the average pet was characterized by different positive and negative traits (e.g., being friendly or annoying). The other measure asked people about their attitudes concerning the treatment of pets, in which they had to rate their agreement with statements like "I think people's pets deserve to be pampered every now and then by going to a pet spa" and "I think it is silly to celebrate a pet's birthday." These statements were designed to assess whether people thought pets deserved special treatment.

On both assessments of attitudes toward pets (positive traits and special treatment), mortality salience had a statistically significant effect. When thinking about giving a speech, highlighting *similarities* between humans and animals led people to attribute more positive traits to pets and to see them as more deserving of special treatment than when human–animal *differences* were emphasized. However, when thinking about the experience of death, this was flipped. Reading about human–animal similarities, in this condition, led people to attribute fewer positive traits to pets and also see them as less deserving of special treatment, compared to when differences were emphasized. In short, reminding people of their mortality, when combined with a reminder of their animal nature, led people to treat pets more negatively.

Accentuating the human–animal boundary is thought to be one of many strategies for providing stability and meaning to human lives. Increasing one's self-esteem has been shown to have a similar effect, repelling mortality salience (Harmon-Jones et al., 1997; Schmeichel et al., 2009; Schmeichel & Martens, 2005). It seems that boosting self-esteem helps people feel that they have value, even if they will eventually die. For example, Harmon-Jones et al. (1997) gave participants false feedback on a personality test designed to increase their self-esteem. This false feedback (which the participants thought was real) reduced the negative effects of tasks that otherwise enhance mortality salience. Similarly, Schmeichel et al. (2009) found that the effects of writing about death were reduced if participants were subliminally presented with the word "I" followed by positive traits (like "handsome" and "smart"). Even this very subtle boost to self-esteem was effective.

This type of defense against mortality salience has also been observed in response to animal stimuli. Consider again the study by Beatson and Halloran (2007) mentioned in chapter 1. They studied mortality salience among an Australian sample. That their participants were Australian is significant because most studies on mortality salience are conducted with Americans and because in other experiments Australians have expressed idiosyncratic attitudes to the human–animal boundary (Haslam et al., 2008; Vaes, Bain, & Bastian, 2014). Nonetheless, in this experiment the results were exactly as one would predict from the main tenets of TMT.

Beatson and Halloran used the method commonly used for eliciting mortality salience, in which participants write about the experience of death. They also used the typical control condition, in which participants write about the experience of dental pain. Participants then viewed a video showing bonobos having sex. In one condition, the similarities between human and animal sex were emphasized, while in another condition the differences were highlighted. Those in the Similarity condition were told to "think about how the behaviours of the animals closely resemble those of human sexual behaviour" and to "Notice, for example, that like humans, animals also engage in face-to-face copulation." Those in the Difference condition, by contrast, were told to "think about how animal reproductive behaviour is very different from human love-making" and to "Notice that the animals do not seem to show any interest or emotion, but rather seem to act automatically to fulfill a survival function." Participants' attitudes to animals were also measured by asking them to rate animals according to general traits, like whether they were good or bad, valuable or worthless, and important or unimportant.

The results were exactly as one would expect from previous studies on self-esteem and mortality salience. For those with low self-esteem, thinking about death and the *similarities* of human and animal sex led to more negative attitudes toward animals. When human–animal *differences* were emphasized, there was no effect at all on those low in self-esteem. This indicates that the human–animal boundary served as a buffer to thoughts about death, which are generally a threat to those low in self-esteem.

Those with high self-esteem, by contrast, actually had more positive attitudes toward animals when thinking about both death and the similarities between human and animal sex. A possible explanation for this is that people high in self-esteem have greater psychological resources to deal with the animal threat, such that the animal threat actually produced a psychological "surplus," leading these participants' attitudes to swing the opposite direction from those with low self-esteem.

These two experiments from Beatson and colleagues illustrate how we deal with threats to the human–animal boundary. Now let's move to the other role for animals in mortality salience: the threats they pose to our physical health. Many experiments on mortality salience have looked at the effects of pathogenic disgust elicitors. These are also frequently combined with explorations of the human–animal boundary, further illustrating the dual role played by animals in mortality salience.

One interesting strand of TMT research has focused on the effects of reminding people about the physical, as opposed to the romantic, aspects of sex (Goldenberg et al., 1999). Highlighting the physical aspects of sex (reading statements like "I like feeling my partner's sweat on my body") seems to trigger thoughts of death. This has also been used in studies of animal stimuli. Goldenberg et al. (2002) found that reading about human–animal similarities prior to reading about the physical aspects of sex led people to think more about death. This was prevented, however, by reading about the differences between humans and animals. Viewing humans as significantly different from animals alleviated the threat posed by the physical aspect of sex.

There is also evidence that thinking about death activates the disgust system, which, as explained already, is responsible for avoiding pathogens. For example, Goldenberg et al. (2001) presented participants with the traditional death prompt, in which people write about the experience of death, and then measured their level of felt disgust. They found that thinking about death increased ratings of disgust most toward things that are considered pathogen-related, including bodily products (e.g., vomit) and animals (maggots, worms, rats, and cockroaches). This indicates that mortality salience activates pathogen avoidance mechanisms that motivate aversion to animals. This is consistent with the exaggerated response to animal stimuli discussed in the last chapter.

One final study on the relationship between physical and psychological animal threats comes from Cox et al. (2007). They too studied the effects of disgust elicitors on thoughts about death. In one experiment, participants viewed either disgusting images (e.g., feces or vomit) or neutral images (e.g., a book or a fork). Those who saw the disgusting pictures were more likely to use death-related words in a word-completion task (e.g., SK_LL and _RAVE). In a second experiment, participants read about pathogenic disgust elicitors (e.g., "It would bother me to see a bowel movement left unflushed in a public toilet") and then read an essay on either human–animal similarities or differences. Again a word-completion task was used to assess death-related thoughts. As one should by now expect, participants who read about the similarities between humans and animals were more likely to use death-related words after reading about the disgusting items. Yet again, reading about human–animal differences provided a buffer to death-related thoughts and prevented this effect from occurring.

These experiments further illustrate the dual role played by animals in mortality salience. Animals present a physical threat that is alleviated by thinking of humans as significantly different from animals. This is, in essence, the psychological response that is central to human attitudes toward animals. They are primarily threatening, and we have developed various mechanisms for suppressing these threats.

This research raises a number of difficult questions, however. Most fundamentally, why do animals make us think of death and not merely motivate aversion? The physical threat posed by animals is clear. But why does this produce additional psychological threats pertaining to our worldviews, specifically concerning the human–animal boundary? Relatedly, why would we have developed ways of *suppressing* the animal threat, as opposed to *eliminating* it (e.g., by just killing animals or removing them from society)?

3.3 DEALING WITH ANIMAL THREATS

How did animals come to be seen as threats? How have we evolved responses to those threats? The evolutionary origins of TMT are much disputed, but discussions of the adaptive value of TMT have not really addressed the role of animals, either within TMT or as psychological threats generally. Many discussions of the evolution of TMT fail to distinguish the adaptive value of *identifying* threats from the adaptive value of *responding* to those threats. As we will see, there are compelling reasons to believe that identifying psychological threats posed by animals likely co-opted systems that had evolved to identify physical threats. The psychology of infrahumanization provides insights into how responses to these threats might have evolved.

3.3.1 Identifying Animals as Threats

The core of TMT is a response to reminders of death and mortality. Many have questioned how this sort of response could have been selected for in evolutionary history (e.g., Fessler & Navarrete, 2005; Tybur, Griskevicius, & Lieberman, 2009). According to TMT, animals pose a very specific type of psychological threat: they remind us of our own mortality. Thus, the main question to address here is why reminders of our animality would have caused thoughts of death for our evolutionary ancestors.

Traditionally, it has been thought that animality is one particularly salient aspect of mortality. Thinking about animals, or being in their presence, is supposed to naturally lead to thoughts about death. Thinking about bonobos having sex, for instance, and how this is similar to human sex will lead to thoughts about our animality and thus our mortality. Because mortality is a fundamental threat to our existence, animals come to be seen as a serious psychological threat.

A general criticism of this proposed role for animals in TMT is that it doesn't have any obvious adaptive value (Tybur, Griskevicius, & Lieberman, 2009). It's not clear what the mortality salience response would have helped our ancestors achieve. It could perhaps motivate avoidance of things that would remind people of death, but this is evolutionary advantageous only if the reminder was also a direct threat to survival. On its own, however, there doesn't seem to be any adaptive purpose to having an emotionally aversive response to thoughts of death.

Most TMT researchers have agreed that it is unlikely that mortality salience was selected for. Arguably the standard account of how animals became psychological threats holds that systems designed to detect physical threats were *co-opted* to perform other functions. The behavioral immune system, described in the last chapter, is one illustration of this. Animals pose a potentially lethal threat to our physical health, as both pathogens and predators. So the behavioral immune system, and other similar systems, has evolved to be precautionary. We avoid certain animals entirely, without verifying the exact risk they pose, because even investigating the risk could be deadly. The aversive response we have to threats to our physical health was co-opted to serve a closely related function—avoiding animals—even in the absence of objective physical risk.

So how would thoughts about death have been co-opted from older threat detection systems? One plausible account of this can be found in Rozin, Haidt, and McCauley's (2008) classic article on the evolution of disgust. They propose that core disgust, which functions to protect the body from pathogens, expanded to become a "guardian of the temple of the body, responding to direct threats of contagion or infection to parts other than the mouth, and also to any evidence that our bodies are really no different from animal bodies" (p. 764). So while the core adaptive function of disgust is to protect the body from pathogens, this adaptive function, they think, was co-opted to protect against thoughts about our animality. This could then have been co-opted further to protect against thoughts of death. As they explain in an earlier version of this article, disgust expanded from its original function to become "a defensive emotion that guards us against the recognition of our animality and, perhaps ultimately, of our own mortality" (1993, p. 712). Treating animals as psychological threats was not itself selected for, on this account. The selection pressure was not against thinking about animality or mortality but rather animals as pathogenic entities. This was then co-opted to respond aversively to animality and mortality.

Another leading hypothesis holds that thoughts about death were a side effect of increased intelligence in our hominid ancestors. As the capacities for memory, imagination, and long-term planning developed, so did the ability to think about death. This would likely have included thoughts about predators and how to deal with them, but it could also have included thoughts about mortality as such. Greenberg, Solomon, and Arndt (2008) propose that the "awareness of ourselves as objects existing in the world, juxtaposed with the capacity to imagine future possibilities, rendered our ancestors aware of a wide variety of potential threats to their continued existence, many of which were fatal and uncontrollable" (p. 116; for a similar account see Landau et al., 2007). Here too aversion to animality and mortality is not seen as being under direct selection pressure. Increased capacity for foresight and imagination led, as a side effect, to a more vivid realization that animal threats were pervasive and could easily lead to death.

I find the co-opt hypothesis to be the more compelling of these two accounts. As others have argued, it's not clear why increased intelligence would lead to anxiety about one's death (Navarrete & Fessler, 2005; Kirkpatrick & Navarrete, 2006). Death might be inevitable, and increased intelligence might lead to a more vivid recognition of this fact; but it's not clear why this would create heightened anxiety about death. Moreover, as our ancestors became more intelligent, they also came into closer contact with animals. This seems contrary to what TMT would predict. Rather than pushing animals away or avoiding them, greater intelligence seems to have led our ancestors to embrace their company.

However, it has been argued that the co-opt hypothesis is equally implausible. Many commenters have wondered how animals would come to trigger thoughts about death. Even if it could be demonstrated that aversion to mortality salience has an adaptive purpose, animals do not seem to provide a unified and coherent reminder of death. As others have argued with respect to disgust, mundane animal behaviors like breathing and sleeping don't seem to elicit the same response as overtly disgusting behaviors, like reproduction or defecation (Nussbaum, 2004; Strohminger, 2014; Tybur et al., 2013). So it does not seem to be animals as such that elicit mortality salience.

As I have argued elsewhere (Kasperbauer, 2015a), the role of animals as carriers of pathogens can help make sense of their role in producing thoughts of death. Rozin et al.'s (2008) basic proposal, that core disgust was co-opted to respond to animal reminders, seems plausible. It also helps identify how very different types of animal reminders could elicit the same response. Many of the stimuli that cause thoughts of death—like sex, corpses, and feces—also have the potential for transmitting diseases. Though few studies exist that could verify this, the same could be true for animals. They trigger thoughts of death because they were a significant threat to the physical health of our evolutionary ancestors. What unifies different types of reminders of animality is their role as sources of disease.

This basic suggestion had also been made by Tybur, Griskevicius, and Lieberman (2009), but they further claim that disgust does not function in any way to avoid reminders of our animality. In contrast, the evidence reviewed throughout this chapter seems hard to deny; reminders of our animality do indeed trigger aversive responses. To respond to a criticism mentioned above, mundane animal behaviors (like breathing and sleeping) may not elicit disgust because they are not sufficiently related to disease transmission. When human–animal similarities are emphasized in TMT studies, many of the physical aspects of bodies are described. The reason human–animal similarities elicit thoughts of death could be that they emphasize sources of disease (e.g., animal blood, eating, and reproduction). Again, as far as I know, none of the research in TMT could confirm this. It would be interesting to test whether mundane animal behaviors would elicit disgust or thoughts about death if it was clearly emphasized to participants that these behaviors might be shared with humans.

Other more direct empirical support for the role of disgust in responding to mortality salience can be found in Kelley et al. (2015). In a series of experiments, they found that people who were more sensitive to disgusting stimuli were more likely to appeal to their worldview to suppress thoughts about death. Disgust-sensitivity made people more attuned to the psychological threat of mortality salience. Conversely, Webber et al. (2015) found that asking people to suppress their emotions while viewing disgusting images decreased the mortality salience effects of reading about human–animal similarities. Reducing the amount of disgust participants felt also reduced the importance of animal threats. Both of these studies further support the claim that basic responses to physical threats could have been co-opted and integrated into broader aversive responses (also see Kollareth & Russell, 2016).

A handful of other explanations have been offered for the evolution of TMT that also feature co-opted evolutionary functions. However, a review of these is not necessary since they primarily draw from the basic idea that TMT evolved out of more fundamental threat detection systems. Perhaps the most prominent alternative account holds that thoughts of death create uncertainty (Greenberg, Vail, & Pyszcynski, 2014; Tritt, Inzlicht, & Harmon-Jones, 2012). Mortality is inevitable, but its timing is unpredictable. Thinking about its possibility might remind us of this and create anxiety. According to this account, thoughts about death are not unique; sources of uncertainty abound. Animals could be a particularly salient source of uncertainty, however, especially given the various physical threats they pose. Unfortunately no research has been conducted on the role of animals in creating uncertainty, so this hypothesis will not receive further discussion.

3.3.2 Suppressing Animal Threats

Identifying animal threats has obvious adaptive value, and responses to those threats would have been under selection pressure for our evolutionary ancestors (as chapter 2 showed). But it has been difficult for TMT researchers to provide a persuasive explanation for the adaptive value of *suppressing* animal threats (for a review of possible evolutionary explanations for TMT and similar psychological processes, see Holbrook, Sousa, & Hahn-Holbrook, 2011). The TMT response to suppressing psychological threats is also somewhat peculiar. Why would adhering to one's worldviews or boosting self-esteem have been selected for? Alternatively, if it is part of a co-opted system, what function might the co-opted system have served in evolutionary history?

Navarette and Fessler (2005) argue that suppressing thoughts of death would have been *maladaptive* for our evolutionary ancestors. Perhaps currently it makes sense to forget about the animals nearby because they are largely non-threatening, but our ancestors would have needed to take them very seriously. Rather than suppressing or forgetting about animal threats, we have clearly evolved responses to eliminate and remove them. Our disgust and fear responses, as well as aggression and predatory behaviors, all had clear adaptive value for our ancestors. Given these robust threat-eliminating responses, what reason would there be to protect ourselves from thoughts about death that animals might cause?

The standard reply to this objection is that psychological threats—like thoughts of death—do not put people in immediate danger and so call for a different type of response than disgust, fear, or aggression. TMT isn't a system designed to remove or eliminate an imminent threat but to cope with a persistent and subtle threat that must be continually monitored (Jonas et al., 2014; Tritt, Inzlicht, & Harmon-Jones, 2012). As Landau et al. (2007) explain, "clinging to one's worldview and self-esteem function to deal with the knowledge that death is inevitable and its potential to arouse anxiety, rather than with specific imminent threats to continued survival" (p. 492). On this account, TMT functions to suppress debilitating thoughts rather than eliminate the cause of those thoughts. Reminders of death are pervasive and unavoidable. Simply reminding someone of his or her animal nature is apparently enough to trigger debilitating thoughts of death. TMT would have thus been adaptive because it enabled normal psychological functioning.

While this reply is persuasive, it does not adequately address the role of animal threats. For our evolutionary ancestors, animal threats would have been much more difficult to avoid than other reminders of death. Corpses could be buried or burned, but unless an animal is killed or injured, it could easily remain within the presence of humans. It thus seems unlikely that the TMT response could adequately suppress the psychological threats posed by animals. TMT research indicates that we elevate ourselves above animals in order to find meaning and suppress reminders of our animality. But it is difficult to see how this could be successful in ensuring normal psychological functioning, given the pervasiveness of animals now and in evolutionary history. To be effective, the TMT response would need to treat animals as imminent threats; but as TMT researchers have argued, that is not its designed function.

Instead, we should look to the psychology of infrahumanization to understand the evolution of TMT (and responses to animal threats generally). Infrahumanization leads us to attribute certain positive qualities to dehumanized animals. Instead of suppressing animal threats, we attribute qualities that make them seem non-threatening and that reaffirm human superiority. This provides a way of coping with pervasive animal threats. We not only adhere to the closely held belief that humans are superior to other animals (a core TMT response) but also modify the nature of the threat. It is easier to live among things that cause thoughts of death (or are generally psychologically threatening) if they possess redeeming qualities.

Besides providing a more effective way of resolving animal threats, infrahumanization also helps account for the fact that many animals were eventually embraced by human societies. At different points in our evolutionary history, we gained significant survival value from living in close proximity to animals. It would have been quite costly to avoid animals or eliminate them, regardless of the physical and psychological threats they posed. Protecting ourselves from these threats, while still living in close proximity, allowed us to continue deriving benefits from animals. The process of infrahumanization would help achieve the outcomes needed to suppress the animal threat without incurring other survival costs.

This sort of explanation is similar to that offered for other things known to elicit mortality salience. Perhaps the most illustrative is sex. The act of reproduction involves a great deal of threat, including the exchange of pathogenic fluids. A number of studies have shown that people are in fact disgusted by the pathogenic aspects of sex. As we saw, people also do not like to be reminded of the physical aspects of sex. Given these responses, we should expect people to avoid having sex! But this of course is not what happens. Instead, it seems that the physical response involved in sexual attraction works to reduce our avoidance responses (like disgust; Ariely & Loewenstein, 2006; Borg & de Jong, 2012). Like infrahumanization, this response allows us to resolve a specific threat in order to gain other valuable benefits.

3.4 CONCLUSION

So, in the end, what conclusion can we reach about threat perception and how it influences our perception of animals? Although they tap into evolutionary threat responses, especially when we are primed to be concerned with our mortality, we find a way to overcome those instincts by infrahumanizing animals. We treat them as members of an outgroup but in a subtle way that can include positive attributions. The positive qualities attributed to infrahumanized animals must not be overstated, however. As the discussion of animal threats indicated, we should expect animals to be treated negatively, even when they receive positive evaluations. Making positive judgments of animals provides a way for us to be comfortable with their presence. This does not entail positive treatment, however.

Infrahumanization can in fact help make sense of animal abuse and mistreatment. Infrahumanized animals will likely receive less attention and moral concern than those in our ingroup (both humans and non-humans). Research on human intergroup relations has shown that infrahumanization still has negative consequences, even if an outgroup is seen as essentially human. For example, infrahumanization has been shown to decrease assistance after natural disasters (Cuddy, Rock, & Norton, 2007) and to lead people to blame victims of intergroup conflict (Castano & Giner-Sorolla, 2006). Infrahumanization should thus be seen as providing insights into why we are often ambivalent toward animals. Our beliefs about animals are often inconsistent; people will claim to value animals while also supporting their mistreatment. Infrahumanization helps explain this phenomenon.

Chapter 4

Dehumanization and Mentalizing Animals

The previous chapter offered an account of how we psychologically rank human beings above other animals. This tendency to rank can lead to an obvious problem: it prevents us from viewing humans and non-humans as equal in some respects, particularly in moral importance. Many ethicists agree that sentient beings are *morally considerable,* or are worthy of the most basic form of moral attention. The reason for this is rooted in a form of equality—namely, that the comparable interests of sentient beings deserve equal consideration, regardless of whether the beings in question are human or non-human (an idea developed most famously by Peter Singer, 1990). A pig's interest in avoiding suffering, for instance, is as deserving of moral consideration as my own interest in avoiding suffering. Not all of my interests are comparable to those of a pig, but aversion to suffering is one that is likely comparable, and thus demands similar moral consideration.

Despite broad agreement among ethicists on this idea, the discussion from the previous chapters indicates that this idea is likely to meet psychological resistance from people generally. As argued in the previous chapter, comparing humans and animals in this way poses a psychological threat. Here we will focus on one main consequence of this threat: the types of mental states we attribute to non-human animals and how they are used to assign moral status to animals.

As just mentioned, ethicists typically use the capacity of sentience to assign moral considerability. As Peter Singer defines it in *Animal Liberation,* sentience is "the capacity to suffer and/or experience enjoyment" (1990, p. 8). Sentience consists of mental states generally characterized as *phenomenally conscious,* which means that their experiences have a subjective quality and feel a certain way to an animal. In this chapter, we will look at the strong psychological link that exists between attributing phenomenal mental states and assigning moral status to animals and how phenomenal mentalizing (the process of attributing phenomenal mental states) is influenced by dehumanization processes.

4.1 USING MENTAL STATES TO ASSIGN MORAL STATUS

4.1.1 Ethical Views

Before jumping into the relevant research on mentalizing, we need a general framework for understanding the different ways mental states might be used to assign moral status. A range of options exists in the ethical literature on animals. A brief review of these options can give us a better idea of where human psychology fits in relation to the proposals made by philosophers.

There are, roughly, three different positions one might take on the relationship between animals' mental states and moral importance (for a fuller discussion of these three positions, see Kasperbauer, 2017). The first we can call *pure phenomenal* views. These use animals' capacity for phenomenal experiences to grant them great moral significance. Emotions are prototypical phenomenal states in that they feel a certain way to the experiencing agent. For instance, animals' ability to feel pain, on pure phenomenal views, is taken to provide a broad-based justification for improving their treatment. Steiner (2008, 2013) and Francione's (2000) animal rights theories typify this view. Phenomenal states can be considered synonymous with what has also been called "experiential" states in the empirical literature. In Figure 4.1, pure phenomenal views are thus high on the Experience dimension.

Pure phenomenal views are polar opposites of the second type of view, which we can call *pure agential* views. There is a range of agential states that might be seen as morally important, including decision-making, planning,

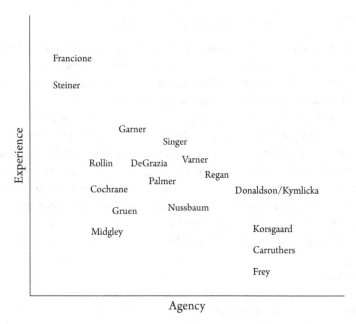

Figure 4.1. Animal ethicists' views on mental states and moral considerability, categorized according to Gray et al.'s (2007) dimensions of mind perception. From Carruthers (1992), Cochrane (2012), DeGrazia (1996), Donaldson and Kymlicka (2011), Frey (1980), Francione (2000), Garner (2013), Gruen (2011), Korsgaard (1996), Midgley (1983), Nussbaum (2006), Palmer (2010), Regan (1983), Rollin (2006), Singer (1990), and Varner (2012).

language, and many others. Pure phenomenal views exclude the importance of agential abilities, while pure agential views exclude the importance of phenomenal abilities. Raymond Frey's (1980) early account of language, according to which language is a prerequisite for moral considerability, typifies this view. In the figure, Frey is high on the Agency dimension. In later works, Frey (2014) treats phenomenal states as having direct moral importance, but for simplicity I am considering only his better-known, early views. The third type of view we can simply call *mixed*. These theories place moral importance on both agential and phenomenal states. Most theories in animal ethics would be classified as mixed, though tending toward the phenomenal end of the spectrum (and thus lie somewhere in between the Experience and Agency dimensions in the figure).

4.1.2 Phenomenal States in Mentalizing

Most current research on mentalizing and moral status judgments draws from Gray et al.'s (2007) two-dimensional account of mind perception. They conducted a survey in which participants compared the mental states of different types of entities. For instance, a chimpanzee and a human fetus might be presented as a pair, and people would have to rate which one was more capable of experiencing pain (or if they were equal). Though this was not specified prior to the study, they found that people naturally attributed mental states according to two features: agential states (e.g., the ability to form intentions and control one's thoughts) and experiential states (what I am calling phenomenal states; e.g., the ability to have sensations and feel emotions). They also asked participants which of the characters it would be more painful for them to harm. The results showed that answers to this question correlated significantly more strongly with experience than with agency.

This research is significant because it suggests that viewing something as morally considerable (which entity people wouldn't want to harm) is strongly influenced by its possession of phenomenal states (like pain and other emotions). As can be seen in Figure 4.1, this psychological phenomenon—using primarily phenomenal states to assign moral considerability—matches well with current consensus in animal ethics. Though ethicists dispute what a phenomenal being is owed, they are broadly in agreement that such a being is owed *something*. However, some theories hold that agential, not phenomenal, states are important for moral considerability. More will be said about this in chapters 7 and 8.

Evidence to support the link between phenomenal mentalizing and moral status judgments has been mounting since Gray et al.'s initial research. Gray and colleagues have subsequently proposed that phenomenal mentalizing and agential mentalizing represent two fundamentally different processes in human moral psychology, applicable to both humans and non-humans (Gray & Wegner, 2009, 2012; Gray, Young, & Waytz, 2012). For instance, Bastian et al. (2011) found that even human beings will receive greater moral concern if described in experiential terms and *less* concern if described in agential terms. Describing a group of people (like athletes, children, or lawyers) as "emotionally responsive" and "warm towards others," rather than "culturally refined" and "rational or logical," increased participants' willingness to intervene if those people were harmed in some way (e.g., if someone broke a promise to them). Experiential descriptions were positively correlated with willingness to take moral action.

This relationship has also been observed in experiments in numerous explorations specifically into the mentalizing of animals. In one of the first published studies from philosophers on this topic, Knobe and Prinz (2008) found that people were much more likely to say that a study of fish pain might be related to moral issues than a study of fish memory (also see Robbins & Jack, 2006). Digging into two other important experiments in greater detail will help draw out the psychological connection between phenomenal mentalizing and animals' moral considerability.

Jack and Robbins (2012) asked people to read stories about the harvesting of lobsters. In one condition people were told that lobsters possessed the sorts of states that would be considered agential in Gray et al.'s sense: they were described as intelligent, able to perform elaborate foraging strategies, and having great memories. In this condition lobsters were also described as feeling little to no emotion. In a second condition participants were asked about states that were consistent with experience in Gray et al.'s study: lobsters were described as possessing the ability to feel emotions such as depression and anxiety but not having much intelligence. Participants were asked to rate how concerned they were about lobsters, how they would feel if they themselves were harvesting the lobsters, and how severe the penalty should be if the harvesting was made illegal. In all three cases, those in the experience condition scored significantly higher than those in the agency condition.

Sytsma and Machery (2012) conducted a study similar to this one but focused on primates. They presented people with a story in which monkeys were being used to test the effects of wound-healing antibiotics and scientists were puzzling over which of five species to use for the experiment. They again varied both experience (described as the ability feel pleasure and pain) and agency (described as the capacity for intelligence and inquisitiveness) in describing the species under question. Participants in all conditions were asked to rate on a 7-point scale whether it was morally wrong for the scientists to use the particular species presented to them. The results showed that people were more likely to judge that the invasive experiment was morally wrong if the monkeys were described in experiential terms than if described in agential terms (these results have also been successfully replicated by Piazza, Landy, & Goodwin, 2014).

All of these studies indicate that attributing phenomenal states to animals is strongly correlated with judgments of moral considerability. They also seem to indicate that agential states are not involved with such judgments or only exert a very weak influence. This research supports what we, for shorthand, can call the *phenomenal account*. The phenomenal account generalizes Gray et al.'s data to claim that moral judgments will diverge as a function of the two dimensions identified. As a psychological thesis, the phenomenal account holds that an animal's ability to experience phenomenal states (of which pain is a perspicuous example) naturally leads people to think it is worthy of the most basic form of moral consideration; it predicts that agents who are attributed experiential mental states will be judged morally considerable.

One might think that surely agential states also have an impact on moral considerability. Though I do not think the empirical evidence fully supports this, there is one important nuance to note: agential states sometimes *entail* phenomenal states, which is consistent with the phenomenal account. This is what we should expect if, psychologically, moral considerability judgments ultimately require the attribution of phenomenal states. This is particularly true for complex cognitive states. Memory and language, for instance, are considered agential states, but they also frequently involve rich emotions. If the capacity for memory or language were to be attributed to an animal, the phenomenal account predicts that the animal would consequently be seen as morally important because the animal can thereby experience phenomenal states.

Empirical support for the link between experiential states and certain agential states comes from an experiment recently conducted by Piazza et al. (2014). They asked participants to rate a wide range of different types of animals (including mammals, reptiles, amphibians, birds, and insects) on 20 different traits indicative of both experience and agency. They found that the correlation between experiential and agential traits was extremely high ($r = .90$, $p < .001$). Moreover, the correlation between experiential traits was higher for agential traits indicative of intelligence ($r = .86$) than agential traits indicative of the basic ability to perform actions, which need not require intelligence ($r = .62$). Participants were also asked whether they thought each animal deserved to be protected from harm, whether each animal deserved to be treated with care and compassion, whether they had sympathy and respect for the animal, and whether it would be morally wrong to harm the target. Responses to these questions were strongly correlated with participants' combined attributions of experiential and agential states ($p < .001$).

These are the basic contours of the phenomenal account. There are other important questions remaining, however. One fundamental question in mentalizing research is what causes these different types of mental state attribution. The experiments above described animals' mental states explicitly, to clearly distinguish phenomenal from agential states. But how are these attributions made in more ordinary circumstances, where the animal's mental states are not predetermined? An important, related question is how people determine which agents are capable of feeling specifically phenomenal states, especially given the link between phenomenal mentalizing and moral status judgments. Of particular interest here is how dehumanization influences mentalizing. Dehumanization research predicts that dehumanized agents will be denied certain phenomenal states. How are these judgments made?

4.2 DEHUMANIZATION AND PHENOMENAL STATES

4.2.1 Effects of Dehumanization and Infrahumanization on Phenomenal Mental States

A few of the basic effects of dehumanization on mentalizing were described in the last chapter. Absolute dehumanization, where another being is viewed in an explicitly negative light, leads to a denial of mental states. Sometimes this occurs along a single dimension, where either agential or phenomenal states are denied but not both. In many other cases dehumanized targets are seen as lacking any mental states whatsoever (neither agential nor phenomenal). This has been observed in people's responses to homeless people and drug addicts, for instance (Lee & Harris, 2014).

Infrahumanization, by contrast, leads people to deny an agent mental states that are considered uniquely human or unique to one's ingroup. With respect to animals, "uniquely human" and "unique to one's ingroup" are one and the same. Animals are sometimes attributed fewer mental states overall—both positive and negative, both agential and phenomenal. Other times, particularly when being dehumanized, they are only attributed negative states. But when they are being distinctly infrahumanized, they are attributed positive states that function to identify their subhuman status, while also being denied mental states that are considered uniquely human.

The experiment mentioned in the previous chapter from Haslam et al. (2008) is one illustration of infrahumanization. In that experiment, animals were denied uniquely human emotions like love and pride but were granted biologically basic emotions like pleasure and anger. Animals were also attributed heightened sensations, like hearing, seeing, and smelling. People do not seem to ascribe these mental states as a result of any sort of investigation but rather make ascriptions based on what they think is appropriate for anything that is categorized as "animal."

There are numerous other effects of dehumanization and ingroup/ outgroup psychological processes generally. The most prominent of these result from how people respond to animals' physical features. Animals' physical features largely signify that they are members of a human outgroup. However, they also possess physical features that lead us to prefer some animals over others. Some animals more closely resemble members of human ingroups than others, and this influences both our mentalizing and our moral treatment of them. Animals exist on a spectrum of resemblance to humans, leading us to treat apes, for instance, differently than we do armadillos or alligators. Let's review some of these effects.

4.2.2 Phenomenal States and Physical Features

Humans possess a strong anthropocentric bias when mentalizing. In other words, animals that physically and behaviorally resemble human beings are more likely to be attributed positive mental states and, as a result, are more likely to be treated well. This basic suggestion has been made by many others. For instance, it is one of the main elements in Plous' (1993,

2003) account of prejudice toward animals. Rarely, however, is it made explicit exactly how this anthropocentric bias influences mentalizing and the assignment of moral status.

Animals share many of our physical features, and this simple fact explains our anthropocentric bias. Horowitz and Bekoff (2007) claim that the most likely beneficiaries of our anthropocentric bias are "animals who bear a superficial physical similarity to ourselves—apes and monkeys— and those who are at least in our taxonomic group—mammals" (p. 29). These animals possess a suite of physical features that are shared with humans, including large foreheads, protruding cheeks, large eyes, colored irises and visible sclera, ability to approximate a human smile, bipedality, and flexible limbs. Many of these features have been consistently found to elicit mentalizing of animals (Herzog, 2010; Horowitz & Bekoff, 2007; Eddy, Gallup, & Povinelli, 1993).

There is a great deal of evidence that animals' physical features influence their popularity with human beings. In an interesting experiment by Sarah Batt (2009), participants were presented with pictures of 40 different species and were asked to rank how much they liked each species in comparison to all the others. Batt also created a ranking of each species according to its biological similarity to humans (using a combination of behavioral, ecological, and anatomical information about each species). She then mapped people's preferences for each species onto the species' biological similarity to humans. The correlation between the two was moderately high ($r = .542$, $p < .01$), indicating that biological similarity did influence general preferences.

Another relevant and clever study comes from Hecht and Horowitz (2015), in which participants were shown 80 sets of two nearly identical dog images and had to choose which they liked best. One of the images in each set was manipulated to enhance certain facial features but not enough for participants to realize what the difference was between the images. Participants showed a preference for dogs with a larger "smile" that resembled that of human beings, as well as dogs with colored irises, large eyes, and a larger space between their eyes. Dogs with these features were selected more than their unaltered versions, indicating an anthropocentric bias. Consistent with this, Protopopova et al. (2012) found that people's ranking of a shelter dog's attractiveness predicted whether it had been successfully rehomed. One would expect, in light of Hecht and Horowitz's experiment, that dogs' human-like physical features are what led people to find them attractive and what made them more likely to be adopted.

Some of the best evidence for the existence of an anthropocentric bias comes from zoos. Relatively large surveys conducted with children at zoos over 40 years ago (Morris, 1961; Surinova, 1971) found that mammals generally, and primates specifically, were the most popular animals (consistent with Horowitz and Bekoff's claim). Reptiles, rodents, and insects were consistently ranked as the least popular. More recently, Moss and Esson (2010) found that mammals typically attract more attention than other taxa at zoos, as measured by attendance and the amount of time spent at each animal exhibit. Clayton, Fraser, and Burgess (2011) also found that people who perceived greater similarity between themselves and animals at zoos were more likely to express interest in animals in both captivity and the wild.

Evidence of anthropocentrism can also be seen in zoos' selection of animals. There has been discussion within the zoo world recently that zoo collections do not carry as many endangered animals as they very easily could (Martin et al., 2014). Instead, zoo collections seem to reflect human preferences. For instance, Frynta and colleagues (2010, 2013) found that people's ranking of an animal's beauty, as well as the animal's body size, were good predictors of whether that animal species would be found in zoos.

So it seems that there is clearly an anthropocentric bias in our preferences for animals. But what impact does this bias have on mentalizing and moral status judgments? First, let's consider two illuminating studies conducted by Clive Phillips and colleagues (these studies are also summarized in Kasperbauer, 2017). Phillips and McCulloch (2005) surveyed people from a large cross-national sample about their views on the sentience of various animal species. People were asked to rate the degree to which each species could feel pain, happiness, fear, and boredom, in comparison to normal adult human beings. Their responses were then combined to create an aggregate sentience score. The final rankings, across all countries, went in the following order: monkey, dog, newborn human, fox, pig, chicken, rat, fish. On the high end, monkeys, dogs, and newborn babies were judged to be about 80% as sentient as normal adult human beings. At the bottom end, chickens and rats were judged to be about 60% and fish 47% as sentient as normal adult human beings. This study clearly indicates that sentience ratings are influenced by our anthropocentric bias.

Phillips et al. (2012) conducted a similar study in which people were asked to rank different animals according to their general capacity to possess feelings (but without specifying individual emotional states). This too involved a large cross-cultural sample, including people from China, the Czech Republic, Great Britain, Iran, Ireland, South Korea, Macedonia, Norway, Serbia, Spain, and Sweden. They did not rank according to percentages, however, but simply by order of ability. The results were thus a relative ranking, indicating animals' sentience compared to other species.

Human infants were included in the sample and were on average ranked above all other animals. The only exceptions were Swedish and Chinese participants, who thought chimpanzees and dogs, respectively, were the most capable of possessing feelings. Following human infants, the average rankings of each species (out of 11) across all countries were as follows: chimpanzee (9.7), dog (9.5), dolphin (8.6), cat (7.7), horse (7.2), cattle (5.5), pig (5.2), rat (4.8), chicken (3.8), octopus (2.7), and fish (2.6). Some tendencies are evident here. Chimps and human infants were clustered together at the very top; chickens, octopuses, and fish all tended to be seen as the least capable of feelings; and cattle and pigs tended toward the middle. These results closely mirror those from Phillips and McCulloch (2005). No formal analysis was conducted in these studies comparing sentience ratings to biological similarity, but the general primate/mammal bias is evident.

To see the implications of this research for moral status judgments, let's look more closely at the combined results. Rats and fish are at the bottom of both scales and in contemporary society are arguably treated without moral concern. Rats, for instance, are widely used in scientific experiments, and in the United States their welfare in these experiments is not protected in the same ways as other animals (because they are not covered by the Animal Welfare Act). Moving to the middle we see pigs, chicken, and cattle. These animals are typically treated with some degree of concern, usually as livestock. For instance, all Western industrialized nations have welfare requirements that must be followed when rearing these animals for consumption. There is some dispute, particularly in the United States, whether these guidelines are sufficient and whether they are adequately monitored; but that the regulation exists at all indicates that they receive some degree of moral concern. They lack the moral significance of primates and companions, however. Dogs and primates were at the top of both scales, which is exactly what would be predicted from the other studies mentioned above. These animals are typically treated better than livestock, for instance, in that their deaths have greater moral significance. Having to put down a family pet is typically considered a tragedy, and some zoos have avoided culling primate species due to public outcry (Kasperbauer & Sandøe, 2016). This makes sense, given the sentience ratings observed here.

There are numerous other experiments that illustrate an anthropocentric bias in our treatment of non-humans. Westbury and Neumann (2008), for instance, found that empathic emotional responses to animals in abusive situations increased according to phylogenetic similarity (as measured by survey as well as skin conductance responses). In a similar experiment, Plous (1993) showed participants pictures of a monkey, raccoon, pheasant, and bullfrog and told them that each animal had been abused in certain ways. Skin conductance measurements detected increased activity in response to the animals' similarity to humans. This is also evident in people's allocation of punishment for animal abuse. In one experiment (Allen et al., 2002), people read about abuse of a goose, monkey, possum, or lizard. They were then asked how much punishment they would give the transgressor. Those who scored highest in empathy gave out harsher punishments, which the results showed were further mediated by similarity to humans. Some people did indeed express moral concern for animals, but this was limited to species nearest to us, most notably the primates.

It seems then that we have a bias toward animals that look and act like us. This bias affects a wide range of attitudes, including our preferences for animals, the mental states we attribute them, and our treatment of them as well. This narrows the types of animals that will be attributed phenomenal states and, as a result, also narrows which animals will be judged morally considerable. To be clear, this does not refute the phenomenal account in any way. The link between phenomenal states and moral status judgments is still very much central. The claim here is that phenomenal states are primarily attributed to animals that look and act like human beings, which therefore limits which animals will be seen as deserving the most basic forms of moral concern.

4.3 DEHUMANIZATION AND USING ANIMALS

Besides animals' physical features, various uses we put animals to also trigger dehumanization processes that affect the mental states and moral status we assign animals. To simplify the analysis, I will focus on two common ways of using animals: as food and as companions.

4.3.1 Mentalizing Food

Categorizing an animal as consumable—existing primarily to be eaten—influences the mental states we attribute them. For example, people who eat meat and animal products attribute fewer secondary emotions to animals (e.g., guilt, regret, nostalgia, melancholy) than those who do not eat meat and do not eat any animal products (Bilewicz, Imhoff, & Drogosz, 2011). Meat-eaters also seem to ascribe fewer mental states to a wide range of animals—not just those they eat—and see fewer animals as deserving moral concern than those who do not eat meat (Piazza et al., 2015).

This does not seem to be specific to heavy meat-eaters but is a general psychological connection people make between mental abilities and edibility. For instance, Bastian, Loughnan, Haslam, and Radke (2012) asked people to rate the extent to which each of 32 animals possessed a mix of phenomenal and agential states. They were also asked how willing they would be to eat each animal and whether they thought eating the animal would be morally wrong. These spanned a wide range of taxa, including mammals, birds, fish, amphibians, reptiles, and insects. Animals that were seen as possessing more mental states were considered less edible, and it was also seen as more morally wrong to eat these animals (for a concise review of the psychology of meat-eating, see Loughnan, Bastian, & Haslam, 2014).

So what's the explanation for this? Arguably the leading explanation for this type of phenomenon is what is known as "cognitive dissonance." The theory of cognitive dissonance was originally developed and formulated by Leon Festinger (1957, 1964). The basic psychological event consists of an aversive affective state that arises when an individual attempts to simultaneously hold inconsistent expectations or beliefs. When dissonance arises, the unpleasantness of the state motivates people to change their beliefs and expectations so that they become consistent (Gawronski, 2012; Harmon-Jones & Mills, 1999).

With respect to consuming animals, one of the main sources of dissonance comes in simultaneously believing 1) beings that can experience pain, suffering, and other phenomenal states should not be eaten and 2) animals are the sorts of beings that possess these mental states. In order to reduce the dissonance between these two beliefs, people must either stop eating animals or attribute fewer mental states to them. Difficulty arises, however, if people have previously consumed meat or used animal products or have grown up in a society where using animals is common. These beliefs tend to take priority when resolving dissonance, providing an "anchor" for people in evaluating other beliefs. As a result, it is psychologically easier to reduce dissonance by denying that animals possess mental states than it is to reject one's history and culture. Though not a direct result of dehumanization, cognitive dissonance is clearly related to many of the dehumanization processes discussed in the last chapter. Harming members of one's ingroup, for instance, is incompatible with how ingroup members should be treated; doing so would create dissonant thoughts. Placing animals in an outgroup, or making it clear that they are beneath humans in some way, makes it psychologically easier to put them to various uses.

Let's review some of the main sources of evidence for a dissonance-based explanation for reduced mental state attribution. First, let's consider evidence for the basic connection suggested above—that attributing mental states to animals conflicts with consuming them. Ruby and Heine (2012) conducted a study with people from Canada, Hong Kong, India, and the United States. Their main task asked participants to rank the mental states and physical appearance of a number of animals. They also asked participants to express their willingness to eat each animal and how disgusted they felt at the thought of eating them. Their central finding was that the *order* of these tasks had a significant impact on the mental states attributed to animals. If people first ranked animals' mental states, they were as a result less willing to eat animals and reported more disgust at the thought of eating them (compared to when the ranking task came last). Dissonance seemed to have arisen simply from going through the process of attributing mental states to animals. Participants seemed to have reasoned, "I have already said that this animal can think and feel, and I wouldn't eat something that can do that."

A number of studies have shown that the opposite relationship exists as well: identifying an animal as food reduces the mental states it is attributed. Let's look at three interesting studies by Steve Loughnan, Brock Bastian, and their collaborators that have illuminated the role of cognitive dissonance in reducing the mental states attributed to animals we eat. The first comes from a study by Bratanova, Loughnan, and Bastian (2011), which showed that humans' role in killing animals isn't nearly as instrumental in creating dissonance as is identifying an animal as a food item. They provided American participants with a description of the Bennett's tree kangaroo, which is native to Papua New Guinea. Being told that the kangaroos were used as food by local people decreased the amount of suffering participants attributed to the kangaroos, but being told that the locals played a role in their deaths had no effect. So even if locals only consumed kangaroos opportunistically (collecting them when they died from falling out of trees), people saw the kangaroos as less capable of suffering than if they were not used for food at all. This also had an effect on the moral concern expressed for kangaroos. When kangaroos were seen as less capable of suffering, people were less willing to say the kangaroos deserved moral treatment.

The role of dissonance here is admittedly indirect. The participants themselves are not involved in consuming tree kangaroos. One might think that they should be more affected by what seems to be the most morally relevant action—killing animals. But that's not what happened. Instead, people seemed to struggle more with the thought that an animal with thoughts and feelings would be used for food. An animal's status as food meant that the cause of its death was relatively unimportant. More important to participants—even though they were not the ones eating kangaroo—was resolving the discomfort of thinking that an animal with feelings was consumable.

Viewing animals as food items also seems to affect how people see animals generally. A widely cited study by Loughnan, Haslam, and Bastian (2010) induced dissonance by asking one group of participants to eat beef jerky while another group ate cashews. After eating the food, they were given a list of 27 animals and asked to "indicate those animals that you feel morally obligated to show concern for." Those who ate the jerky identified fewer animals ($M = 13.5$) than those who ate cashews ($M = 17.3$). Eating meat reduced *general* concern for animals.

Like the tree kangaroo study, the role of dissonance is somewhat unclear here since the animals being assessed in the study were not the ones being consumed by participants. Another part of the experiment, however, provides a more direct demonstration of the role of dissonance. Since participants were told they were eating *beef* jerky, in another task they were shown an image of a cow in a pen and asked to rate the cow's ability to experience a range of mental states. They were also asked whether the cow deserved "moral treatment." Though participants in both the jerky and the cashew conditions reported that the cow deserved moral treatment, those in the cashew condition granted greater moral concern than those in the jerky condition ($M = 6.08$ compared to $M = 5.57$, on a 7-point scale). No significant relationships were observed between mental states and moral status of the cow. However, there was a positive correlation between eating the jerky, attribution of phenomenal states to the cow, and the number of animals identified as deserving moral concern in the first task. That is, those who were induced to express moral concern for fewer animals (by eating jerky) tended to see the cow as less capable of phenomenal states.

This study indicates that eating beef jerky creates dissonance that reduces the mental states attributed to the type of animal being consumed, which in turn reduces moral concern for the animal, and also seems to decrease concern for animals generally. Bastian, Loughnan, Haslam, and Radke (2012) replicated these results with an interesting twist on the methodology. First they replicated the general phenomenon we have been discussing: simply describing a cow or a sheep as being raised for slaughter (compared to living in a pen with other animals) led people to see cattle/

sheep as less capable of having mental states. In another task, participants were asked to describe the processes involved in bringing beef or lamb to grocery stores. In one condition they were told they would be asked to eat pieces of meat, while in another condition they were told they would be eating fruit. Bastian et al. found that, as expected, writing about rearing animals for slaughter led to fewer ascriptions of mental states to cows and sheep but *only* for those who expected to eat meat. Those who expected to eat fruit showed no effect.

A good explanation for these results is that eating meat created a psychological conflict. Those who were preparing to eat fruit did not experience the conflict, even though they had written about the processes involved in meat production and animal slaughter. Presumably writing about meat production created some degree of discomfort since the participants in the study claimed to be meat-eaters. But the possibility of actually consuming meat was much more significant, providing a situation where people felt the need to attribute less of a mental life to cows and sheep, in order to reduce dissonant thoughts.

These three experiments provide strong support for the role played by meat—and seeing animals as meat—in leading people to attribute less mentality to animals. These experiments do not, however, look directly at what people think about the moral status of eating meat. Participants in these studies do make the general connection predicted by the phenomenal account of mentalizing: namely, that animals possessing phenomenal states are less suitable for consumption. But these studies tell us relatively little about whether carnivorism, as such, creates dissonant thoughts.

One final study that addressed this question comes from Rothgerber (2014). He found that simply reading a story about a vegetarian affected people's attitudes toward animals. Compared to a control condition, people who read about someone who avoids meat for moral and health reasons were more likely to say that a wide range of mental states were unique to human beings (e.g., nostalgia, self-control, and melancholy). A dissonance-based explanation for this is that vegetarians remind those who eat meat that they might be doing something bad. Because people like to see themselves in a good light, the existence of someone who chooses not to eat meat for moral reasons creates dissonance, leading them to search for justifying reasons for eating meat.

Whether the vegetarian was described as consistent or not also had interesting effects. If the vegetarian was consistent in his or her food habits and never ate meat, participants reported eating less meat in their own diet. However, this also had the effect of increasing participants' score on a measure of their beliefs about the moral justification for meat. After reading about a consistent vegetarian, participants were more likely to agree with statements like "It violates human destiny and evolution to give up eating meat" and "Meat tastes too good to worry about what all the critics say." Consistent vegetarians posed a psychological threat to participants, such that they wanted to distance themselves from eating meat while also justifying the use and consumption of animals and animal products.

The reason for choosing vegetarianism also mattered to participants. People seemed more threatened if vegetarianism was chosen for moral and health reasons than if it was necessary because of a food allergy. Confronting vegetarianism that was a result of choice made people more likely to deny that animals can feel pain and more likely to approve of the process of meat preparation, agreeing with the statement "Meat is processed so that animal pain and discomfort is minimized and avoided." It also made people more likely to approve of the nutritional value of meat, agreeing with statements like "Meat is essential for strong muscles."

These studies provide good evidence that eating animals and attributing them mental states are psychologically incompatible and, as a result, create cognitive dissonance. To alleviate the dissonance, we dehumanize animals, in order to emphasize their inferior status. Once we've convinced ourselves that animals are not "like us" in any relevant sense, it becomes much easier to use them as food.

4.3.2 Companionship and Mental States

In the last chapter I suggested that the animals we live with as companions are granted honorary ingroup status among human beings. Even if they do not look or act like human beings, they possess other features that lead us to judge them positively. For example, the features that make them "cute" (e.g., large eyes) are also what lead us to judge that they possess warmth (according to Susan Fiske's dimensions of warmth and competence).

If this is right, we should expect pets to be attributed mental states and be assigned moral status consistent with human ingroups. One experiment in support of this comes from Angantyr, Eklund, and Hansen (2011). They presented participants with a story describing a situation in which a man, woman, cat, or dog had been found lying on a street with broken ribs and a punctured lung. In other conditions, the same situation was described but for a human child, a human infant, and a puppy. Participants were then asked to rate 16 emotions they were feeling toward the target. One of these emotions was empathy, which is generally taken as an indicator of emotion sharing between two agents and is also known to be preferentially attuned to members of one's ingroup (Kasperbauer, 2015b). Empathy for humans and animals across conditions was positively correlated, which suggests that people did not discriminate against animals based on their outgroup status; if they empathized with one group, they also empathized with the other. The researchers also found a partiality effect for empathy: parents showed more empathy for infants, and pet-owners showed more empathy for puppies. This difference did not show up for the adult pets or for the human child. So not only were dogs and cats treated as ingroup members, but the animals with enhanced cuteness (puppies and infants) elicited particularly strong ingroup responses.

Other support for the ingroup status of pets comes from research on animal personality traits. A number of studies have found that animal behavior across many taxa can be understood in terms of consistent underlying psychological traits (Weiss, 2017). This is similar to long-standing research on human beings. Rankings of dogs and cats on the Big Five personality traits (neuroticism, openness, extraversion, conscientiousness, agreeableness), for instance, are consistent across multiple different types of judges, including the animals' owners, strangers, and animal behavior experts (Gosling, Kwan, & John, 2003). Personality traits of course have implications for the mental states attributed to animals, and likely impact our treatment of them as well.

The aspect of this research most pertinent here is the finding that we often project our own thoughts and feelings onto pets but that we do so in ways similar to when we project our thoughts and feelings onto other human beings. This further suggests that pets are treated as ingroup members. Kwan, Gosling, and John (2008), for instance, asked dog-owners at a dog park to evaluate the personality traits of other dogs and their owners, as well as their own dogs. These included questions about, among other things, their kindness, sympathy, warmth, anxiety, creativity, and intelligence. They also completed a test measuring their own personality traits. Although there was evidence that dog-owners tended to project their own traits onto their dogs, this was not significantly different from the projections made onto other dog-owners.

A related, surprising result from recent research is that attributions of guilt to dogs seem to be largely a projection of human feelings. It is often thought that dogs express specific behaviors indicating that they feel bad about having done something wrong. However, in experimental settings, dogs who have committed a misdeed (e.g., eating food they were instructed not to eat) do not seem to act significantly different from obedient dogs (e.g., those who did not eat the food they were told not to eat). What seems to matter more is the behavior of the owner. In Horowitz's (2009) study, for instance, some owners were falsely told that their dogs had misbehaved. These dogs expressed more "guilty" behavior after their owners scolded them than the dogs that actually misbehaved but received no scolding. So it seems that "guilty" behavior is more a response to owners' reactions than to dogs' causal role in creating a certain outcome (also see Hecht, Miklosi, & Gacsi, 2012).

More direct evidence that this involves projection of human feelings onto dogs comes from Brown and McLean (2015). They asked people to read descriptions of dog behavior that were ambiguous but could be interpreted as depicting guilt (e.g., avoiding eye contact after knocking over and breaking a plate). Participants were also given standard measures of their own disposition to feel guilt. The results showed that those who were prone to feel guilt were more likely to interpret the ambiguous behaviors as depicting guilt.

These studies are important for two reasons. One is that they suggest that dogs are treated as ingroup members. Their behavior is interpreted as expressing the familiar human emotion of guilt, despite apparent ambiguity. The second is that this has implications for our treatment of animals. Attributing guilt to dogs sometimes involves punishment and is in many cases likely central to the dog–owner relationship. Projecting guilt onto dogs may thus lead to poorer treatment and in some cases negative welfare. This is not specific to guilt, however. There are presumably numerous other emotions projected onto dogs, some of which could have positive implications for their treatment. For example, suppose that what has been found with guilt is also found for dogs' "happy" behavior. The sorts of things people do for dogs that produce what is interpreted as happiness might improve dogs' well-being, regardless of whether they are founded on inaccurate or exaggerated interpretations.

In addition to suggesting that pets and other companion animals are considered honorary ingroup members, the previous chapter suggested that becoming close with animals presents a psychological threat. This is particularly true when we bring animals into close physical contact with ourselves. We have a natural defense reaction to the presence of animals that requires us to demean them and make their subhuman status clear. So even though pets are granted ingroup status, they will still be infrahumanized.

One piece of evidence for this is that pets are often mistreated. For instance, dog abuse and abandonment is still quite high in the United States, despite overall positive attitudes toward dogs. Throughout the 1980s and 1990s, an estimated 12–20 million dogs and cats were euthanized every year in the United States, a rate that has decreased only recently to around 3–4 million (HSUS, 2014). Some are euthanized on welfare grounds (e.g., to prevent extreme suffering), but a significant number are euthanized for no reason except that their owners could not keep them and shelters could not (or would not) find a home for them.

We can also see this in the effects of mortality salience on attitudes toward pets. The experiment by Beatson et al. (2009) discussed in the last chapter found that people treated their pets differently depending on the level of mortality salience and "animal threat" they experienced. When thinking about something that involved no animal threat, like giving a speech, reading about human–animal similarities actually improved people's attitudes toward pets. They were, for instance, more likely to say that pets deserve to be pampered. Emphasizing human–animal similarities had the opposite effect, though, if people read about death. Reading about death combined with thinking about human–animal similarities led to more *negative* attitudes toward pets.

The explanation for this, as mentioned previously, is that all of these factors pose animal-related threats. To spell this out, there is a threat from

1) treating pets as if they were special in ways that humans are special, 2) thinking of non-humans as similar to humans, and 3) thinking of death, which activates the same threat response system as animal threats. So while companions receive positive mental state attributions, as a result of being seen as ingroup members, their ingroup status can also pose a threat, leading to negative mental state attributions. Where and when this occurs are relatively unexplored, however, in the empirical literature.

4.4 CONCLUSION

This chapter wraps up a discussion begun in the introduction to the book about the ways in which we compare ourselves to animals. The psychology of dehumanization and infrahumanization alters how we view animals, particularly through the mental states and moral status we assign them. Sometimes this leads us to deny a degree of moral concern for animals, like when we justify our consumption of them by attributing them fewer mental states. Other times this leads us to treat them well, by taking them into our homes and treating them as members of our family. Even in this latter case, however, we take actions to emphasize their inferior status. This is one of the main consequences of the psychology of infrahumanization, which is at the heart of our relationship with animals.

One might wonder, however, how exactly the psychological factors identified thus far relate to moral psychology more broadly. Thinking about animals is of course not the only thing we do in our moral lives, and many of the phenomena described are not obviously related to moral attitudes at all. This chapter has introduced one general psychological process—mentalizing—and discussed the way it relates to moral attitudes toward animals. But there are many others. Rather than canvass them all, in the next chapter I look specifically at psychological processes that pose *obstacles* to moral thinking and explain how they might apply to thinking specifically about animals.

Chapter 5

Diagnosing Moral Failures

The story of human morality is a story of failure. Moral change (on basically any metric) is slow and occurs piecemeal, almost never yielding where we most expect or desire. This may sound bleak, but it is difficult to see any way of escaping this conclusion.

The reality of moral failure must be explained and accounted for. The previous chapters have provided more than enough reasons to suspect that moral change involving attitudes to animals will be difficult. More will be said in chapters 7 and 8 about how these obstacles might be overcome. The task here is to lay out some basic features of moral psychology that are not specific to animals but are important for understanding why our treatment of them does not change in the ways we desire.

The factors identified here are not uniformly prohibitive—sometimes they can indeed facilitate moral change—but nonetheless present major obstacles in our moral lives. By "moral failures" I generally mean that these factors make it difficult for people to act or change, either in the ways desired by agents themselves or in the ways prescribed to them by others. Moral prescriptions can come from friends, politicians, professional ethicists, or whoever has an interest in changing moral behavior. Even with determined effort from these people, or from agents themselves, the factors identified present obstacles to change.

5.1 MORAL EMOTIONS

The main obstacle to moral change is that much of our thinking—moral and otherwise—lies outside our conscious awareness. This is not to say, however, that if we were aware of *everything* that was happening in our brains, we would thereby be capable of moral change; automatized unconscious processing is in fact good for many things, and conscious reflection often leads to disaster. But increased control and cognizance of our unconscious processing would undoubtedly make certain types of change easier. As a consequence of our unconscious lives, we often lack control over things we would very much like to change and sometimes don't even understand the content of our own thoughts and beliefs.

One of the best examples of this is implicit bias. Research in psychology has shown, for instance, that people will express negative attitudes toward races that are different from their own, even though they claim (genuinely, it seems) that their real attitude is quite the opposite (e.g., Jost et al., 2009). These and other examples will be explored first by looking at the role of emotions and situational variables in moral psychology. These factors are grouped together because they are pervasive, often operate below conscious awareness, and are difficult to control.

5.1.1 The Unconscious and the Recalcitrant

There is no question that emotions play a strong role in moral psychology (Huebner, Dwyer, & Hauser, 2009). Emotions are observed prior to, concurrent with, and immediately after making moral judgments (Prinz, 2006). They also amplify and strengthen moral judgments (Avramova & Inbar, 2013; Guiseppe, Claus, & Singer, 2012). There is little question, at least among researchers working in the brain sciences, that a great deal of emotional processing occurs unconsciously. Gantman and Van Bavel (2015) recently proposed that moral thinking should be viewed as analogous to sense perception. Like stimuli affecting touch, taste, or vision, moral stimuli can influence the way we see the world as a whole, independent from cognitive reflection about morality. Much of their evidence comes from research on emotions. We cannot, without instruments, detect when or how emotions are being processed, nor are we directly aware of when they affect our behaviors. Emotions are not unique in this respect. They are just one of many types of information that have evolved to operate automatically, without requiring any cognitive or conscious control (Carlson et al., 2014; Dijksterhuis & Aarts, 2010; Winkielman & Berridge, 2004).

There are two important features of emotions that indicate why they pose obstacles to moral change:

(1) Emotions are *intransigent*: they often do not change easily.

(2) Emotions are *subtle*: their effects are difficult to detect, and in particular their long-term consequences for moral behavior are often surprising.

Underlying both of these features is the fact that emotions are resistant to our rational control. Emotions are often automatic responses that occur without any input from conscious reflection. Even when they are not so encapsulated—say, when unconscious emotional processing has effects on conscious emotions—we lack the ability to simply modify our conscious emotions through private reflection, at least not in a way that would have a substantial impact on the underlying response.

Situational variables possess similar features as emotions, though these will not be addressed directly until after we plunge a bit deeper into the psychology of emotions. But just to preview the eventual conclusion: situational variables are also subtle, and though situations themselves are not always intransigent, the effects they have on us are. What's more, situations often have an impact through emotions. The relationship between emotions and situations partly explains why they both have these features. People have relatively stable emotional responses, for instance, when situations remain stable. More on this in a bit.

These features of emotions have long been recognized by psychologists and neuroscientists. Many philosophers first became aware of research on the relationship between emotions and morality from Jonathan Haidt's (2001) classic paper, which argued (among other things) that emotional responses drive moral reasoning. Perhaps the most memorable aspect of Haidt's paper is its synthesis of previous decades of research. Haidt drew a thread unifying his own research and many other classic studies back to Zajonc's (1980) paper on "affective primacy." Though relatively controversial at the time, the idea of "affective primacy" has become a central piece of social psychology and much of cognitive neuroscience. Zajonc's basic idea was that emotional input always takes priority over other types of informational processing. Given the way emotions have evolved, the way they mature in human beings, and the way emotions are processed throughout the central nervous system, we should expect that other types of information processing, like high-level cognition, will follow in the steps of emotions and yield to them when there are conflicts.

Some of the best evidence for affective primacy comes from research showing that emotional stimuli elicit a rapid response, even when presented subconsciously. For instance, one of the most salient types of emotional stimuli for human beings are other human faces (Axelrod, Bar, & Rees, 2015). The emotion system detects signals produced by human facial expressions easier than many other signals, and when it does it activates a swift response. For instance, we have long known that flashing images of smiling faces or faces with a furrowed brow (indicating anger) to people will activate brain regions responsible for emotion processing (Whalen et al., 1998). Smiling faces that are shown for only 30 milliseconds (.03 seconds) will also elicit activity in the zygomatic major of the perceiving subject within 1 second after being shown (Dimberg et al., 2000). The zygomatic major is a muscle in the face responsible for producing the smile, indicating that even very simple facial expressions can quickly elicit a reaction in human perceivers.

Presenting facial expressions faster than can be consciously detected also has effects on broader types of behavior. Winkielman and Berridge (2004) report an experiment in which the presentation of smiling faces made people drink more water immediately after, even though the participants did not report any change in their emotions. Their explanation for this is that the emotion system interprets social signals, like happiness, as indicating things that would be good for us, even when the signals are received unconsciously.

5.1.2 Automatic Influences on Morality

The primacy of emotions has been studied in a number of ways in relation to morality. Most recent discussion among philosophers has focused almost exclusively on research by Jonathan Haidt and Joshua Greene. This narrow focus is unfortunate since it has led philosophers to overlook a lot of interesting research. The discussion of Haidt and Greene will thus be brief.

Haidt is arguably best known for his research on "moral dumbfounding" (Haidt, 2001). The basic finding of this research is that people's immediate reactions to moral wrongdoing, which are plausibly driven by emotions, have a strong influence on their subsequent moral reasoning. This leads people to staunchly defend their initial reactions, instead of reconsidering their merit or revising them in light of new information. Greene's research is complementary to Haidt's. Greene et al. (2001) found, through functional magnetic resonance imaging (fMRI), that people's immediate reactions to moral dilemmas were correlated with brain areas responsible for emotional processing, while areas responsible for working memory were correlated with slower and possibly more reflective responses. Haidt and Greene's research programs are both frequently taken to show that emotions control a great deal of our moral lives, including parts often thought to be more dispassionate and controlled by reason. More will be said in a bit about disputes over this research. Since these studies are well-worn, though, let's turn to other research on the role of emotions.

Recently the intransigence and subtlety of human psychological processes have been discussed in reference to "dual process" theories of the mind (often described in terms of dual "systems"). One of these systems, System 1, is fast and automatic. The other, System 2, is slower and often characterized as more reflective. The types of emotional processes we are focusing on here are often associated with the automaticity of System 1 thinking (Evans & Stanovich, 2013; Kahneman, 2011; Sloman, 1996). There are many well-known criticisms of dual process theories (e.g., Keren & Schul, 2009; Kruglanski & Gigerenzer, 2011). However, these criticisms do not question the main principles discussed here: they do not question that some processes are fast and unconscious, nor do they question that attempts are made to control these fast judgments but often fail (though see Newell & Shanks, 2014).

System 1 has been described by many (including Greene and Haidt) as presenting a challenge to moral thinking. We do not have to appeal to dual process theories to see why. System 1 processes operate quickly and independently of rational control, influencing behavior in ways we often do not realize. No matter how many other systems there are, they all will be competing with System 1 processes. It has also been argued that System 1 is our default mode of thinking. The suggested reason for this is that we are "cognitive misers": we don't think about something unless we have to (Kahneman, 2011; Stanovich, 2010). Instead, we use heuristics to solve problems quickly and easily (Sunstein, 2005). These are thought to be largely driven by System 1 processes.

There is also general recognition, among dual process theorists, that attempts to control System 1 processes often fail. Positing a slower, more reflective system is often meant to capture the range of processes that attempt to do this. System 1 operates automatically, without *requiring* input from System 2 (or slower processes generally); but System 2 will attempt to intervene in System 1 processes when there is reason to think that System 1 might make mistakes (Evans & Stanovich, 2013). But research has shown that we often fail to sufficiently control System 1 processes. We might do this by failing to identify mistakes in System 1 processes, identifying mistakes but failing to activate a correction response, failing to fully suppress System 1 mistakes, or suppressing System 1 mistakes but failing to provide any other correction (Stanovich, 2010, pp. 99–100). So not only are System 1 processes given some psychological priority, but they are difficult to control once enacted.

Though System 1 thinking often serves as a useful guide, it can also lead to obviously incorrect conclusions with potentially disastrous consequences. One of the best sources of evidence for this is the literature on risk perception. Classic research by Paul Slovic has shown that people tend to determine the likelihood and potential impact of risks based largely on emotional responses (Slovic & Peters, 2006). One way this "affect heuristic" operates is by crudely leading people to see a risk as uniformly positive or negative, depending on their emotional response to the risk. For instance, if people have an overall positive feeling when they think about a risky event, they assume that the consequences of that event coming about will be uniformly positive—that only benefits could come from it, and nothing harmful. The opposite occurs if they have a negative feeling toward the risk. It has also been suggested that System 2 processes are generally inadequate in controlling this bias. Tests of intelligence, for instance—which are thought to measure System 2 capacity—indicate a positive correlation between intelligence and the tendency to view risks as uniformly negative (not involving any benefits; Stanovich, 2010, p. 133).

An illustration of the affect heuristic, with implications for attitudes toward animals, comes from Siegrist and Sütterlin (2014). They had participants read a story about an oil spill that killed 1,200 birds, which resulted either from a human cause (drilling) or a natural cause (cracks in rock formations). Participants were asked what sorts of emotions they felt as a result of the event (positive or negative). They were also asked how bad they thought it was that so many birds died and how much animal suffering they thought was caused by the oil spill. The results showed that answers to all three questions varied according to condition, indicating that the causal role of human beings made people feel worse, made the event itself worse, and increased animal suffering. Moreover, further statistical analysis found that negative emotions mediated people's judgment of the badness of the event and the amount of suffering involved. That is, people felt worse about the oil spill when it was human-caused, which led to more severe ratings of things that would seem to be equal between the cases. This heuristic clearly led to implausible conclusions. There's no reason to think that the amount of animal suffering, for instance, would be worse just because it was human-caused.

This is not directly an illustration of how moral change is difficult but rather that our attitudes toward animal suffering are clearly influenced by factors of which we are not fully aware. To probe deeper into the role of emotions in moral psychology, let's look more closely at a specific emotion.

5.1.3 Moral Disgust

The emotion that best exemplifies the features identified above (intransigence and subtlety) is disgust. Evidence has been steadily mounting over the last 10 years for the role of disgust in moral judgments (Chapman & Anderson, 2013; Kelly, 2011). There have been some significant challenges to the evidence (Kayyal et al., 2015; Landy & Goodwin, 2015; May, 2014), but none of the challenges have questioned that disgust plays a role in at least *some* important set of moral judgments.

The link between disgust and morality was first developed in Shweder et al. (1997) and Rozin et al.'s (1999) CAD theory of moral emotions. CAD stands for Community–Autonomy–Divinity and corresponds (coincidentally) to emotional responses of the same acronym, Contempt–Anger–Disgust. These emotions are hypothesized to be domain-specific: contempt is elicited by harms committed against the community, including violations of social hierarchies; moral anger functions as a response to harm done to individuals, primarily to oneself; and moral disgust is elicited when people feel as if they have somehow been contaminated by the deeds of others or by violations against the natural order of things. Though CAD is not the focus here, it continues to be influential on empirical research into morality (Hutcherson & Gross, 2011).

Another way of describing the function of moral disgust is that it responds to *purity* violations. For instance, in Haidt's research cited above, purity violations consisted of acts like eating off of a toilet, having sex with a dead chicken, and wearing a uniform once worn by Nazis. There is a great deal of evidence to support the role of disgust in responding to these sorts of purity violations. Horberg et al. (2009, 2011), for instance, found that reading about disgusting acts and watching disgusting video clips (e.g., involving fecal matter) increased disapproval of purity-related transgressions (e.g., having sex with a dead chicken) and increased approval of purity virtues (e.g., becoming a vegetarian). These purity-related transgressions had no impact on judgments concerning transgressions not related to purity (e.g., theft).

Purity violations are sometimes seen as *harmless* transgressions. There is some dispute over whether purity violations might implicitly involve harm (e.g., Gray, Schein, & Ward, 2014). But that the harm is seemingly indirect raises a puzzle: why are these actions moralized if they do not cause harm? I will not directly defend the claim that disgust responds to harmless moral transgression (I take up the issue again in chapter 7). But disgust does often lead us to disapprove of things that we do not, on reflection, actually disapprove of. And one plausible explanation for why we might disagree with our disgust-based judgments is that they do not actually track harm to other people. Disagreeing with one's disgust-based moral values is of course a problem for moral progress if disgust is difficult to modify.

Evidence to support the intransigence of disgust comes from Russell and Giner-Sorolla (2013). They argue that among the moral emotions, disgust may be the most difficult to modify. In one of their experiments, they compared the flexibility of disgust to moral anger (Russell & Giner-Sorolla,

2011). They presented participants with scenarios designed to elicit either disgust (eating a dog and a sexual relationship between people of very different ages) or anger (kicking a dog and abusing one's power in a workplace relationship). Afterward, participants filled out ratings of their moral judgment of the act as well as their level of anger and disgust and were asked to list things that could change their moral judgment. For instance, someone might think that kicking a dog is justifiable if doing so stopped the dog from attacking a young child or that eating a dog is justifiable in cases of extreme and otherwise inescapable hunger. Participants were asked to imagine that those changes had taken place and then filled out the emotion and moral judgment measures again, keeping those changes in mind. As a result of these imagined changes, anger was reduced, but not disgust. Moreover, the change in anger was positively correlated with a change in moral judgment. So not only was disgust unresponsive to justifying conditions, but any change in attitude was due primarily to a change in anger.

Eating one's dog is arguably unrepresentative of the range of people's disgust-based judgments concerning animals. But disgust does likely influence many of our judgments about which animals are appropriate to eat. As the evidence reviewed in chapter 2 indicated, our disgust response evolved primarily as a response to animal pathogens. One would thus expect that our judgments of which animals should be eaten, and whether animals should be eaten at all, will be largely determined by disgust. As Russell and Giner-Sorolla's research suggests, we should thus expect that these judgments will be difficult to modify.

There's no reason to dwell on this here, however. The intransigence and subtlety of emotions should be relatively clear. To further explore how emotions can present moral obstacles, we turn now to how emotions interact with situational factors.

5.2 EMOTIONS INTERACTING WITH SITUATIONS

Situationists in philosophy and psychology claim that the pervasive causal influence of situational factors speaks against a strong role for certain psychological traits in human behavior (most famously, within philosophy,

John Doris, 1998, 2002, 2010; and Gilbert Harman, 1999, 2009). Within philosophy, situationists have criticized virtue ethicists for adhering to an empirically indefensible conception of such traits. Situationists have claimed that the character traits thought to underlie virtues are not as broad or as behaviorally efficacious as they're supposed to be. However, situationism applies to many ethical theories, not just the psychological foundations of virtue ethics. Situational factors are often problematic for moral thinking because they are seemingly so trivial. They also interact with emotions in surprising ways. Together they form a strong challenge to the role of reason in guiding our moral lives.

5.2.1 Situationism Applied to Animals

There are numerous cases in the empirical literature of people being influenced by seemingly trivial situational factors to do things they otherwise disapprove of. One classic example comes from work derived from Stanley Milgram's famous shock experiments. In these experiments, participants were instructed to deliver increasingly painful shocks to someone who was ostensibly just another participant. Across a wide variety of different experimental conditions, people readily delivered the shocks, even when the target (who was actually a confederate enlisted by Milgram) explicitly asked not to continue and in some cases showed signs of harm, even apparent death.

Sheridan and King (1972) conducted a variation on this experiment in which they replaced the human confederate with a puppy. However, for this experiment, the puppy received *actual* shocks. Sheridan and King found that 77% of participants were willing to deliver shocks to the puppy. Though the shocks were deemed to be harmless, they were jolting enough to occasionally elicit howls from the puppy. Apparently, this was not enough to motivate people to desist from following the instructions to shock.

A common explanation for Milgram's results is that people readily conform to authority. People who have been brought into a laboratory environment are primed to follow instructions and submit to the authority of experimenters. They may also place particular trust in the experimenters as experts. As a result, participants readily follow directions that they would otherwise resist.

A similar explanation could be applied to the puppy experiment: the authoritative structure of an experimental setting may have made it easier for people to deliver shocks to the puppy. One might think that these circumstances are too artificial to have relevance to real-life behaviors. However, one can see similar authoritative structures in many industries where animals are often said to be treated cruelly (e.g., in laboratories and in intensive livestock production). And if people cannot overcome situational factors to respond to actual puppy howls in an experimental setting, we probably cannot expect them to overcome real-life situational factors to respond to animal harms that are likely less vivid and less personally relevant.

5.2.2 Predicting Emotions Within Situations

The Milgram experiment is just one of many experiments illustrating that trivial situational factors influence our moral behavior—often not for the better. One of the leading explanations for why trivial situational factors are so powerful is that we struggle to anticipate how we will react when faced with moral decisions. Morality is a highly emotional enterprise, as discussed above, and what we think our future selves will do during more dispassionate moments just doesn't seem to correlate with what we actually do.

The general phenomenon of predicting one's behavior when emotions change, as a result of changing circumstances, is known as *affective forecasting*. Research on affective forecasting has found that people are generally poor at predicting their future emotional states. People struggle to accurately predict how they will feel in the future and subsequently how they will act (Miloyan & Suddendorf, 2015; Wilson & Gilbert, 2005). A classic example of this comes from Woodzicka and LaFrance (2001). They asked female college students to predict how they would respond if asked inappropriate questions during a job interview. These included questions about whether they were single, whether people find them desirable, and whether they thought women should wear bras to work: 28% of these students predicted they would either leave the interview or confront the interviewer for asking these questions, and 68% predicted they would refuse to answer at least one of the questions.

In a separate experiment, they conducted an *actual* interview using these questions (as well as others to make the interview seem realistic) with a different set of female college students (these students thought they were being interviewed for a research assistant position). The behavior observed in this realistic setting was very different from what women predicted in the previous experiment. Here *not a single* student refused to answer the offensive and inappropriate questions, compared to 68% in the previous experiment who said they would; 36% asked the interviewer why those questions were being asked, but none of these responses were confrontational; and 80% of those who inquired did not do so until the end of the interview.

The structure of an interview is arguably similar to an experimental setting like that described in Milgram's study. The interviewee, like the research subject, is in a position of subordination, which makes it more difficult to object when something is happening that people would disagree with outside of that context. However, again one might object that this is an artifact of unique situations—life is rarely like an interview. But this is shortsighted. We frequently confront events that elicit strong emotions. This is particularly the case when pursuing moral change. One need not see an interviewer as an authority figure to feel uncomfortable when voicing objections to his or her behavior. Responding to any question an interviewer asks—no matter how ridiculous—might just be seen as "the way things go." Many people likely have a similar reaction to the ways we treat animals. In more dispassionate moments, the status quo might seem an easy target for critique, and we might convince ourselves that we would speak against it if given the chance. But when actually faced with the task, our emotions dictate a different course of action.

Woodzicka and LaFrance's experiment illustrates that responding to others' moral behavior can be suppressed by situational factors. What about our own moral behavior? A number of experiments in the situationist literature indicate that our own moral behavior is similarly influenced by seemingly trivial external factors.

An illustrative example comes from a classic study by Batson et al. (1999). In this experiment, participants were asked to assign themselves and another participant to two different tasks, one of which provided the opportunity to win $30. They were also given a coin to help them make the decision fairly. Out of 40 participants 28 chose to flip the coin. However, only 4 of these 28 assigned the other participant to the money-making task. Assuming the coin was equally weighted, many of these people were clearly ignoring the coin flip in order to give themselves a chance to win money. This is somewhat surprising, given the relatively modest amount of money they could possibly win, as well as the fact that success was still far from guaranteed. Moreover, 24 of the 28 coin-flippers indicated afterward that they thought the coin flip was the fairest way of determining the task assignment. These people were, as Batson et al. state, "moral hypocrites."

Perhaps more interesting, however, were the results of a second experiment. They were able to replicate these results except among people who had a mirror placed in front of them during the experiment. Using mirrors and pictures of faces has been shown to prompt people to behave as if their actions were being monitored (see a review in Doris, 2015). Of 26 people who were facing a mirror, 10 chose to flip the coin, and of these, 5 assigned themselves to the money-making task and 5 assigned the other partici- pant. The mere addition of a mirror was enough to make people follow their own professed beliefs about what was fair.

This again shows that trivial situational factors impact our moral behavior. To bring it back to the role of emotions, a possible explanation for these results is that people do genuinely believe that flipping the coin is the right thing to do, but the possibility of losing the option of winning $30 is too emotionally aversive, leading them to ignore the results of the coin flip. Introducing a mirror somehow balances out this aversiveness (perhaps being observed doing the right thing makes us feel good).

A reaction one might have to this experiment is that people are tre- mendously stupid—why lie just in order to have a chance at winning $30? Affective forecasting research, however, suggests an alternative explana- tion: we are just very bad at monitoring our emotions. As a result, when faced with emotionally charged moral decisions, we act contrary to what we think we ought to do.

One final demonstration of affective forecasting, which also nicely depicts the interaction between emotions and situations, comes from Teper et al. (2015). In a series of experiments, Teper et al. asked partici- pants to perform long and boring math problems. Participants were told that they could find out the answer to the problems by pushing a button on their computers, but they were requested not to do so. They were also given a small incentive ($5) for getting more than 10 of the math problems correct.

Though they were asked not to cheat by pushing the button, participants did so, on average, 1.19 times. Some participants were also given false feedback about their heart rate, indicating either that they had a slow and steady heart rate or that they had an increased heart rate. These participants were also asked to predict how many times they thought they would cheat in the task. Participants who were told they had an increased heart rate were more accurate in their predictions of cheating—closer to the 1.19 average—than those who were told their heart rate was steady. Teper et al.'s explanation for this is that those who were given false feedback thereby became better at simulating how they would actually feel while completing the math questions and therefore were more accurate in their predictions.

Support for this came in another experiment they conducted in which participants consumed an herbal supplement. In one condition, they were told the supplement could cause jitteriness and anxiety, while in another condition, no possible side effects were described. Those who were told that the supplement would cause anxiety were more likely to push the button to reveal the answer, but they were also more likely to *predict* that they would push the button. Here again those who received false feedback, which led people to expect more intense emotional arousal, were better at predicting their future moral behavior.

Again, a likely explanation for this is that people realize to some extent that they act differently when in altered emotional states, particularly when they are feeling anxious. Normally people fail to realize that they will be in these emotional states when confronted with the decision to cheat (as illustrated in this experiment as well as Batson et al. above). The false feedback helps people better predict their future behavior by prompting them to expect an altered emotional state.

Without emotions we would be lost in making moral decisions. In some cases not feeling emotions, or not the right ones, does in fact hurt our decision-making. But as is hopefully now evident, subtle influence from emotions (and situational factors that operate through them) poses significant problems for improving our moral behavior.

5.2.3 The Power of Reason

The position just outlined on the role of emotions and situations in moral psychology is not new. It arguably represents a consensus view among researchers across the cognitive sciences. However, there are also many detractors from this position. There have been numerous critiques of the idea that emotions and situations undermine moral change. This opposition can roughly be summarized as claiming that people are sufficiently competent at controlling these factors through private reflection. There are reasons to disagree with this view, but more needs to be said about what these criticisms amount to and why they fail (a good discussion of these criticisms can be found in Doris, 2015, ch. 3).

None of the views discussed here deny that emotions play a strong role in our moral lives. Nor do they deny that emotions occasionally cause problems. They largely deny, rather, that emotions are intransigent. Advocates of these views see a larger role for reason in shaping our emotional responses, particularly with respect to moral behavior. To make sure nobody is being treated unfairly here, let's take some time to review a handful of the most prominent positions.

Some of the harshest critics of the role of emotions in moral psychology are neosentimentalists. Neosentimentalists are, at their core, sentimentalists: they think emotional responses are integral to moral judgments. However, they further think that emotions with *merit* are important, and this requires a regulative role for reason. Justin D'Arms (2005), for instance, says our emotions are "responsive to reason" (p. 10). He further claims that it is "not implausible" (D'Arms, 2013, p. 6) that we can develop control over our emotions. Other times (e.g., D'Arms & Jacobson, 2003, p. 144) neosentimentalists assert that we are capable of controlling our emotions to a sufficient degree, even while acknowledging that emotions are elicited automatically and frequently outside of conscious control.

Neosentimentalists have not put forth much effort in defending their position with empirical evidence, however. So let's look at other, more concrete proposals. The position most closely aligned with neosentimentalism comes from Cordelia Fine. Fine (2006) asserts that "the link from an automatic evaluation to a corresponding judgment—can be disrupted by controlled processes, in accordance with the individual's consciously held personal motivations or values" (p. 85). Kennett and Fine (2009) argue that this sort of intervention from reason is *required* for true moral judgments.

This position has been echoed by many others. Hanno Sauer (2011, 2012a, 2012b, 2014) has built a case for the role of reason in modifying our emotional responses. He, like Fine, accepts a strong role for emotions in moral psychology but nonetheless thinks private reflection is capable of having adequate influence on our moral lives. He thinks emotions do respond to reason, claiming "Although emotions are often beyond our rational control, they can still be rationally amenable" (2012b, p. 103). Sauer (2012a) characterizes the sort of position staked out above as the "automaticity challenge" to moral philosophy. He claims in reply to this challenge that automatic processes can also be rational, in that they reflect legitimate concerns. That a process is automatic does not mean that it is irrational. For instance, with respect to dual process theories (as described above), he claims that System 2 informs System 1 such that the content between them is roughly congruent.

More recently, Peter Railton (2014) has provided an account complementary to Fine and Sauer's. He argues that the emotions are part of "a flexible, experience-based information-processing system quite capable of tracking statistical dependencies and of guiding behavioral selection via the balancing of costs, benefits, and risks" (p. 833) and that "the affective system has come to be viewed, not in contrast to representational, cognitive, evaluative, and decisional capacities, or as disruptive of forward-looking cost-benefit calculation, but as an integral part of them" (p. 835). Emotion science provides a foundation for practical rationality, he thinks, because it has shown that emotions respond to environmental input and direct us accordingly. So our emotionally based moral intuitions, fast though they may be, are sufficiently rational. This is enough to give us reason to think we have "reliably good intuitions" (p. 840) in our moral lives. If Railton and the others are right, perhaps the factors identified thus far are not obstacles but instrumental to moral progress.

The problem with these proposals is that they lack evidence to support a *sufficient* role for reason. It is totally uncontroversial to claim that it is *possible* for intuitions to be modified through reason or to find cases where seemingly intransigent emotional responses did eventually yield to reason. But rare instances are not of much assistance if our goal is to improve ourselves.

What we need is evidence that the factors identified already can be modified with *regularity* and *efficacy*. In other words, we need to frequently make the changes we aim to make. This basic suggestion has also been made by Neil Levy (2006) in response to some of the above criticisms. He argues that it doesn't really matter if reason *can* play a regulative role if it never actually does so; automatic processes continue to do their thing. Moreover, he suggests, we need evidence that reason doesn't just reintroduce aspects of automatic responses that are thought to pose problems when meeting moral goals (like various biases). Replacing one unwanted automatic process with another would count as just another way that reason is inefficacious.

So what evidence do these different proposals offer for the role of reason? Fine (2006), as well as others, draws from research by Margo Monteith on the regulation of prejudice. Very briefly, this research has found that people's negative attitudes about others can indeed change. However, it also has found that this requires people to be highly motivated and to have significant assistance in making these changes.

This suggests a *resource* criterion: we need evidence that the identified factors can be modified with the resources normally available to people. This will of course vary across contexts, but what we need to ask ourselves is whether the resources in any situation are enough to overcome the factors already identified. There may be many cases where very strong implicit biases, for instance, can be overcome with vast resources, but this does not affect the claims made about obstacles to moral change. That an obstacle can be overcome with vast resources does not thereby make it less of an obstacle in normal circumstances.

Fine (2006) admits that attitude change requires substantial resources: "Where the individual is motivated to form accurate judgments, and has the attentional resources available to do so, automatic intuitions can be over-ridden and accurate judgments formed" (p. 97). Kennett and Fine (2009) make a similar claim: "while a person's incidental mood or emotional state can 'contaminate' her moral judgments . . . this bias can be corrected more or less accurately . . . when the individual's attention is drawn to their mood as a possible source of bias . . . or she is motivated to be accurate" (p. 88). Fine and colleagues conclude from this research that unwanted emotional influences can be overcome. But they do not address any of the criteria just mentioned: they do not ask whether these unwanted influences are corrected regularly or efficaciously or whether these resources are available to ordinary moral agents (e.g., how people would become informed about the source of various biases).

Many others have drawn from similar research as Fine in order to respond to the claim that emotions pose a problem for moral reasoning (e.g., research on altering racist attitudes; Pizarro & Blum, 2003; Liao, 2011). But this research also does not show that change is easy or without obstacles. Quite the contrary: it shows that moral change requires determined effort, usually from a combination of factors that are beyond the agent's control. Sauer (2012a), for instance, claims that "the most spectacular evidence for how subjects can educate their intuitive judgements comes from research on social prejudice and stereotype activation" (p. 268). In support of this, he cites a single study from Rudman, Ashmore, and Gary (2001), in which students had to take a class on social prejudice taught by a black professor in order to change their implicit attitudes about black people in general. This study only reaffirms that emotions and situational factors are the main drivers of attitude change. People did not reason their way to the conclusion that people of other races are non-threatening. They had to be forced into a situation very different from what they would normally experience.

Fine and Sauer also cite research on "implementation intentions" to support their claims about the role of reason. Implementation intentions are basic if–then commands that are aimed at changing one's behavior. For instance, consider a study by Gallo et al. (2009), which Sauer (2011) cites in support of the revisability of disgust. What the results of this experiment showed was that telling oneself "If I see blood, then I will stay calm and relaxed!" decreased disgust responses to pictures of blood, but "I will not get disgusted!" had no effect. An identical phenomenon was observed with fear of spiders.

Here too the results seem to suggest that emotions can be modified only through great effort. Disgust is revisable, but only with significant support. Implementation intentions, at least in this experiment, *prepare* the participant for the oncoming stimulus and dictate a specific response. Desiring to change one's emotional response and even making a concerted effort to do so are insufficient. Without the right "coaching" or some form of properly informed external support, it is unlikely that individuals would be able to modify their disgust response. Moreover, why should we expect that external support like this is easy to come by or can be sustained? As Doris (2015) concludes on the inadequacy of implementation-intentions, "the prospect of fragility remains" (p. 128). Even if specific goals help in revising our attitudes, they remain easy to disrupt through situational factors, and there is little reason to think that external support in resisting these will be available.

In short, the evidence cited by critics does not seem to provide good reason to think emotions and situations can be easily overcome in our moral lives. Their evidence does not meet the specified evidential criteria and therefore does not provide reason to think that private reflection can revise our moral psychologies under ordinary circumstances. Rather, the studies they cite suggest that rational influences can have an impact but only in certain rare and exceptional cases where people have resources that are not normally available to them.

Supporting evidence for the importance of resources also comes from research on System 2 control of System 1 processes. Stanovich (2010, p. 124), for instance, reviews evidence that intelligence does in fact correlate with a range of tasks indicating successful control of System 1 processes. However, Stanovich further notes that this is primarily the case in tasks where people are *prompted* to suppress System 1 activities. This, he suggests, overestimates the efficacy of System 2 control in ordinary life because normally this sort of prompting is unavailable. As he says, "people of higher cognitive ability are no more likely to recognize the *need* for a normative principle than are individuals of lower cognitive ability. When the former believe that nothing normative is at stake, they behave remarkably like other people" (Stanovich, 2010, p. 154). Stanovich's conclusion is that there is no method based in one's powers of reflection that can consistently control automatic processes. We are generally poor at controlling automatic processes without having some form of external assistance, and it's not always clear what form of assistance will be effective.

To briefly return to one of the claims made at the outset of the chapter, the challenge presented by automatic responses is that they often resist our control. If we could properly train these responses to do what we wanted, they would be quite helpful. But that's not what actually happens. We do in fact disapprove of certain automatic biases, for instance, and when we try to control them we often fail. This very basic fact about human psychology has gotten lost in the disputes between philosophers and psychologists like Greene and Haidt. By singling out Greene and Haidt for criticism, philosophers have obscured the extent to which their arguments conflict not only with a handful of recent studies but with several decades of solid research that forms the basis for much of the cognitive sciences.

An objection some of the critics cited here might have is that the investigation thus far has unfairly assumed that people are irrational. By assuming irrationality as the explananda, the irrational factors identified here are much more obviously relevant than the rational factors promoted by Railton, Sauer, Fine, etc. The general thrust of this objection is reasonable, but it's easy to turn it back around on the critics. Many philosophers have unfairly assumed that people are rational and further assumed that they can therefore just gesture toward the possibilities for moral change in cases of apparent irrationality. Philosophers need to take evidence for human irrationality more seriously. As we will see in later chapters, there remains much for philosophers to do once we have outlined where our moral psychologies fall apart—particularly with respect to treatment of animals.

5.3 SELF-CONTROL FAILURES

Some may read about situationism and emotion science and remain unconvinced that they pose significant obstacles to moral change. Many of the experiments described above indicate that there are individual differences in how these factors affect us; certain people do indeed avoid unwanted influences from unconscious factors, at least some of the time. A possible explanation for this, one might think, is improved *self-control*. Sure we may all be subject to biases, but some of us are better at controlling these biases. Emotions and situations, we might think, are only an obstacle to those who lack the strength to overpower irrational unconscious influences.

Self-control is often conceptualized as a classic dual process conflict: self-control is a System 2 process that explicitly attempts to control the mistakes made by automatic processes in System 1. For example, we can make plans, inhibit our impulses, resist distractions, or make conscious decisions to change something about ourselves—these all involve self-control. The last decade of self-control research has found that controlling System 1 processes in this way depletes System 2 resources. Performing one self-control task undermines performance on subsequent self-control tasks. As a result, self-control processes are limited and, in many cases, easily defeated. This poses an additional obstacle to moral progress.

5.3.1 Ego Depletion

Perhaps the best-known explanation for why self-control often breaks down refers to what psychologists call *ego depletion*. Research on ego depletion uses the ego as a hypothetical construct to capture *whatever it is* that is responsible for a range of self-control processes. The most prominent model of how ego depletion works is the resource model, as developed by Roy Baumeister and colleagues (Baumeister, Vohs, & Tice, 2007; Muraven & Baumeister, 2000). This model conceives of the ego as a limited resource that is reduced by every act of self-control. Subsequent acts of self-control are increasingly difficult and less effective as this resource is depleted. Self-control failures, on this account, are a consequence of depleted psychological resources.

The main source of evidence for the resource model comes from research using what is known as the *sequential task paradigm*. In these studies, participants are given a sequence of tasks designed to deplete mental resources, and—as the resource model predicts—performance declines with each act of self-control. Hagger et al.'s (2010) meta-analysis of 198 studies using the sequential task paradigm supports the consistency of this basic phenomenon (for some criticisms of this meta-analysis, though ones which do not seem ultimately convincing, see Carter et al., 2015).

Further support for the basic tenets of the resource model of ego depletion comes from Hofmann, Vohs, and Baumeister (2012). They asked people to record every time they experienced a desire to do something (like eat cake or use the Internet) as they went about their normal lives, as well as whether they attempted to resist that desire and whether they were successful. They found that repeated attempts to resist desires earlier in the day reduced the ability to resist desires later in the day and that this was particularly true when these acts of self-control occurred in rapid succession. This supports the inference that the results of sequential task research, as conducted in the lab, also apply to everyday life.

Research using sequential tasks has also found that ego depletion impacts moral behavior. For instance, being asked to control one's emotions (an ego-depleting activity) reduces the amount of guilt people feel after causing harm to another person, and reduces charitable giving (e.g., being asked to donate money to people with AIDS; Xu, Bégue, & Bushman, 2012). There is also evidence that ego depletion increases dishonesty (Gino et al., 2011; Mead et al., 2009).

Mead et al. (2009) provide a nice illustration of the effects of ego depletion on dishonesty. They used a common technique designed to deplete self-control resources, which required people to write a story about themselves without using the letters "a" and "n." Across a range of tasks where participants could win small amounts of money, this sort of ego-depleting task caused people to be more dishonest in order to improve their chances of winning. For instance, after writing the story, participants were asked to perform a task where they had to search within a number matrix to find three numbers that would add to 10. The prize for a correct answer? 25 cents. When participants were allowed to self-report their score on this task, those who were ego-depleted were significantly more likely to exaggerate their scores, indicating that reduced self-control led to more dishonesty.

In a second experiment, using a different ego-depleting task, participants were told they would receive 10 cents for each correct answer to a short quiz. They were also told that the experimenter had only two quizzes left and that although the correct answers were lightly visible on one of the papers, they could use that one if they desired. Results showed that ego-depleted individuals were more likely to choose the cheat-sheet and were also more likely to use the lightly visible answers on the sheet.

Research on ego depletion and self-control thus helps identify an additional obstacle to moral progress: we are severely limited in our capacity for self-regulation. A single act of self-control reduces our future abilities to self-regulate. This has implications for moral behavior and the achievement of moral goals.

5.3.2 Challenges to Self-Control

One challenge that arises in our moral lives as a result of self-control failures is in *establishing* new moral goals. A plausible starting point in improving one's moral self is fixing past mistakes and altering the goals that have been pursued in the past but are now disapproved of. Modifying one's goals in this way clearly requires self-control. Van Dellen et al. (2014) found that reduced mental resources affect goal prioritization and often lead to excusing behaviors. To elicit ego depletion, they asked people to write a text from memory without using a space bar or the letter "e." They were then asked to identify broad life goals. People who had undergone the ego-depletion task were more likely to agree with statements like "I'm not worried about making progress on this goal now because I know I will have time to progress on it later" and "Sometimes I think this goal is too lofty." This illustrates that goal-setting is more difficult when mental resources are depleted.

Research on ego depletion has also found that changing one's current goals is itself a resource-depleting act. It seems to be particularly difficult to change one's goals by *avoiding* past goals, compared to pursuing new goals (Elliot et al., 2014). For example, thinking "I really do not want to eat meat" is likely more resource-depleting than "I'd like to be kinder to animals." Although the latter goal might be a step forward, it is arguably unhelpful in avoiding unwanted behaviors, thus making it difficult to change one's past behavior.

Another challenge raised by self-control failures is in attempting to *improve* our self-control abilities. There are two ways this has been studied: through practicing self-control and by affirming the strength of one's self-control abilities. First, on practice: there is indeed evidence that self-control can be improved with practice, but there are limitations. Bertrams and Schmeichel (2014), for instance, found evidence that the positive effects of practicing self-control dissipated within 1 week. They had people practice self-control by asking them to pay close attention to logical consistency when writing about controversial moral issues (e.g., physician-assisted suicide). This type of training immediately improved performance on an anagram task (i.e., solving anagrams), compared to those who were allowed to write whatever came to mind about the controversial topics. But this effect did not persist when measured 1 week later.

There is also some evidence that optimism about one's self-control and willpower is enabling (Job, Dweck, & Walton, 2010; Job et al., 2015). That is, beliefs about ego depletion impact actual ego depletion. For instance, receiving reasons to think one's mental resources have been artificially increased—even if they actually have not—can lead to better self-control (Clarkson et al., 2010). This is a classic illustration of the power of self-deception. Tricking ourselves into thinking that we are strong-willed might help us overcome depleted mental resources.

However, these self-conceptions also have limited efficacy. They provide extra resources but not unlimited resources. Muraven (2010), for instance, found that perceptions of one's effort and the strength of one's self control on a task had no effect on improved self-control. Reducing consumption of desserts for 2 weeks and squeezing a handgrip twice a day improved performance on a task where people had to control their responses (either hit a key or not hit a key when a square appears on a screen). By contrast, practicing math problems and writing in a diary about acts of self-control had no effect on performance on this task. Participants' ratings of how much effort they put into these things also had no correlation with improvement. It was only real acts of self-control—through resisting desserts and practicing hand strength—that had any impact.

Optimism about one's willpower also has certain negative consequences. Vohs, Baumeister, and Schmeichel (2012) found that believing one has unlimited willpower has short-term benefits but long-term costs. They primed people to believe either in unlimited willpower (by reading statements like "Sometimes, working on a strenuous mental task can make you feel energized for further challenging activities") or in limited willpower ("Working on a strenuous mental task can make you feel tired such that you need a break before accomplishing a new task"). Participants then completed up to four different tasks, each designed to deplete mental resources. For instance, one task instructed them to watch segments of *Eddie Murphy Raw* without laughing. After these tasks, they completed two additional tests aimed at measuring what remained of their self-control abilities. One measured how much they would delay a monetary reward, and the other asked them to estimate various quantities of things (e.g., the weight of a dozen apples). The results from these two tests showed that those primed to believe in unlimited willpower were exceptional after two of the four tasks but then declined rapidly by the fourth task, performing worse than those primed to think willpower is limited. They put so much into the first two tasks that they had nothing left for the third and fourth tasks.

So although optimism about one's willpower can help muster additional resources when necessary, it does not actually increase overall willpower. If one is expected to engage in multiple acts of self-control, it would actually be better to believe in limited mental resources, so as to save one's energy. Job et al. (2015) found that people who believe that willpower is limited do in fact tend to rest in between repeated acts of self-control. The research above suggests that this is a good strategy.

To sum up, research on ego depletion has identified prominent obstacles to self-regulation. Our psychological resources are drained rather easily, and when they are drained, we struggle to establish new goals for ourselves and pursue goals with adequate willpower. These obstacles obviously apply to moral goals pertaining to animals. The psychological processes identified in the previous chapters would likely need to be suppressed in order to enact certain forms of moral change. The research discussed already indicates that any sort of suppression is extremely difficult.

5.3.3 Objections to the Resource Model

There have been a number of objections to the resource model of self-control. A prominent alternative to the resource model is the *process* model (Inzlicht & Berkman, 2015; Inzlicht & Schmeichel, 2016). This model differs from the resource model in holding that self-control resources are not finite and can be restored more easily than is often supposed. If this is right, then self-control failures along the lines I am envisioning may not turn out to be a major obstacle to moral change.

One of the main claims of the process model is that exercising self-control causes the mind to reorient in motivation and attention (Inzlicht & Schmeichel, 2012; Inzlicht, Schmeichel, & Macrae, 2014). This explains the phenomenon of ego depletion without appealing to limited reserves. Rather, our psychological resources are dependent on the type of tasks we are pursuing. According to the process model, acts of self-control motivate us to shift between tasks; any individual act of self-control makes us reconsider our priorities. Ability to self-regulate is thus depleted as people perform acts of self-control that are not psychologically rewarding to the agent (e.g., the boring experimental tasks used in most ego-depletion research). The agent loses motivation to pursue these tasks, leading to the classic ego-depletion phenomenon. The problem of self-regulation is not then a matter of depleted resources but rather agents' motivation to perform particular tasks. On the process model, agents could undergo traditional ego-depleting tasks (like resisting desserts) but still successfully exercise self-control if performing a task that is psychologically rewarding to them (e.g., working on a novel that they really enjoy).

Regardless of whether one endorses the process model, there is indeed a great deal of evidence that is hard to understand within the resource framework. Masicampo, Martin, and Anderson (2014) summarize evidence indicating how easily ego depletion can occasionally be reversed. Sometimes the factors that restore psychological resources also seem somewhat trivial. For instance, being allowed to choose between two topics in a writing task is less ego-depleting than being given a topic (Moller, Deci, & Ryan, 2006). Since this seemingly does not involve any additional act of self-control, it is not clear why there would be any downstream effects on self-control processes. Psychological resources are also restored—under conditions when they should be depleted—when people are asked to perform acts of self-control regarding important personal goals (Inzlicht, Legault, & Teper, 2014). This is presumably a result of being more motivated to act on highly valued goals, but it's not clear why motivation would have an effect if mental resources truly were depleted.

These sorts of results and the process model generally do cause problems for the resource model of ego depletion, but they don't work against the claim that self-control failures pose an obstacle to moral progress. That psychological resources are easily restored in some conditions—like when pursuing valued goals—does not mean that our psychological resources are *unlimited*. Our mundane everyday acts of self-control are likely to be limited just as the resource model predicts. Moreover, cases indicating that we can replenish our resources by acting on highly valued goals do not show that these acts are performed without struggle.

Evans, Boggero, and Segerstrom (2015), for instance, provide reasons to think that we can experience fatigue even when we do in fact have sufficient resources to complete a task. For illustration, they cite evidence that people who think exercise is fun do indeed have better stamina during exercise but that this does not mean that these people *don't get tired* or that they could exercise continuously. Willpower, mental resources, ego—or whatever you want to call it—is limited in some way, even if there are strategies for stretching those limits in certain circumstances.

As we saw already in the discussion of emotions and situations, an important question is whether our behavior can be controlled to the extent required to meet important moral goals. Even if we can self-regulate better than the discussion here has indicated, we must still ask if our psychological abilities are sufficient. And again, it should be noted that self-regulation for moral goals requires substantial assistance. In order to regulate moral behavior we must realize that self-control is required in the first place, and this likely requires the help of others (see, e.g., Sheldon & Fishbach, 2015). This raises the bar for what individuals are psychologically capable of when pursuing moral goals.

5.4 CONCLUSION

This chapter has identified some of the most problematic features when attempting to enact moral change, both in our moral lives generally and specifically with respect to the treatment of animals. Emotions and situations influence our moral behavior in ways we often do not realize. When we try to redirect these influences—for instance, with our powers of self-control—we often fail to make the changes required.

The psychological factors discussed here and in the previous chapters give us reason to pause before making certain ethical prescriptions regarding animals. Given the moral psychology of human attitudes toward animals, some actions will be difficult, if not impossible. Arguably the consensus view among ethicists, however, is that psychological constraints are irrelevant to ethical prescriptions. Psychological difficulty says nothing about moral rightness. In the next chapter, we will look more in depth at how these psychological factors must inform our treatment of animals.

Chapter 6

Psychological Plausibility
for Animal Ethics

The story of human morality, as mentioned in the last chapter, is a story of failure. But does routine moral failure impact our moral obligations? Though there are reasons to be pessimistic about human moral capacities, there are also reasons to be confident that *some* positive account can be given in support of many important moral goals, especially those pertaining to animals. Unfortunately, those who write about animal ethics have paid little attention to moral psychology, especially to the "darker" elements of our attitudes to animals. Consequently, there is little awareness of which obligations to animals are realistic and which are not.

Many people (particularly philosophers) are suspicious of the claim that moral obligations are limited by our psychology. This suspicion is somewhat understandable. One hears often enough that transitioning to vegetarianism is impossible, for instance, because "meat is just so delicious." Such crude excuses should not be used as a guide for moral truth. However, there is also a great deal to say about the occasional inflexibility of human psychology (including gustatory preferences). Psychology is often taken to be irrelevant to ethics because people assume it is easily changed. Here we will outline the implications when this is not so clear—what follows from having good reasons to think psychological limitations are present and how our obligations to animals must be responsive to these psychological factors.

6.1 "OUGHT IMPLIES CAN" AND
INDIVIDUAL ETHICS

The model most commonly used for thinking about psychological constraints on moral obligations is known as "ought implies can" (OIC). The basic idea behind OIC seems pretty simple: I have a certain moral obligation (like refraining from eating animals), only if I can actually meet that obligation. There is significant difficulty, however, in understanding what "can" means in the context of moral behavior.

6.1.1 Incremental Cans

Perhaps the broadest and most general understanding of "moral cans" is in instrumental terms. This view holds, in short, that I can meet a moral obligation if I can take the steps necessary to meet my final goal. There might be 5 or 500 steps; they may take only a few days or instead a few decades; and each step might be easy or hard to meet, but so long as I can take steps to meet a moral obligation, then the obligation is within the realm of what I can do. Difficult moral goals are rarely, if ever, achieved in a single sweeping action. Instead we should say that ought implies "can take the next step" in meeting a moral goal (Stocker, 1971). So long as I can take the next step, whatever it might be, then I can meet my moral obligation and ought to fulfill it.

Pursuing moral goals in incremental steps, over potentially long periods of time, reduces the psychological demands on human agents. This consequently seems to reduce the ethical implications of psychological limitations. Anyone, it might seem, can take some incremental step toward meeting a moral goal, especially so, we might think, if they must meet an important moral goal, which is more likely to receive the attention it deserves.

There are reasons for skepticism, however. The psychological limitations identified in the previous chapters are pervasive. They will be part of any incremental step we might take toward meeting moral goals involving animals. There are also numerous other pervasive psychological constraints on moral behavior—documented in detail in the empirical literature—which suggest that we can't count on moral behavior to improve over time. Humans are rarely on their best behavior. Why should approaching moral ideals incrementally help avoid this problem? Instead of making moral life more manageable, incrementally pursuing moral goals may just multiply our opportunities for failure.

Much of the philosophical literature on OIC focuses on single-shot cases where an agent is limited in some respect in achieving some goal. The pursuit of moral goals does not consist solely of single-shot opportunities, but the incremental approach just alluded to does suggest that each individual step matters a great deal. These single-shot cases can thus help us get a grip on what is important about psychological limitations.

One illuminating case comes from Bart Streumer's (2007) defense of OIC. He describes a man, Bob, who we are told is uniquely capable of preventing a plane crash. The plane, which is carrying hundreds of passengers, is rapidly descending due to an engine failure, and Bob is the only person with the requisite skills to fix the engines. However, Bob is on the ground, and the plane crash is imminent. We might think that Bob has a reason to save the plane because saving the passengers is a good thing. Because of his unique abilities, we might also think he has an obligation to do so; if not him, then who else? But being an ordinary human being, it is impossible for Bob to fix the engines in time to save the plane. So if we accept that ought implies can, Bob does not have any obligation or reason to save the plane. To claim otherwise—that Bob does have an obligation—would be to reject ought implies can, and it is not clear what such a rejection would be grounded in.

Now how might the incremental approach apply to Bob's case? Consider the possibility that Bob is feeling optimistic and ambitious and decides to sprint up to the top of the nearest building. Supposing he is very fast and the buildings in his vicinity very tall, he could perhaps cut the space between him and the plane considerably. By doing this he has, in a sense, brought himself closer to achieving the goal of saving the plane. He has made some progress toward meeting his goal. And if ought merely implies "can take the next step," then perhaps Bob does have an obligation to save the plane after all.

A problem, one might think, is that this step seems inadequate. Running up a tall building is a false sense of progress. Bob has not actually made an incremental step toward his goal. Heuer (2010) objects to this case (and others like it) because there is no opportunity for a "real try," or a legitimate attempt at fixing the plane. Because the task is in fact impossible, any action Bob takes will be futile. There is no efficacy in any of his actions with respect to the ultimate goal. Any measure of progress is thus misleading.

Heuer's point is not an objection to the case, however, but an indicator that incremental progress is not always sufficient to revive moral obligations. In everyday life, we frequently take steps that bring us closer to our goals but not in quite the right way. We make "real tries" only to recidivate, stall, give up, etc. There's no need to quantify how often this happens; presumably readers will find it a familiar experience. And for OIC, every step counts: even if we make a single effective step toward a goal, our work is not done; we must ask at every step whether we have made real progress.

6.1.2 Implications of Incremental Failure

The main implication of the case just described is that when we are routinely constrained in meeting moral goals, we are not required to meet those moral goals. This seems to follow straightforwardly from OIC. If we truly cannot make real progress toward meeting a moral goal, then according to OIC, we are not obligated to pursue that moral goal.

This might seem uncontroversial, perhaps trivial; but it has radical implications for ethics and moral thought. Ethicists frequently fail to specify how individuals ought to go about meeting their moral obligations. They typically assume that there will be difficulties in achieving moral goals, that overcoming these difficulties will require help from others, and that many goals will require people to work cooperatively. But because ethicists often do not specify how this should be done, they do not consider the consequences if external support and cooperation are unavailable.

Bob's case illustrates a common occurrence when individuals lack the resources to meet important moral goals. Given the psychological processes discussed in the previous chapters, we should expect individuals to be routinely constrained in a similar way as Bob. The discussion of self-control from the last chapter perhaps illustrates this best. Any single step toward meeting a moral goal depletes the psychological resources available to an agent in taking the next step. Receiving assistance from others will make this easier, but if that assistance is unavailable, then the agent remains limited in what he or she can do to meet moral goals.

In this context, we can consider Peter Singer's (2015) comments on the demandingness of morality: "You have approximately 80,000 working hours in your life. While this might feel like a lot, it's not much when compared to the scale of the problems in the world" (p. viii). Though this is not Singer's intention, one might read this quote and wonder how people can be held to a moral obligation even if a *whole* life's work is incapable of satisfactorily addressing the underlying issue. Even if a life devoted to a particularly important moral cause produces certain good consequences, it is difficult to see how this involves an *obligation* if no real progress is made toward meeting the overall goal.

Again, this conclusion might seem trivial, and indeed in a sense it is. We are starting with a simple claim: human beings frequently cannot take steps toward achieving certain moral obligations, and this has implications for how we should think about the nature of those obligations. But this is just the core of what will be developed throughout this chapter. There are other implications that are much more controversial.

Though the implications of OIC just discussed seem inescapable, it must be admitted that cases like Bob's leave much to be desired. In particular, there are a wide variety of "tryings" that must be explored. Let's consider some objections people are likely to have to the discussion thus far.

6.1.3 *Future Change*

A great deal of moral discourse is explicitly aimed at ideal agents: hypothetical versions of ourselves who are better than us along some morally important dimension (like kindness). Sometimes the ideal presented to us is intended not as something we should strive to be but rather as something we can look to for general guidance (e.g., someone who possesses the classic virtues of honesty, patience, or justice). However, we can set aside this view for now because in many cases it reduces to a view where general guidance is seen in instrumental terms, where the ideal is in fact promoted in order to help us achieve a certain goal.

Explicitly instrumental conceptions of moral ideals promote ideals as something we should strive for because—who knows—perhaps we can change in the way prescribed. This view is inherently optimistic: even if we fail a thousand times, we may yet succeed; and this is important when striving to meet important moral goals. This is in fact a common refrain in the literature on moral psychology. Nobody wants to shut off the possibility of change. And when change happens, we want moral discourse to reflect what we think is right, not what we think is psychologically realistic. For instance, Owen Flanagan (1991) argues that psychological realism is ultimately a poor guide to ethics because current psychological profiles tell us neither what sort of future psychological profiles we should pursue nor what might be bad about future psychological profiles that we should avoid. They just tell us what is.

There are different ways of allowing for psychological change on this instrumental view. One we can call the *optimistic* approach. For instance, we might say that ought does not "conversationally" imply can. In conversation, and in moral discourse, we may disregard what we are capable of in order to more directly assess what we ought to do. Sinnott-Armstrong (1984), for example, argues for the claim "if cannot, might yet be true that I ought." As the world changes, so does moral psychology. So even if I currently cannot take effective steps to meet a moral obligation, perhaps eventually I could, or perhaps other human beings could, and if this happens we should be morally prepared. Similarly, Holly Lawford-Smith (2010) discusses "unowned oughts." Perhaps nobody currently can meet certain moral obligations, but we want those obligations to stick around because they seem so important. When conditions change, perhaps those oughts will become owned.

However, this optimistic approach seem unhelpful. It is not clear what work this sort of optimism is doing without some reason to think that human beings will in fact change in the way desired. Moral psychology is arguably more likely to change in ways unanticipated by ethicists. The trajectory of historical and societal change is notoriously difficult to predict. So why think that people are *more* likely to become able to meet the ideals set forth by professional ethicists than any other ideals?

We do not need to dwell on objections to this particular position, however, because there is a related view that is more deserving of critical attention. We can call this the *social* approach. To give the optimistic view more bite, many have suggested that we focus specifically on the impact of social and political changes; these are the factors that make it more likely that oughts will become owned. Holding out for future change might be hopeless, but with the right social circumstances some of the changes we want to see may indeed be realized. Focusing on the role of broader forces, like those provided by the governments of states and nations, can give us some idea of which changes are likely to occur and, thus, help us hone in on what moral obligations individuals can and cannot meet.

Given what follows from individual limitations (if we accept OIC), the social approach is the only way to retain many moral goals. Broader forces are required in order for individuals to be able to work toward their moral obligations. However, psychological limitations still apply at the level of collectives, including the governments of states and nations. Many who adopt the social approach have overlooked this.

6.2 SOCIAL SUPPORT AND CRITERIA FOR PSYCHOLOGICAL PLAUSIBILITY

6.2.1 The Social Approach

Psychological limitations become problematic, we might think, only when individuals are abstracted away from the communities they operate within. Individuals can pursue moral change only as members of certain communities and societies, so why be surprised that they are limited when attempting to act alone? A more psychologically realistic approach to moral change, then, is to primarily address social change and the role individuals might play as part of societies. Individuals acting alone, as in Bob's case—and indeed in many of the cases discussed in philosophical ethics—shouldn't be taken as representative of how moral change occurs in the real world.

The main benefit of thinking about moral change in this more social way is the increased availability of time and resources. Communities have much greater access to resources and much more time to pursue change than do individuals. Time and resources were severely limited in Bob's case. They are also severely limited in many cases where individuals are pursuing moral change on their own.

Consider, for instance, the phenomenon of ego depletion, as discussed in the previous chapter. At any given time individuals have a relatively set amount of psychological resources they can use in meeting their moral goals. That these resources are limited for each individual matters much less, however, if we consider the amount of resources available to all members of a group in aggregate and how long that group will pursue a particular goal. The limitations are not only distributed over many people over a long period of time, but proper coordination may enable groups to use those resources more efficiently. For instance, there would be less individual ego depletion if the burden of difficult self-control tasks (whatever those might be) were shared evenly among people.

The moral duties of groups and how we should understand group decision-making have been the focus of much recent theorizing (e.g., Huebner, 2013; List & Pettit, 2011; Sunstein, 2014). Highly structured groups, with shared decision-making procedures, are referred to as "collectives." Collectives are the type of groups that are most likely to be able to pursue specific moral goals. They are capable of understanding what individuals must do to satisfy their ultimate desires and can coordinate the behavior of members of the collective in order to achieve shared goals.

There are many different types of collectives. The governments of states and nations can be considered collectives, as can small groups consisting of just four or five people who are responsible for very specific tasks. There are also many different ways a collective can function. Some possess a top-down control structure, where decisions made by a single individual or a small set of individuals at a higher level dictate what individuals must do at lower levels. The methods by which top-down structures control individuals can also vary. Instead of dictating actions, those in charge can put policies in place to regulate behavior or can put in place an infrastructure to encourage and enable some behaviors instead of others. While this is still a top-down structure, it offers more flexibility for individuals in how they might act in accordance with the decisions of those at the top. Other collectives possess a bottom-up structure, where individuals acting independently influence what the collective does. Voting behavior can be seen as a bottom-up structure like this.

The idea behind the social approach is that any type of collective will help individuals meet moral obligations (though of course some may be more effective than others). Let's consider one proposal for how collecti-vization might affect our moral obligations, from Gilabert and Lawford-Smith (2012). They focus on the issue of feasibility in social and political change, or whether a political ideal can be achieved, given certain real-world constraints. Moral psychology is relevant here because feasibility seems to include questions of psychological difficulty. Whether a moral ideal can be achieved psychologically is part of the question of whether the ideal is feasible.

Gilabert and Lawford-Smith argue that most ideals are feasible if con-sidered over a long enough time span. It is a mistake, they think, to assume that short-term infeasibility indicates what sort of social and political change is ultimately possible. As they say, "The inaccessibility, at a certain time, of a certain institutional scheme does not entail either its instability or the infeasibility of the core principles it implements. Principles range over, and orient, long-term political trajectories" (p. 821). Because social and political changes are meant to take place over a long period of time, the only ideals that should be ruled out are ones that are absolutely impos-sible to achieve—not ones that are merely difficult.

Another way to think about this sort of position is in terms of a scale of possibility. If we consider the possibility of social changes on a scale of 0 to 100, Gilabert and Lawford-Smith's view is that anything with a pos-itive probability—greater than 0—should be considered feasible. Ideals should be discarded only on moral grounds, not because they have a low probability of being realized (also see Lawford-Smith, 2013a). This is meant to provide a large scope for future change. Especially with signif-icant resources, we could make ideals with low probability become more probable.

But is this approach satisfactory? Maybe not. Though the greater time and resources available to collectives do make them more capable of achieving low-probability ideals, this is not enough to avoid problems presented by OIC. That something is in principle possible does not mean that we can reach that ideal in a way that would satisfy OIC.

One reason to be skeptical of the sort of view espoused by Gilabert and Lawford-Smith is that it is too generous in what it considers feasi-ble. As Stephanie Collins (2013) points out, pursuing changes with a low probability of success is likely to end in failure. The claim that something is feasible if there is a non-zero chance of it being realized fails to take seriously the "can" in ought implies can. Collins focuses on cases where, according to OIC, individuals have a duty to collectivize because they cannot achieve certain moral obligations on their own. But groups too must be held to OIC, "the group cannot have a duty to φ if it is very likely that, if it tries (i.e., has φ as a collective aim and members attempt to perform their role), the collective does not φ" (p. 239). This is a more rigid standard than Gilabert and Lawford-Smith propose. Collins thinks that we should discard more than just those ideals that are absolutely impossible. An ideal that only has a 1% chance of being realized, for instance, is not sufficient to be considered feasible with the normally available resources.

A related reason to be skeptical is that time and resource constraints still apply to groups. OIC applies to groups in much the same way as it does to individuals—namely, that severe limitations on meeting each step in a long series of steps have similar implications for moral goals. If a group frequently fails to take steps toward meeting its moral goals—even if in principle it could—then according to OIC the group is not obligated to meet those goals. Gilabert and Lawford-Smith's view can be understood as a form of the optimistic approach but applied to groups. They want to hold out for the possibility that a group could eventually achieve an ideal, given that circumstances can change, thus increasing the chance that an ideal will be realized (assuming non-zero probability). But this is inadequate. If an ideal has a low probability of being achieved, we need some reason to think its probability will increase. Without that, it's not clear why we would think it is within the realm of what we "can" do. Moreover, it is insufficient to say that the ideal can be achieved with vast amount of time and resources. Without some idea of where the resources would come from, this just looks like wishful thinking.

Gilabert and Lawford-Smith might respond to these objections by distinguishing between the creation of ideals and their implementation. They might accept that psychological limitations should limit the implementation of moral ideals but deny that it should impact their construction. If in trying to realize a certain social policy we determine that it would be too psychologically difficult to adhere to (whatever that might mean), then they might agree that the policy shouldn't be implemented. They seem to express such a view by saying "it must be sufficiently likely that institutional schemes satisfying the core principles can be reached by agents in a certain context" (p. 820). But if agents cannot satisfy the core principles within the relevant contexts, then in what sense do those principles constitute moral obligations? The distinction between creating and implementing ideals is helpful in constructing more realistic policies but not in constructing realistic ideals or showing why unrealistic ideals might be useful.

In summary, it is not enough for a social or moral goal to be in principle achievable. We need evidence to think that we can actually make progress toward a goal. When we cannot make progress toward a goal as individuals—which is the case for many moral goals—then we need evidence that we can make progress within groups and as collectives. That collectivization makes it easier to achieve difficult goals does not reduce this requirement. Collectives possess limitations just as individuals do, and our moral obligations must be responsive to these limitations.

6.2.2 Ideals Are Just Guides

An objection that must be addressed pertains to the way the social approach is framed. As mentioned, moral ideals are sometimes presented as something that we can look to for general guidance, rather than as a goal to be pursued. One might thus object to the way the social approach has been framed in instrumental terms. Instead, moral ideals should be seen as providing general guidelines that inform social and political changes but are not meant to be pursued as a final endpoint.

Brownlee (2010), for instance, argues that cases like Bob's draw from an overly instrumental conception of ideals and ignore all the ways in which ideals restructure our lives without specifying any particular path or endpoint. Ideals, she argues, are "models of genuine excellence around which we can shape our lives and our commitments" (p. 434). This general idea also seems reflected in Gilabert and Lawford-Smith's claim that "Principles range over, and orient, long-term political trajectories." Ideals have practical implications, but that is not the ultimate aim. As a result, one might think that psychological limitations are less relevant. If the goal isn't to achieve moral ideals, then why be concerned if they are not in fact achievable?

We should push back against this objection. Moral ideals frequently *are* used to provide concrete moral goals, even when this is not the ultimate intention of their promotion. Recommending compassion toward animals, for instance, is a broad feature of our personality that might be worth cultivating regardless of the positive outcomes it creates. But cultivating compassion does have some sort of outcome that can be assessed. And some people do in fact recommend compassion as a virtue of character because they think it will provide concrete benefits for animals (Bekoff, 2013, 2014). Specific expressions of compassion are identified as plausible endpoints, even if that is not the ultimate goal.

Even if ideals are importantly non-instrumental in some cases, those who promote explicitly non-instrumental ideals are simply ignoring the question of psychological realism. Ideals may indeed be valuable because they give us a sense of meaning or assist us in achieving clarity on how to think about important moral issues. But this does not mean they produce moral obligations. According to OIC, putting forth a moral obligation entails psychological abilities to meet that obligation. A moral ideal that is not meant to say anything about those psychological abilities then is not satisfying the conditions of OIC.

If our moral ideals are not meant to achieve any particular moral goal, we also open up the possibility of pursuing moral change through numerous other means. For instance, Mark Alfano (2013) argues that although certain moral ideals cannot be achieved, promoting them can sometimes lead to other desirable outcomes. He describes this as moral fictionalism. Instead of creating moral ideals that are responsive to psychological reality, professional ethicists could devise "tactically deployed *fictions*" (his emphasis, p. 13). Moral ideals might be informative here, but they might not. It would ultimately be an empirical question of what meets our moral goals most effectively. So again the question of psychological realism must be addressed in order to pursue moral change.

Regardless of how we conceive the social approach then, we must consider the psychological abilities of human beings when making moral prescriptions. This is the only way to satisfy OIC. We must know more about how human beings operate in order to make meaningful moral goals.

6.2.3 Criteria for Psychological Plausibility

We have seen why psychological profiles matter for ethical theorizing. However, the discussion thus far has been largely critical, showing why common ways of constructing moral ideals will be deficient if they are not sensitive to moral psychology. Let's now shift to a more constructive mode and show *how* moral ideals can be sensitive to moral psychology, in order to create *psychologically plausible* moral ideals.

The classic account of why psychology matters for ethical theory is Owen Flanagan's (1991) *Varieties of Moral Personality*. This is where Flanagan introduces his widely influential principle of minimal psychological realism (PMPR), which states "Make sure when constructing a moral theory or projecting a moral ideal that the character, decision processing, and behavior prescribed are possible, or are perceived to be possible, for creatures like us" (p. 32). A problem with the PMPR is that its conception of possibility, at least as discussed by Flanagan, is far too broad. Flanagan claims later in the book that the "PMPR requires only that the recommended ideals be possible under some conceivable social arrangement or other" (p. 201). Only requiring a "conceivable social arrangement" to meet an ethical theory's ideals sets a very low bar for psychological plausibility. As a result, the PMPR doesn't seem to place any meaningful constraints on ethical theories.

Ethicists should adhere to stronger criteria for minimum psychological plausibility. Here are three such criteria that are particularly helpful for analyzing ethical claims regarding animals:

(1) *Impact*: An ethical theory is psychologically plausible if the ideas it promotes are capable of having the intended psychological effect on currently existing human beings.

(2) *Achievability*: An ethical theory is psychologically plausible if it promotes ideas and actions that are achievable by human beings, if not now then at some point in the future.

(3) *Transition*: If an ethical theory requires currently existing psychological profiles to undergo significant modification, that ethical theory is psychologically plausible only if it can explain how the psychological transition could occur, given current understandings of human psychology.

These criteria are essentially temporal in nature: *impact* refers to a theory's current effects, *achievability* to effects in the future, and *transition* to how current impacts relate to achievability at some point in the future.

Let's begin by exploring impact in more detail. The impact criterion holds that an ethical theory must have some effect on currently existing human agents who make up that theory's primary audience (e.g., some segment of the population). Importantly, this does not pertain solely to actions. A theory that *only* requires a change in attitude, for instance, can be assessed according to its likelihood to influence attitudes.

While impact refers to the component of a theory that can influence currently existing psychological profiles, achievability refers to what profiles might exist at some point in the future. If an ethical theory cannot currently have an impact in action or attitude, then, according to the achievability criterion, we must ask whether it could *ever* influence human beings. Psychologists frequently uncover aspects of our moral psychologies that will likely persist into the future. Achievability requires ethicists to use this research to explain how their prescriptions can be expected to impact on human beings in the future.

The transition criterion links future achievability to currently existing human beings. It asks how human psychology is supposed to change in order to meet a theory's ideals. While achievability asks ethicists to specify future psychological profiles, transition asks how the psychological change entailed by those future profiles might occur. It is important that this criterion not be interpreted too strictly. *Thorough* understanding of the psychological transition is not necessary to make an ethical theory psychologically plausible. The claim is merely that ethicists should have at least some idea of the attendant psychological demands implied by the theory—to explain how current psychological impacts are connected to future ideals.

These criteria place much more meaningful constraints on ethical theories than the PMPR. For instance, there would seem to be numerous morally commendable psychological profiles that *could* exist under *some* conceivable social arrangement, as the PMPR promotes. It is not clear, however, why such potentialities should be taken seriously if 1) they have no psychological impact on currently existing human beings, 2) the social arrangements themselves cannot be achieved, or 3) there is no explanation for how such potentialities are to be attained. These criteria complement the arguments laid out previously against the optimistic approach to moral change and Gilabert and Lawford-Smith's conception of the social approach.

To illustrate the applicability of these criteria, consider recent debates over the psychological plausibility of virtue ethics. As mentioned in the last chapter, critics of virtue ethics have claimed that the empirical evidence demonstrates that character traits are frail and fragmentary—they are easily influenced by situational factors and are strongly expressed in only particular situations (Doris, 1998, 2002, 2010; Harman, 1999, 2009). Virtue generally requires character traits that are robust across situations, and thus it appears that being a virtuous agent is extremely difficult, if not impossible. In essence, these critics have challenged virtue ethicists to explain whether virtue is achievable and to explain how human psychology is supposed to change over time to create virtuous individuals. Advocates of virtue ethics have, in turn, attempted to meet this challenge by providing an account of virtue that coheres with current research on moral psychology (Miller, C., 2013, 2014; Russell, 2009; Snow, 2010). In doing so, they have acknowledged the importance of creating psychologically plausible theories (and significantly enriched discussions of virtue).

Something similar would be useful for ideals in animal ethics. Perhaps many ideals would turn out to be psychologically plausible. It is hard to say though until more work has been done to assess the relevant evidence. We can do so by applying the criteria just mentioned to prominent ideals in animal ethics.

6.3 NON-IDEAL ETHICS FOR ANIMALS

6.3.1 Non-Ideal Theory

People writing about animal ethics do not, for the most part, pay attention to human moral psychology. Sometimes for simplicity ethicists focus on the obligations of individuals, without aiming to specify what form of social support would be required to make those obligations realizable. Other times ethicists adopt the social approach, as outlined already, but again without specifying how social changes are to be achieved. The arguments outlined earlier in the chapter have hopefully provided good reasons to think these approaches are problematic.

A view within political philosophy that explicitly aims to take into account real-world constraints and the realizability of moral ideals is known as *non-ideal theory* (Simmons, 2010; Stemplowska & Swift, 2012; Valentini, 2012; Wiens, 2012). Contemporary discussion of non-ideal theory primarily draws from Rawls' (1971) discussion of ideal and non-ideal theories of justice. While ideal theory is exclusively forward-looking and attempts to identify the conditions of justice without regard for current limitations or constraints, non-ideal theory "asks how this long-term goal [of justice] might be achieved, or worked toward, usually in gradual steps" (Rawls, 1971, p. 246). Moral goals within non-ideal theory are constrained by real-world conditions, including (among other possibilities) "imperfect compliance, corruption, poverty, greed, self-interest, apathy, bureaucracy, and also uncertainty" (Lawford-Smith, 2013b, p. 653).

Criteria for psychological plausibility are relevant here because psychology is clearly an important real-world condition that must factor into non-ideal theories (for further discussion of the role of psychology in non-ideal theories, see Kasperbauer, 2015c). As Lawford-Smith expresses in the previous quote, human greediness and self-interest will limit what we can expect people to do. The psychology behind these phenomena—and many others—must factor into the moral ideals we promote, if we expect them to actually have an impact on ordinary human beings.

6.3.2 Abolitionism in Non-Ideal Theory

One recent attempt at constructing a non-ideal theory for animals comes from Robert Garner (2012, 2013). Garner's primary target is abolitionism, as espoused by Gary Steiner (2008) and Gary Francione (2000; Francione & Garner, 2010), which he criticizes for being too idealistic. Abolitionists hold that it is impermissible to sacrifice animals' interests for that of humans, and so, abolitionists argue, all human use of animals must cease (though there are some qualifications which are not important here). According to Garner, abolition of human use of animals is so unrealistic that there are no non-ideal versions that abolitionists could use as stepping stones to reach their goals.

Garner's aims are transitional in nature. Non-ideal theories, on his view, should be constructed with ideals in mind and should be used to take efficient steps toward meeting broader societal goals (which will likely include ideals). So he endorses the use of ideal theories, as long as they inform the construction of non-ideal theories that can be used for real social change. His own ideal theory, he thinks, has more promise in this regard than those of abolitionists. His ideal theory holds that "animals have a right not to have suffering inflicted upon them" (2013, p. 15) and "the lives of animals can only be sacrificed if very significant human benefits accrue" (2013, p. 133). Though he acknowledges that these too are highly ambitious, he thinks they are more easily accommodated in the actual, non-ideal world than the abolitionists' claim that it is impermissible to sacrifice animals' interests for that of humans.

There are, generally, two claims abolitionists have made in response to the charge that abolitionism is unrealistic (Francione, 2000; Francione & Garner, 2010; Steiner, 2013). Both are aimed at theories focused on animal welfare, which hold that our primary moral responsibility is to reduce the suffering caused to sentient animals but not to discontinue human use of animals (except insofar as it causes suffering). Their first claim is that welfare theories are not demanding enough and serve only to excuse morally impermissible practices. Second, they claim that welfare theories further entrench current exploitation of animals, obstructing more effective abolitionist measures.

The problem with both Garner's view and abolitionism is that they rely on psychological claims that neither side has attempted to substantiate with evidence. For instance, Garner's position assumes that a significant portion of the population thinks that sentient animals are morally considerable and should not be harmed. If that turns out to be false, then his position would seem to be no more realistic than abolitionists'. Similarly, abolitionists assume that people are capable of meeting, or taking sufficient steps toward, the more demanding moral duties advocated by Steiner, Francione, and others. They smuggle in a certain view of moral psychology by assuming that regardless of what people *currently* believe, people are *ultimately* capable of realizing that killing animals for human benefit is wrong and that this can eventually motivate a change in behavior. Their claim that reducing animal suffering only reinforces current low standards of treatment also involves a number of psychological assumptions. Most problematically, it seems to assume that *only* ideal theorizing is capable of motivating people toward the proper moral goals.

In short, the problem with both of these views is that their proponents have not established that their moral goals are psychologically plausible. They have not offered reasons to think that human psychology can change in the way envisioned by their theories. This is particularly problematic for Garner because he openly aims to take real-world constraints into account. Non-ideal theory would seem to entail a commitment to addressing *all* relevant causal constraints on realizing moral goals, including constraints presented by human psychology. As David Wiens (2013) argues, if our aim is to implement moral ideals in the real world, the content of our normative prescriptions must incorporate "the actual causal processes that limit the range of feasible alternatives" (p. 326). Garner excludes abolitionism from the range of feasible alternatives, but he does not adequately address the possibility that his own view should be excluded as well.

Psychological plausibility of course also poses a problem for abolitionists. However, abolitionists are not committed, as Garner is, to taking real-world constraints into account when forming moral goals. A possible objection abolitionists might make to my position on psychological plausibility (and to non-ideal theory in general) is that psychological limitations are merely potential costs or obstacles to change and are thus irrelevant to the content of normative prescriptions. As Gilabert and Lawford-Smith (2012) argue, psychological limitations are like certain social and economic conditions in that they are "soft constraints" and can be modified through altering one's circumstances. The only real challenge is constructing a transition strategy to enact the changes.

In order to further illustrate this objection, consider the practice of meat-eating. Animal welfarists often argue that it is permissible to kill and eat animals, so long as they are not made to suffer in the process. But in making concessions to meat-eating, Steiner and Francione might claim, animal welfarists fool us into thinking that we are making moral progress, when in fact things have not improved much at all. They would maintain that our moral goal should be to cease all human consumption of animals.

A passage from Donaldson and Kymlicka (2011) illustrates how abolitionists might view the obstacles present in making this change:

> In the transition period there can be a sense of deprivation of past
> freedoms and opportunities, and a powerful awareness of the bur-
> den of new practices. So there needs to be a transition strategy to
> deal with this (e.g. incremental changes, lots of experimentation,
> compensations, and so on). But in judging what are reasonable
> efforts to bring about the circumstances of justice, the fundamental
> issue is not the transition costs (which can be offset), but whether
> the transition leads to fair and sustainable practices in the long term.
> (p. 202)

So long as we have identified the right moral ideal, this passage seems to
suggest, even the cost of achieving the transition is unimportant. Many
abolitionists are likely to agree with this claim, particularly with respect to
the treatment of animals. In many cases where animal lives are at stake, we
should be willing to absorb any costs.

But this in fact assumes a certain conception of psychological plausibility. In order to pursue a transition strategy, abolitionists must inevitably
rely on some process of determining what it would take to reach the endpoint. Not all states of justice are achievable, even with considerable time
and resources to reach the endpoint. So the only way to make sense of
Donaldson and Kymlicka's passage above is to assume that one is working
with a moral ideal that *is* achievable. The criteria for psychological plausibility are important because they set a standard for making such a deter-
mination. The very idea that we can offset psychological changes through
"transition costs" assumes something like the achievability and transition
criteria. Only by establishing how human psychology might change can
we understand what it would take to get to the next stage in meeting a
moral goal.

Another possible objection that either Garner or abolitionists might
make is that the criteria for psychological plausibility set too high of a bar
for psychological change. In putting the burden of proof on ethicists to
explain why we should expect human psychology to change, perhaps the
criteria are unfair to the flexibility of individuals and implicitly assume

that change is unlikely. As Gilabert and Lawford-Smith (2012) have remarked, to treat psychological limitations as intractable in this way is a form of "cynical realism."

Although individuals certainly can and will change, the potential to change is not unlimited. Saying this, however, is not cynical realism. In making normative prescriptions, ethicists are committing themselves to some view about the psychology of human beings. The criteria of psychological plausibility set a *minimum* condition for ethicists to explain why their views are compatible with human psychology.

For further illustration, consider a spectrum of positions one could take on the normative implications of psychologically difficult moral ideals:

> *Cynical Realism*: Individuals can never change, and there is no use asking them to try.
> *Optimistic Realism*: Individuals probably will not change, but that should not stop us from asking them to try.
> *Practical Idealism*: Individuals can change, but we should focus on the most realistic options when asking them to try.
> *Starry-Eyed Idealism*: Individuals can change; it just takes time and effort.

Both of the extremes here should be rejected, with the most reasonable position arguably lying closest to practical idealism. It would be particularly starry-eyed to maintain that psychological possibilities are *irrelevant* to individuals' moral obligations. The basic claim that psychological plausibility has normative implications does not, however, make one a cynical realist.

In contrast, the abolitionist claims mentioned above seem to be instances of both starry-eyed idealism and cynical realism. Abolitionists seem particularly starry-eyed in arguing that animal welfarism is not sufficiently demanding but that their own ideals are within the realm of achievability. And they come off as cynical realists in assuming that animal welfarism will be the last stop for improving animal treatment. Garner, in further contrast, seems to embrace practical idealism but does not provide good reasons to think he has identified psychologically realistic ideals. Garner assumes greater psychological inflexibility than abolitionists (which moves him away from the starry-eyed end of the spectrum) but doesn't have anything to ground this in. The minimal criteria of psychological plausibility are helpful here. Garner needs to establish that his own ideals currently have an impact on people, or if they do not, whether we could expect them to have an impact in the future, given current understandings of human psychology.

6.3.3 Final Objections

There are a few lingering concerns one might to have to the arguments thus far. An initial thought someone might have is that criticizing abolitionism is an easy target. Abolitionists hear often enough that their ideas are unrealistic. I have tried to sharpen this sort of criticism and identify what abolitionists should address with respect to moral psychology. But this may have come too easily. Aren't there are any other ideals, beyond abolitionism and Garner's critique of abolitionism, that have psychological plausibility problems?

The issue of psychological plausibility takes as its target not abolitionism as such but any view where a moral ideal makes steep psychological demands without an investigation into whether these demands are achievable. The core idea is that psychology matters for ethical theorizing about animals. Arguing for this does not require numerous examples; what goes for abolitionism will go for similar ideals. The main point is that ideals— and moral goals generally—must be responsive to human psychology. Ethicists who are interested in changing attitudes toward animals must consider whether the specific goals they promote meet minimal criteria for psychological plausibility.

Most of the psychological plausibility problems within animal ethics also arise out of general psychological processes and are not directly a result of responses that are specific to animals. Because the cause of the problem is general, there will also likely be general implications. There are some problems that face any theory in animal ethics.

For example, one broad challenge is accounting for moral change over time. Animal ethicists have been remarkably silent on this issue. The only relevant debate within the field, as far as I can tell, is over the role of reason in changing our attitudes to and treatment of animals. Perhaps the most prominent moral psychological claim found in the animal ethics litera-ture, commonly attributed to Peter Singer and Tom Regan, is that human agents need only use the faculty of reason to recognize their moral duties to animals. From an individual perspective, that is, people should be able to reason their way through any psychological obstacles to see what is required of them.

Consider, for instance, Regan's (1991) argument against care ethics. A key feature of care ethics is that our moral duties arise out of our close relationships with others. We owe more to our offspring, for example, than we do to strangers. Regan (1991, pp. 96–98) claims that this is not only morally objectionable but also psychologically implausible. He argues that human beings, as rational agents, are psychologically constrained by morally arbitrary principles—we recognize and want to avoid them. And showing partiality toward others, he argues, is one of these morally arbitrary principles. For example, in the case of pain, Regan does not see how we could say that the pain of one person matters more than the pain of another (including other animals). Pain is undesirable always and eve-rywhere, and rational agents should realize this. If someone's emotional attachments are causing unreasonable partiality, Regan suggests that we work to bring our sentiments in line with our reason—our reason can tell us who to care for.

Regan's assertions raise a number of important moral psychological issues. He is making falsifiable moral psychological claims (e.g., reason resists moral arbitrariness, partiality can be reduced through reason, pain is perceived to have equal and fundamental moral importance wherever it is found) and is also arguing against another normative theory's moral psychology (the partiality presupposed by care ethics is easily modifi-able). However, the main motivation behind his approach seems to be the objectionable consequences that follow from the moral psychology of care ethics. Suppose he is right about this, and care ethics does indeed present an undesirable picture of human psychology. The burden would still be on Regan, it would seem, to demonstrate that his own moral psy-chological claims are at least minimally plausible.

Regan's views on the function of reason in producing moral change seem to be quite common in the animal ethics literature. Many animal ethicists assume that reason can alter behavior and reign in our emotions to the degree required by their theories. What is significant, and somewhat surprising, is how rarely the proponents of these claims provide evidence in their support. Hundreds of studies, some of them including classic, widely cited experiments, could be cited to illuminate the role of reason in producing (or failing to produce) moral change, but they are entirely absent from the major publications in the field (the single exception I'm aware of is Varner, 2012). So to summarize the response to the initial objection: there are numerous ideals with psychological plausibility problems within animal ethics, but perhaps a bigger problem in the field is addressing general psychological constraints. The potential role of reason is a big one, but any of the psychological processes described in the last chapter would also be good candidates.

Another thought one might have is that the discussion thus far is too pessimistic about moral psychological change. Pessimism has been addressed already, but here I have in mind a more historically oriented formulation of the objection. From looking at human history, we know that moral psychology will change. Moreover, we know that we have been wrong about many perceived psychological obstacles in the past. For example, achieving gender and racial equality has at different times been seen as psychologically implausible in the United States. Someone could object that I am making the same mistake as those who opposed gender and racial equality by assuming that human psychology is so inflexible. Even if we have evidence that some ideals are unachievable, why should that matter? Shouldn't the presumption be in favor of radical psychological change? Don't we already know that persistence can eventually overcome psychological constraints?

A thorough answer to this objection will come in the next chapter. Here it is sufficient to make a couple simple points about achievability in history. The history of moral change indicates that moral psychology is flexible but not that it is *infinitely* flexible. For instance, improvements in gender and racial equality have been achieved through some routes much more easily than others. Coercive laws and complex methods of social change are often required and only over long periods of time. Certain past claims about psychological resistance may thus in some cases have been quite accurate. That apparent psychological obstacles in the past were eventually overcome does not mean that people were wrong to claim either that psychological obstacles existed or that moral goals should be promoted with these obstacles in mind.

Similarly, equality for animals (whatever that might mean) may indeed be achievable but not by just any route. Some methods of moral and social change will meet significant psychological resistance. The criteria outlined here are meant to encourage ethicists to work to determine which routes those are. In many cases, identifying one possible route for change will not be sufficient. As moral psychology changes, so must transition plans for further psychological change.

Some moral changes also *accommodate* psychological obstacles rather than changing them. This produces the appearance of moral change but without substantial modifications to underlying psychology. For instance, it is still much disputed whether certain improvements in gender and racial equality are merely apparent. There are laws and policies in place to prevent egregious harms, but these may not reflect people's core attitudes. As a consequence, these attitudes may just find other outlets that are not so easily regulated by the law. Consider, for instance, Derrick Bell's (1992) famous statement of the inevitability of racism in America: "Black people will never gain full equality in this country. Even those herculean efforts we hail as successful will produce no more than temporary 'peaks of progress', short-lived victories that slide into irrelevance as racial patterns adapt in ways that maintain white dominance" (p. 373). I do not intend to argue for the animal equivalent of Bell's "racial realism" here. The point is just that we must be wary of false achievability. If we have good reasons to think that a moral goal is unachievable, then the standards should be higher—not lower—for evaluating whether that goal is in fact achievable. The evidence reviewed in the previous chapters suggests that we should be cautious about certain claims regarding moral change in our attitudes toward animals.

A closely related idea that someone might have is that moral change is typically haphazard. When we look at the history of moral change, rarely do we see anyone closely following a long-term plan—similar to the sort of criteria outlined here—in order to *effectively* create moral change. Social and moral change comes about accidentally, if at all. As sociologist Erik Olin Wright (2010) summarizes momentous social changes in human history, "Mostly people were not deliberately trying to change the world; they were trying to deal with concrete problems they encountered as they made their lives as best they could" (p. 299). Supposing this is true, shouldn't we just give up on constructing psychologically plausible moral goals? Why care about realistic moral goals if moral change is determined by numerous other non-moral factors?

This presents a difficult challenge. The fundamental premise of the objection is reasonable. If moral judgments are strongly influenced by factors outside of our control, as argued in the last chapter, then we should indeed expect moral change to occur haphazardly.

However, there are opportunities to initiate pockets of change, and there are indeed people currently trying to make those changes. This is reflected in the social approach outlined earlier. More will be said about potential changes that could be made in chapter 8. For now it is enough to note that insofar as attempts are made to initiate social change, it is preferable to do so with psychologically realistic methods and goals. This includes accounting for the various unconscious influences on our moral behavior, as well as structural and political conditions that would enable certain changes. If we are going to pursue moral change over time, then we must pursue these changes incrementally. The arguments here have hopefully shown why we need to look to moral psychology in order to do this effectively.

6.4 CONCLUSION

While the previous chapters have mainly been concerned with how we actually think about animals, here we have looked a bit more at how we ought to think about our moral goals concerning animals. In the next chapter we return to certain crucial empirical issues. As mentioned in the previous section, human history poses a challenge to the idea that that there are any significant obstacles to moral change. Historical changes in our attitudes toward animals might indicate that treatment of animals has radically improved and will likely continue to improve. This might further suggest that moral attitudes toward animals are extremely flexible, in which case much of what has been said thus far will seem misguided. To address this issue, we must look more closely at the relevant evidence for attitude change historically and across cultures.

Chapter 7

Animals and the Expanding
Moral Circle

Changing moral attitudes toward animals are often attributed to an expanding "moral circle." The idea can be found in Peter Singer's (1981) classic *The Expanding Circle*, and more recently Steven Pinker (2011) has argued that improved treatment of animals closely parallels other rights movements and will likely continue to do so. Rarely, however, is the concept of an expanding moral circle explored in any detail, as either a historical or a psychological phenomenon.

If an expanding moral circle can account for our moral attitudes toward animals, then the arguments in the last chapter might seem misguided. Though often understood as a metaphor, we can interpret the expanding moral circle as making both predictive and explanatory claims. It identifies certain factors that predict that our moral attitudes to animals will improve in some sense, leading to better treatment for animals, and it explains past improvements in attitudes toward animals according to these same factors. If these claims are accurate—presently, historically, and across cultures—then those factors had better be featured in any adequate account of moral attitudes toward animals. The previous chapters, however, have not suggested anything like an expanding moral circle. Indeed, an expanding moral circle would seem to fly in the face of dehumanization because an expanding circle suggests that animals are increasingly viewed as deserving treatment equal to human beings.

The concept of an expanding moral circle, as we will see, does not adequately explain changing attitudes toward animals. Moral concern toward animals has increased in some sense but not in the way suggested by an expanding moral circle.

7.1 THE EXPANDING MORAL CIRCLE HYPOTHESIS

7.1.1 Main Tenets and Challenges

Let's begin by exploring the expanding moral circle hypothesis in more detail: what it is, what predictions it makes, and what moral psychological changes it seems to entail. There are three main features that form the core of the expanding moral circle. These are not official doctrine; nobody has explicitly characterized the expanding moral circle by these features. But they should be seen as mostly uncontroversial. It should be noted that many proponents of the expanding moral circle hypothesis do not explicitly use it as an explanatory device. Nonetheless, it can be taken as such. The content of the expanding moral circle hypothesis makes compelling claims about human moral psychology that deserve further scrutiny.

Arguably the most important feature is a quantitative claim about the number of different types of entities we show moral concern for. The most basic idea captured by the expanding moral circle is that more entities are being treated better than they were previously. This includes both overall number of entities and number of different *types* of entities. The moral circle doesn't expand by adding more members of traditionally included groups. It expands by adding groups that are traditionally seen as outside the circle and adding more and more members of those groups.

This first feature seems to be about moral considerability, or moral status. As discussed in chapter 4, entities with moral status meet a minimum threshold for moral concern. The expanding moral circle hypothesis claims that historically there is an increase in the number of different types of entities for whom we have shown moral concern. It also predicts that this trend will continue.

In addition to this quantitative claim, the moral circle hypothesis seems to involve a qualitative claim. The moral circle hypothesis claims that the change in treatment is morally important, or makes a moral difference. This is the main point of contention between abolitionists and welfarists, as described in chapter 6. For example, a new law that prevents livestock animals from physical abuse would be seen as morally important in the right way for welfarists but not for abolitionists. Abolitionists would object that providing livestock with better welfare does not mean they have entered the moral circle because ultimately they are used for human purposes. Abolitionists are thus contesting what sort of change in treatment qualifies as morally significant.

This provides an interesting wrinkle to the classic distinction between moral considerability and moral significance (as outlined by Goodpaster, 1978). The quantitative claim, which seems the most common way of framing the moral circle hypothesis, appears to be about moral considerability; it claims that an increasing number of different types of entities receive basic moral concern. This qualitative claim, however, suggests that entities can be morally considerable without really being part of the *human* moral circle; they are comparatively morally insignificant. An animal can be the proper target of moral concern but still be seen as undeserving of treatment comparable to human beings. The moral circle hypothesis thus also seems to claim that there is a qualitative shift in treatment toward animals. There is not just *any* improvement but one that really matters, morally speaking. As we will see, determining when the right sort of change has occurred poses a significant challenge in assessing the evidence for moral expansion.

The expanding moral circle hypothesis also identifies the source of moral change in previous social, moral, and political movements. Certain well-known social movements have altered a number of criteria used to determine membership in the moral circle—including gender, race, religion, class, and many others. Species and phylogenetic classification might be next on the list. Whether an entity is considered non-human may eventually be recognized as morally irrelevant.

This social aspect of the moral circle hypothesis differs from the quantitative and qualitative claims in that it points to possible causal mechanisms for expansion. Whatever caused the success of previous movements should, according to the expanding moral circle hypothesis, eventually influence attitudes toward animals as well. The moral circle hypothesis does not say exactly what the mechanisms are, but it suggests that scholars should be able to identify possible causes based on the history of social and moral change.

From looking at the history of moral change, there seem to be two main ways of becoming a member of the moral circle. One way is for the qualifications for membership in the circle to change. For example, instead of being white or male or highly educated, we could take the moral circle to require humanness. Anything non-human would thus be excluded. We could, for instance, also recognize sentience as a qualifying feature, in which case some non-humans would count. As mentioned above, however, there may be further distinctions once inside the circle. Some entities in the moral circle might be more morally significant and so be owed more.

Another way to change membership in the moral circle is by discovering that certain entities possess the necessary qualifications for membership, though previously this was not recognized. For instance, if intelligence is a qualifying condition, then some animals could be added by virtue of their sophisticated cognitive abilities. Here an entity becomes morally considerable because it is seen as possessing properties that other entities already in the circle also have.

Both methods of moral expansion involve exploration of things both inside and outside of the circle. They often work in tandem in order to revise group membership. For instance, studies of animals have uncovered previously unrecognized capacities. But deeper analysis of what we take as morally important about human beings has also changed. Sentience, for example, may have come to be seen as important for this reason. What matters is how things feel to us, not our language, intelligence, and so on; and this is further reinforced as we learn more about animals' capacity for feelings.

These two routes to inclusion in the moral circle constitute the main explananda of the expanding moral circle hypothesis. To understand what causes the moral circle to expand we must investigate how we learn about and recognize new moral properties and how we attribute to entities moral properties that they were previously thought to lack. These factors will drive the analysis throughout the rest of the chapter.

To briefly summarize, we have identified three features that constitute the phenomenon of the expanding moral circle. The expanding moral circle is 1) an increase in the number of different types of entities seen as morally considerable, 2) a change in treatment that is morally important, and 3) part of a connected series of changes in moral treatment. This is a somewhat stipulative definition. It is mainly intended as a starting point for the investigation. Let's now look in more detail at how others have attempted to explain how entities are added to the moral circle.

7.1.2 Proposed Causal Factors

In historical analysis, it is often difficult to separate outcomes from causal factors. For example, increased legal rights is likely both an outcome and a cause of increased moral concern for animals. What we really want, though, are the causes. We want to know what exactly has caused changes in treatment of animals and whether there is any reason to think these causal factors will continue to have an effect. Increased legal rights, for instance, might be a result of some other causal factor; perhaps animals have become more valuable in a monetary sense, thus giving litigants a reason to grant increased protections over them as property. That would not necessarily support the expanding moral circle hypothesis.

Distinguishing between causes and outcomes provides a solution to the more general problem of getting beyond facile recognition that treatment of animals has improved. For the moral circle hypothesis to be important or interesting, it has to make a claim about how and why moral change occurs. This requires specific proposals for what has caused past changes in treatment of animals as well as predictions for how changes will occur in the future.

One proposed explanation for the expanding moral circle can be found in Singer (1981). His basic claim is that over time human beings have become more altruistic and less self-interested. We have become more interested in pursuing and protecting the well-being of others, even without accruing benefits for ourselves. Animals are not the sole beneficiaries of this process but were high up on the list of things we began caring about as soon as we stopped caring mainly about ourselves. On a scale from pure selfishness to altruism, the prediction is that we first care about our own interests, then things that are closely related to us (like family and friends), and then things that seem to be closely related to us (like certain animals); and eventually this comparison to ourselves will drop out completely.

This explanation seems unsatisfactory, however, because the transition from selfishness to altruism remains unexplained. It is not much of an explanation, for instance, to say that treatment of animals has improved because we care about them more than we used to. The question is *why* this might have occurred. In the terminology just mentioned, the selfishness to altruism hypothesis seems more of an outcome than a cause. No clear causal mechanism is contained in the mere observation that altruism has increased. Attributing the change to altruism seems like a mere redescription of the process instead of an identification of relevant causal factors.

Another possibility is based in human reason and the power of good arguments to change minds. Perhaps over time the arguments in favor of the moral importance of animals have improved. Or perhaps in parallel people have become better at reflecting on the moral properties of animals or the legitimacy of criteria used to determine who is owed moral status. There are overwhelming reasons to be skeptical of this sort of proposal, as discussed in chapter 5, so we will set it aside.

The large majority of proposed explanations for the expanding moral circle are non-rationalist. For instance, the philosopher Robert Solomon (1999) proposes that empathy is the primary cause of the expanding moral circle. He argues that, "what allows the circle to expand is not reason . . . but rather knowledge and understanding in the sense of coming to appreciate the situations and the circumstances in which other people and creatures find themselves" (p. 75). His proposal roughly follows the phenomenal account presented in chapter 4. There is a psychological connection between seeing something as capable of feeling and seeing it as deserving moral concern. So as we have come to see more and more animals as capable of emotional awareness, we have also as a result come to see them as having moral status. As Solomon explains the process, "We *learn* to perceive chickens, cows, and warthogs as sentient beings with real emotions, and we learn to conceive of our uses of animals as a moral choice, not, first of all, because of any rational principles but because of our cultivated and expanded emotional awareness" (p. 76).

This basic proposal has also been put forth by a number of psychologists. Sherman and Haidt (2011), for instance, focus specifically on cuteness: "we propose that cuteness expands the moral circle and that it does so by motivating sociality, which in turn activates processes of mind perception" (p. 248). This proposal also closely follows the reasoning behind the phenomenal account presented in chapter 4, as well as the evolutionary account outlined in chapter 2. Some animals, they acknowledge, are disgusting and as a result are denied certain mental states, which furthermore leads us to deny them moral status. However, other animals we perceive as cute because they share features with human infants. These features motivate us to engage with them as we would human children, leading to the sort of phenomenal mentalizing that is psychologically linked to moral considerability judgments. Cuteness is one important determining factor in this process, but there are also others, including compassion, love, and gratitude (a similar proposal pitting empathy against disgust has also been made by Pizarro, Detweiler-Bedell, & Bloom, 2006).

A problem with both of these proposals is that empathy and cuteness are more attuned to ingroup members. Much of the evidence for this was reviewed in chapter 4. Empathy does increase moral concern but mainly toward animals that look and act like human beings. We should thus expect any expansion in the moral circle based on empathy to be quite limited. There is also evidence that empathy often fails to produce a change in behavior when there is a discrepancy between two parties in terms of status and power (Zaki & Cikara, 2015). This is of course highly relevant to interactions between humans and non-human animals.

Empathy and cuteness thus seem to predict very small pockets of moral expansion. A prediction we can make from these proposals is that animals considered outside of the moral circle will only be brought in if they possess heretofore unrecognized neotenous features. However, this will consist of an expansion not in our moral concepts but in which animals possess the necessary criteria for membership. Furthermore, the only criterion that would really matter, in such cases, is one's capacity for experiencing phenomenal states. This is perfectly consistent with the account from chapter 4, but it is not clear how this provides support for the expanding moral circle hypothesis. The underlying moral psychology does not seem to predict steady or significant increases in moral concern for animals.

An important criticism of these empathy and cuteness proposals comes from Steven Pinker (2011). Though he agrees that there is a psychological connection between perceiving animals as cute and allowing them in the moral circle, he does not think that this provides an adequate explanation for improved treatment of animals. He emphasizes the importance of mutually beneficial relationships that have developed between human beings and various non-human animals. With respect to humans, he argues, this is often what leads to changed ingroup status (p. 581). Ultimately, however, he thinks that what has expanded are legal protections, not necessarily our moral sensibilities:

> What really has expanded is not so much a circle of empathy as a circle of *rights*—a commitment that other living things, no matter how distant or dissimilar, be safe from harm and exploitation. Empathy has surely been historically important in setting off epiphanies of concern for members of overlooked groups. But the epiphanies are not enough. For empathy to matter, it must goad changes in policies and norms that determine how the people in those groups are treated. (p. 591)

The "epiphanies of concern" Pinker mentions could refer to either of the expansion strategies mentioned above. For instance, perhaps people have begun to care more about animal sentience, or perhaps more and more animals are seen as sentient. Either way, Pinker seems to suggest, these factors only matter if they lead to concrete changes in laws and policies aimed at protecting animals.

Pinker's claims pose a general challenge for any explanation of the expanding moral circle that is based in human psychology. Psychology pushes us in some directions rather than others, but what we want is something with staying power. *Maybe* something in our psychologies has caused improved attitudes toward animals (whatever that might mean), but maybe instead it's something rooted in the way laws and policies have changed over time. For instance, as Pinker argues, perhaps democracies have made it increasingly difficult to engage in aggression and violence. Human beings are the main beneficiaries of these laws, with animals receiving protection as a side effect. Attitudes toward animals may thus have changed as a consequence of rules created for human gain. If that's true, then moral psychological changes were not the primary causal factor in expanding moral concern for animals.

However, changes in laws and policies also frequently fail to have staying power. Legal rights aren't obviously reflective of any moral psychological change. As Wagman and Liebman (2012) state in their book on animal law, "The existence of a law shows only that some group was able to harness the machinery of government to effectuate its ends" (p. 18). Moral attitudes toward animals may not have changed so much as they are now being managed better. Whether this is part of an expanding moral circle depends on its efficacy over time. For instance, perhaps explicit harm to animals has just become more difficult and is penalized more often. This does not mean that there is less of a desire to harm animals.

So while Pinker's challenge must be addressed, it remains an open question whether changing legal protections do indeed provide support for an expanding moral circle. As mentioned above, legal rights are both causes and outcomes of changing attitudes. Legal rights do seem to provide enduring protections, but that doesn't mean they have caused expanded moral sensibilities.

Thus far we have taken a broad perspective on the moral circle and looked a little bit at the predictive and explanatory claims of the expanding moral circle. But the historical evidence, one might think, is what is most important. As an entryway into that discussion, we will look in more detail at the most recent changes and critically evaluate whether they provide support for an expanding moral circle.

7.2 CHANGING ATTITUDES TOWARD ANIMALS

The psychology of dehumanization indicates that we overlook the suffering of outgroup members, particularly animals. This is part of seeing something as inferior to us. Seeing something as subhuman requires us to view its pain and suffering as less important than that of other human beings.

However, the expanding moral circle would seem to predict that harm to animals has come to be seen as morally problematic. We should expect that active harming of animals has decreased and active protection against harm has increased. This is part of seeing animals as morally considerable. But does the evidence support these claims? Do recent changes in attitudes to animals support the existence of an expanding moral circle?

7.2.1 Evidence of Expansion

It is difficult to deny that we are currently experiencing a great level of moral concern directed at a wide range of animals. One must tread carefully when analyzing very recent history, but it also seems that this change has been building over the last 50 years. Reject the moral circle if you must, the reader might think, but surely you cannot deny that things are improving for animals.

One type of evidence often cited in support of an expanding moral circle concerns the use of animals in laboratory research. Rowan and Loew's (2001) review of trends in the late 20th century found that use of animals in laboratory research had been steadily declining, after having peaked in the 1970s and 1980s (mainly in Britain and the United States). Similar trends have recently been reported for the United States. In 2014, 834,543 animals covered by the Animal Welfare Act were used in laboratory research, the lowest recorded since 1973 (U.S. Department of Agriculture, 2015). Similarly, the European Union's (2014) report on animal use found that the downward trend has continued, with 11.5 million animals used in 2011, down from around 12 million used in 2008. All of these statistics could be cited as evidence of an expanding circle of moral concern.

It has been suggested, however, that the use of laboratory animals is vastly underreported. In the United States, the majority of animals used are rats and mice, which are not covered by the Animal Welfare Act and so do not figure into the numbers reported above. In the United Kingdom, around 90% of the animals used are mice and rats. A similar percentage, or more, is likely in the United States. A recent analysis by Goodman, Chandna, and Roe (2015) suggests that when mice in particular are included, it is clear that animal use in America is increasing. They found that over a period of 15 years, institutions that had received a significant amount of money from the National Institutes of Health had increased their use of vertebrates, from just over 1.5 million to just over 2.5 million. This trend may not reflect use by other institutions in the United States, but it does give reason to wonder whether there is expanded moral concern for animals. We should also consider the total number of animals being used. Even if the trend is downward, the European Union alone is using over 11 million animals every year. Good data on global trends are hard to find, but in 2005 it was estimated that over 100 million animals were used annually across 179 countries (Taylor et al., 2008). If there is an expanding circle of moral concern for laboratory animals, these data suggest that it is expanding very slowly.

We might also point to meat consumption as evidence of an expanding moral circle. In 2012, annual worldwide meat consumption was expected to reach 455 million tons by 2015 (Alexandratos & Bruinsma, 2012). Though global meat consumption is increasing, the *rate* of meat consumption is declining. Overall meat consumption increased 2.6% from 1980 to 2006 but is expected to increase only 1.6% between 2005/2007 and 2030 (Alexandratos & Bruinsma, 2012, p. 46). Much of this decline will be seen in Western countries, which have traditionally been heavy consumers of animals reared in objectionable conditions. The overall *amount* of meat consumed in developed countries has actually already started to decrease. This could perhaps be cited as evidence in favor of an expanding moral circle.

However, there are reasons to be skeptical. Although meat consumption is slightly decreasing in Western developed countries, this is more than made up for by increases in developing countries, especially in Asia (Alexandratos & Bruinsma, 2012, p. 44). China, Brazil, and India, for instance, are all expected to significantly increase their rates of consumption through 2050 (p. 58). There are many causes of this, including decreasing costs of production, population growth, and malnourishment. These factors are unlikely to go away. Moreover, agricultural intensification is increasing and projected to continue increasing. From 1997 to 2007, for example, world beef production increased by 1.2% a year, but total number of cattle increased by only .5% (Alexandratos & Bruinsma, 2012). This means that efficiency of cattle use improved by .7%. From an animal welfare perspective, it might seem that this is a good thing: a .7% increase in efficiency means that fewer animals are brought into existence purely to be killed for our consumption. There is a downside to this, however, in that intensification likely entails worse lives for the animals. Killing fewer animals is only an improvement if their lives are not made worse off.

Arguably the best evidence for an expanding moral circle is the huge increase in laws and legal rights granting increased protection for animals. Rowan and Rosen (2005) argue that legislation for animals in the United States was met with failure for most of the 20th century but eventually reached great success in the 1990s, at both the state and federal levels. Since 2005 things have really taken off. Just to review some highlights: in 2008 the EU Court of Human Rights considered, for the first time anywhere, whether a chimpanzee could be considered a person. In 2009 the Lisbon Treaty, passed by the European Union, included the requirement that all EU nations protect the welfare of sentient animals. Since 2013 animal cruelty has been a felony everywhere in the United States (Tauber, 2015, p. 133). The 2015 report by the Animal Legal Defense Fund (ALDF, 2015) determined that 43 of the 50 American states and 6 territories surveyed had improved their legal protection of animals within the last year. This included increased penalties for mistreatment and improved standards of care, among many other types of legislation aimed at protecting animals. And in November 2015 the U.S. National Institutes of Health decided to end all biomedical research on chimpanzees. This is far from an exhaustive summary of recent landmark legislation, but it is enough to indicate that animals are now seen as legitimate recipients of legal rights.

As mentioned previously, it is difficult to determine whether increased legal protections are motivated by positive moral attitudes toward the party receiving legal protections. It is often noted that animals have traditionally been seen as property within the eyes of the law (Favre, 2011; Tauber, 2015). Protection against harm to animals is still treated roughly along the lines of damage to property—namely, as a criminal act against the owner, not the animal. This might be changing, but there are still reasons to think it will be difficult for most legal traditions to incorporate animal interests and weigh them equally against those of humans. Tauber (2015, p. 62), for instance, notes that the U.S. federal government has tended to litigate *against* animals. He reports that when the federal government has participated in cases involving animals, it has adopted a position opposed to animals in 48% of cases and protected or advanced animal interests in about 8%. He also argues that the federal government tends to be much more successful when litigating against animals. Animals also haven't fared well in the U.S. Supreme Court. In one notable ongoing case, the court ruled in defense of ritualistic animal sacrifice and selling videos depicting animal cruelty, on the grounds that they are protected by the First Amendment (Tauber, 2015, p. 87). This suggests there might be strict limits to legal protections for animals. Increased legal protections are certainly important for showing moral concern for animals, but it is not clear how to account for the limitations just outlined in the expanding moral circle story.

Many legal experts have echoed this skepticism about the ultimate impact of animal protection legislation. As Wagman and Liebman (2012) summarize the history of legal changes for animals, "as the laws expanded by increasing the potential defendants and number of animals included within the laws' purview, they significantly shrunk in terms of coverage of potential acts of cruelty" (p. 151). They note how exemptions have arisen in response to anti-cruelty laws in order to permit traditional uses of animals in agriculture, scientific research, and many other areas. As this has played out in the United States, they claim, "a set of laws supposedly aimed at providing oversight and enforcing humane values—and preventing the worst cruelty—now does not cover the largest number of acts that cause the greatest amount of animal suffering" (p. 151). Brian Leiter (2013, p. 531) similarly suggests that animal legislation has strong limits because exploitation of animals continues to be instrumental for improving human quality of life and supporting various cultural traditions. As a result, it is unlikely that courts will proactively extend protection to animals.

Laboratory research, meat consumption, and legal regulations might all be seen as only remotely connected to public perception of animals. If we want to know whether moral concern has expanded, one might think we should look at studies of what people actually say about animals. Herzog, Rowan, and Kossow (2001) argue that surveys conducted throughout the late 20th century indicate a definite improvement in attitudes toward animals among Americans. On pretty much every area of animal use, more people supported improved protection for animals at the end of the century than at any time in the previous 50 years. This trend seems to have continued. A Gallup poll conducted in May 2015 found that American attitudes toward animals improved between 2008 and 2015 (Riffkin, 2015). Specifically, there was an increase from 25% to 32% in the percentage of respondents who said that animals "deserve the same rights as people to be free from harm and exploitation." There was a corresponding decrease in the number of people who said that animals can be used for human benefit, so long as they are not harmed or exploited. This suggests a shift in attitudes about whether animals can be used for human benefit—a seemingly significant moral change.

More animals—and more types of animals—do seem to have moral status than ever before. We can make that conclusion based on many different studies, including Herzog et al.'s above. This is not reflected in the Gallup poll, however. The number of people reporting that animals "don't need protection" remained stable at 3% from 2003 to 2015. This makes it difficult to conclude that we are experiencing a moral expansion—that we should expect a continued increase in the number of animals seen as morally considerable. Past changes in attitudes toward animals seem to support the quantitative claim of the expanding moral circle, but recent changes do not.

It's also unclear how we should interpret the increase in people who think animals cannot be used for human benefit (from 25% to 32%). Pet-keeping, for instance, might count as "keeping animals for human benefit." But it seems unlikely that a third of Americans object to pet-keeping. This raises the more general issue of how respondents understand the terms used. For instance, consider their interpretation of "harm and exploitation": 94% of people thought animals deserved some degree of protection from harm and exploitation. However, another question in this poll found a much smaller percentage of people who expressed concern about the ways animals were treated as pets (68%), in zoos (78%), and as livestock (80%). These more pointed questions had not been asked previously, preventing any historical comparison. But the lower numbers should make us wonder whether people are applying a relatively narrow conception of harm and exploitation. A significant portion of respondents (20–30%) apparently does not think *any* harm or exploitation is involved in pet-keeping, captivity, and intensive agriculture. This too makes it difficult to conclude that current attitudes to animals are part of an expanding moral circle.

This review of different areas of possible expansion has hopefully identified good reasons for skepticism. It is not obvious that treatment of animals is significantly improving or that we can expect this to change in the near future. Making strong claims here is difficult—it would be foolish to think treatment *can't* improve—but the most recent shifts don't seem to provide evidence for a significant expansion in moral concern. In the last 50 years, more different types of animals have come to be seen as worthy of the most basic level of moral concern. But I emphasize *basic*. Harming some of them clearly has come to matter, morally speaking, but it's not clear how widely this concern has spread (i.e., to which animals), nor what people think counts as harm.

The issue of harm is particularly important for the expanding moral circle. A plausible hypothesis is that we have become more sensitive to animal harms and that this will only continue. If true, this would seem to provide support for the expanding moral circle. The claims just reviewed provide some reasons to be suspicious of this hypothesis, but more investigation is needed.

7.2.2 Perceiving Harm to Animals

Jonathan Haidt's moral foundations theory has interesting implications for the perception of harmful transgressions against animals. Haidt and his colleagues have proposed that harm is one of six basic foundations in our moral psychologies. Though harm-based transgressions are central to our conception of morality, according to Haidt, there is also much else. For instance, he thinks that there are such things as harmless transgressions and that the sphere of morality goes far beyond harm, to include violations of purity, loyalty, and much else. Canvassing this theory is important because it provides clues as to why harm to animals sometimes fails to elicit moral reactions.

According to Haidt and his colleagues (Haidt & Graham, 2007; Haidt & Kesebir, 2010), human morality is determined by six moral foundations:

(1) care/harm
(2) fairness/cheating

(3) loyalty/betrayal
(4) sanctity/degradation
(5) authority/subversion
(6) liberty/oppression

These domains were identified from a series of surveys and experiments conducted over the last 25 years. According to Graham et al. (2013, p. 108), these are considered "foundational" because they are common in judgments of others, emotionally based and automatic (as described in chapter 5), found across diverse cultural contexts, likely connected to innate dispositions, and evolutionarily based.

Although these foundations are supposed to be universal, Haidt's research is perhaps best known for showing that some human groups express some of these more strongly than others. Haidt's main finding, primarily in an American context, is that political liberals prioritize fairness and caring (the first two domains) more than loyalty and dominance hierarchies, while political conservatives tend to prioritize loyalty, purity, and other values associated with dominance hierarchies (foundations 3–5; Graham, Haidt, & Nosek, 2009; Haidt & Graham, 2007). Though this difference is most extreme in the United States, it has also been found in many other countries. For instance, Graham et al. (2011) found evidence for this basic phenomenon in 12 different world regions (United States, United Kingdom, Canada, Australia, Western and Eastern Europe, Latin America, Africa, Middle East, South Asia, East Asia, and Southeast Asia). So regardless of other political and social circumstances, there are significant differences between people who tend to prioritize fairness and care and people who tend to prioritize loyalty, authority, and sanctity (also see Van Leeuwen & Park, 2009).

A potential problem caused by this difference is that it predicts significant disagreement over which types of moral transgressions are most serious. Harm is not of ultimate importance for everyone. For instance, in one classic study, Haidt, Koller, and Dias (1993) found that Brazilians tended to treat violations of conventions (like failing to wear the right school uniform) as *morally* wrong but denied that anyone was harmed by these transgressions. People in Western societies, in contrast, only saw such acts as a transgression of conventional norms, without any harm or moral wrongdoing. Transgressions that do not obviously cause harm tend to be moralized more frequently by those in non-Western societies and people who are low in socioeconomic status, according to Haidt, and as a result have been overlooked by many Western scholars. But Haidt points out that harm is not the overriding concern even among affluent Westerners. For instance, one study found that people think harm is involved in around 30% of the instances where people think they or someone else has done something immoral (Hofmann et al., 2014).

This disagreement about the role of harm in moral transgressions is particularly important here because of how animals factor into moral foundations theory. One of the questions on the Moral Foundations Questionnaire explicitly asks about harm to animals (Graham et al., 2011). It states, "One of the worst things a person could do is hurt a defenseless animal." Participants' level of agreement with this statement contributes to their score on the care/harm foundation. That is, people's responses to this question tend to be positively correlated with responses to similar questions (e.g., their thoughts about killing human beings and showing compassion to people who are suffering). And as mentioned, responses to these questions about care/harm tend to be further correlated with responses to questions about fairness, which ask about things like fair treatment and justice.

The psychological difference between political liberals and conservatives thus has implications for attitudes to animals; measuring people's attitudes toward harm/care also taps into their attitudes about harming animals. The psychological difference in harm perception revealed by moral foundations theory predicts a parallel psychological difference in how people perceive harm to animals. Those who value care and fairness should show greater concern for animals, while those who value what are called the "binding foundations" (loyalty, authority, sanctity) should prioritize other interests over those of animals.

People who draw from the binding foundations are not particularly uncaring or unkind. Rather, moral foundations theory indicates that they place greater value on cultural and social stability and are more likely to think that certain forms of inequality are justified (e.g., due to their beliefs about dominance hierarchies). These two factors often work in tandem: inequalities that are firmly established in social and cultural traditions are more likely to be valued by those drawing from the binding foundations. This of course also has implications for animals. Animals are traditionally seen as inferior to human beings in many human cultures and are also central in many food customs. Those who draw more from the binding foundations are likely to endorse the inferior status traditionally ascribed to animals as well as the traditions that justify their consumption.

This is exactly what empirical research has found. For instance, scores on the harm/care foundation predict vegetarianism and disapproval of biomedical research on animals, while authority scores predict carnivorism (De Backer & Hudders, 2015; Koleva et al., 2012). One way the binding foundations have been studied in relation to animals is by measuring "social dominance orientation." People who score high on social dominance are more likely to agree with statements like "Superior groups should dominate inferior groups" and "Some groups of people are just more worthy than others." Responses on this measure correlate with a range of negative attitudes and behaviors toward animals. To briefly review: people high in social dominance orientation are more likely to think it is justified to use animals for human benefit (e.g., in biomedical research or to be raised for consumption) and are more likely to consume animal products (Dhont & Hodson, 2014; Dhont et al., 2014; Hyers, 2006). They are also more likely to see vegetarianism as a threat (agreeing with statements like "The rise of vegetarianism poses a threat to our country's cultural customs") and to think that animals are inferior to human beings (agreeing with statements like "The life of an animal is just not of equal value as the life of a human being"; Dhont & Hodson, 2014). They are also more likely to believe that animals and human beings are fundamentally different (Costello & Hodson, 2010). This belief in the difference between animals and humans is also correlated with scores on the related measure of right-wing authoritarianism (agreeing with statements like "The only way our country can get through the crisis ahead is to get back to our traditional values"; Motyl, Hart, & Pyszczynski, 2010).

Another pertinent finding is that people who score high on the binding foundations are more hostile and discriminatory toward outgroups (Kugler, Jost, & Noorbaloochi, 2014). This too has significant implications for attitudes toward animals. As should now be evident, animals are generally seen as members of an outgroup. This is supported by evidence showing that people who think in terms of social dominance are more likely to dehumanize other human outgroups and to see them as "less evolved" than those in their own ingroup (Kteily et al., 2015). They are also more likely to explicitly see both animals and other human outgroups (e.g., immigrants) negatively (Dhont et al., 2014). These results are similar to the comparisons made between humans and animals in the experiments reviewed in chapter 3.

As should now be clear, research on moral foundations theory indicates that people who draw from the binding foundations, particularly authority and loyalty, tend to disvalue animals and view them negatively. This is not a result of the *absence* of harm-based moral concern but the prioritizing of other concerns. The general structure of moral values, as determined by the binding foundations, is partly responsible for this prioritization. As Dhont et al. (2014) summarize much of the research discussed above, "attitudes toward both human and non-human animal outgroups are grounded in a generalized desire for group inequality and hierarchically structured group relations" (p. 106). This prioritization also results from the unique role of animals within human traditions, which dictate that they have a certain place within human hierarchies that demands certain types of treatment.

So how is this research relevant to the expanding moral circle? It shows that there will be significant obstacles in expanding moral concern for animals within any human culture. Past expansions, as well as changes observed currently, may be better explained as changes among people drawing from certain foundations. For example, perhaps coming to see harm to animals as morally important must be preceded by seeing harm as of ultimate moral importance for human affairs.

Moral foundations research also suggests that people will significantly differ in how they interpret and perceive harms to animals, depending on which foundations they draw from. Those who draw more from the binding foundations remain sensitive to harm, but their attention is directed more at harm to their cherished traditions and social structures. This poses additional obstacles to expanding moral concern for animals.

To see further implications of this targeted understanding of harm, consider a study by Prickett, Norwood, and Lusk (2010). They found, in an American context, that people who vote Republican are less likely to be interested in improving welfare for farm animals or in regulating farms generally. However, there was still strong support from Republicans: 64% agreed that the government should provide good welfare for farm animals, compared to 84% of Democrats. This majority support might be seen as indicating consensus agreement that something should be done to improve animal welfare.

However, we can still expect significant disagreement between Democrats and Republicans about what form this should take. The policies produced by this disagreement may ultimately be dissatisfying to one or both groups, despite it being done in the name of animal welfare. This possibility is evident in the responses Prickett et al. received to questions about animal welfare. They found three different conceptions of which conditions and behaviors were important for welfare: some cared primarily about "normal" behaviors and having access to outdoors, others cared mainly about reducing prices for consumers while also providing the most basic necessities for animals (e.g., water, food, treatment of diseases), and others cared only about providing the bare minimum of water, food, and treatment of diseases. There was no calculation of the correlation between these responses and political orientation, but we can still see that these different conceptions of welfare will likely conflict, plausibly due to different moral values. For instance, providing animals the conditions in which to perform a range of normal behaviors is costly and will make it difficult to reduce prices for consumers. Those drawing from the binding foundations are likely to place the interests of human beings (i.e., the consumers) over those of animals. So they might see themselves as caring about welfare but would ultimately disagree with more ambitious proposals for promoting animal welfare, beyond providing basic needs. Moreover, given the way moral foundations seem to function, these disagreements are not likely to be easily resolved.

In short, harm may be central to our moral lives, but there are many other considerations that are also very important and occasionally trump harm. This poses an obstacle to expanding moral concern for animals. Harming animals will likely be overlooked when other important human interests are at stake.

Before moving on, one challenge to moral foundations theory must be mentioned. There have been many criticisms of moral foundations theory, but perhaps the most prominent (at least the most data-driven) comes from Kurt Gray and colleagues (Gray Schein, & Ward, 2014; Schein & Gray, 2015). They argue that liberals and conservatives do not differ as much as Haidt's research has suggested. Instead, they argue, harm is at the center of all moral judgments.

Gray et al.'s criticisms don't seem to create overwhelming problems for the arguments here, as we can see from Haidt, Graham, and Ditto's (2015) reply to Gray et al. They argue that Gray and colleagues' data actually support the claim that harm is clearly not the only type of moral concern. Purity, subversion, disobedience, and fairness are also common. The core insights of moral foundations research also do not directly rely on the claim that there are harmless transgressions. Harmless transgressions do help illustrate the problems identified throughout this chapter, but more important is the prioritization of other interests over those of animals. It is abundantly clear that harm to animals is not an overriding concern for many people, and research on moral foundations provides a good explanation for this: some people place other values above harm, particularly when the harm in question is done to animals.

7.3 ATTITUDES TO ANIMALS HISTORICALLY AND ACROSS CULTURES

As discussed in chapter 4, attributing emotional capacities to animals— and capacity for phenomenal states generally—is central in seeing them as morally considerable. A prediction we can thus make is that part of the expanding moral circle is seeing animals as more capable of phenomenal states. This could follow either of the explananda noted previously: certain phenomenal states (e.g., pain) could have increased in moral importance, or instead phenomenal capacities that were always important were suddenly recognized in animals. Looking to historical debates about animal mental capacities can give us a better idea of the major watershed moments in thinking about phenomenal states and harm to animals.

7.3.1 The Western Trajectory on Pain and Suffering

Brian Leiter (2013) states that "the increasing moral importance assigned to the experience of pain and suffering . . . is also one of the stunning changes in the moral sensibility of modernity" (p. 513). The psychological connection between moral concern and phenomenal states like pain and suffering was discussed in chapter 4. But where did this psychological connection come from? Might the origin story of the phenomenal account provide support for the expanding moral circle?

A widely accepted explanation for expanding moral concern places the locus of activity in late 18th- and early 19th-century Britain (French, 1975; Passmore, 1975; Ryder, 1989; Turner, 1980). There are competing views about which movements were most important, but the standard narrative is that shifting attitudes around this time eventually made their way to the United States, and then eventually to other nations as well. This is not to say that concern for animals was born at this time. Rather, the largest and most influential movements seen today seem to have their roots in legal, moral, and political movements of late 18th- and early 19th-century Britain.

Laws passed in Britain at this time are often taken to be the marker of a significant change in moral sentiment. The first big law in Britain against cruelty to animals was passed in 1822. The Martin Act, as it came to be known (after Richard Martin, who presented it before the House of Lords), prevented explicit abuse of animals. The law still viewed cruelty to animals as damage to property, but it is widely seen as the first in an important series of steps toward preventing cruelty to animals (including the 1876 Cruelty to Animals Act). This was succeeded by the formation of the Society for the Prevention of Cruelty to Animals in 1824, which in 1840 became the Royal Society for the Protection of Cruelty to Animals (RSPCA). Though not a legal shift, the RSPCA was instrumental in the enforcement of anti-cruelty laws throughout the 19th century. Similar anti-cruelty societies and legislation soon appeared in the United States as well (Favre & Tsang, 1993).

There are many hypotheses for exactly how and why these changes occurred at this time. Some place the beginnings of the shift earlier in the 18th century. For instance, the historian Keith Thomas (1984) has asserted that pain only achieved moral significance once pet-keeping became popular in 18th-century Britain (eventually spreading to other countries as well). Anita Guerrini (1989) and Richard Ryder (1989) argue that dissection experiments, common throughout the 17th century but not formalized institutionally until the 18th century, were what led to the enhanced salience of animal bodies and their possession of morally significant mental states. There were movements against animal experimentation in the 1690s in France (and England soon after), but these did not gain sufficient momentum without public concern about pain and suffering. The subsequent increased use of anesthetics in Great Britain, which spread rapidly throughout the rest of Europe, seems to have raised pain to the status of a legitimate moral issue (Guerrini, 2003).

These historical accounts uncover certain problems with the expanding moral circle hypothesis. The main problem is that it seems moral concern has been remarkably slow to expand to animals, given the nature of the shift seen in the 18th and 19th centuries. The changes that occurred seem to have put in place the foundations of a moral psychological profile that would grant moral concern to a wide range of animals. So why did it take 150 years for animals to receive significant legal protections?

One possibility is that we have been steadily building on this foundation over the last 150 years. For instance, the next shift often cited comes in the 1960s and 1970s. Peter Singer's *Animal Liberation* was published in 1975, but before that was Ruth Harrison's (1964) *Animal Machines*, which prompted the Brambell Report (1965). The Brambell Report is often identified as a watershed moment in protections of animals because it expanded the concept of animal welfare, particularly for livestock. Whereas livestock had previously only been protected from pointless cruelty, the report initiated protection from overuse and neglect. Furthermore, the report's inclusion of "normal" behaviors as a strategy for preventing frustration and thereby suffering was seen as broadening the traditional conception of suffering (Mench, 1998).

But this explanation seems hopeless, given that animal pain and suffering were supposedly significant by at least 1900. We can find concerns similar to those expressed in the Brambell Report going back to the 17th century. The Brambell Report, as well as work by Harrison, Singer, and others, should have been seen as piling on to what had already been established hundreds of years earlier. Given that they were not, perhaps they should be seen as *rediscovering* insights produced by dissection experiments, pet-keeping, and other 18th- and 19th-century events. Animal use in experiments and agriculture, for instance, increased dramatically in the 20th century. The moral circle may have been contracting rather than expanding.

So where does that leave the expanding moral circle hypothesis? We might instead appeal to the increased legal rights granted to animals in the late 20th century. As mentioned above, Steven Pinker's view is that what we have experienced is an expansion in legal rights, not moral sensibility. However, even looking just at legal rights, we can see problems with the expanding moral circle hypothesis. Jones (2013), for instance, argues that most policies governing the use of animals fail to recognize scientific consensus on which animals are sentient. If legal rights have worked in tandem with the increased importance of phenomenal states, we should expect this to change. Perhaps it will, but that it hasn't yet makes it hard to see how we're currently experiencing an expanding circle of moral concern. And as argued above, we should expect limits to legal protections, especially when humans stand to gain from animal exploitation.

We might also appeal to the social aspect of the expanding moral circle, that moral concern for animals will increase as it has for other marginalized human groups. The history of legal changes in the 20th century suggests that the animal movement has indeed built on the success of previous movements. There are problems, however. As we have seen repeatedly, animals are a somewhat unique outgroup. Human beings are much more likely to extend ingroup membership to other human beings than they are to animals. It's also not clear whether legal protections of animals have involved any strong moral psychological change. Suzanne Staggenborg (2012, p. 63) argues that the civil rights movement in the 1960s put in place a "rights frame" that subsequent movements have drawn from. Once the rights framework was in place, radical moral psychological changes were arguably unnecessary. Highly motivated special interest groups are all that were required to increase legal rights for animals. As Silverstein (1996) suggests, the connection between the animal movement and previous movements was in the use of rights terminology because "rights language happens to be one of the most common and accepted ways of heightening awareness of marginalization and mistreatment" (p. 51). But effective use of rights language does not depend on convincing people or gaining consensus about the moral status of animals.

In summary, the increased importance of phenomenal states in the last 150 years is limited in its support for the existence of an expanding moral circle. Phenomenal states are important for moral considerability, but they don't grant continuously increasing moral protections. Though this has not been the focus of this chapter, the psychology of dehumanization can help account for the limited impact of phenomenal states. One main route for dehumanizing animals is to attribute certain qualities they share with humans while denying others that justify poor treatment. It is possible for more animals to be attributed phenomenal states—thereby receiving moral status—but also be treated as inferior to human beings because of other dehumanization factors. As this brief review has indicated, animals have been denied improved treatment, and one likely cause is their presumed inferiority to humans. Though there is no question that attitudes toward animals have changed in many ways, it's not clear that this has been caused by any fundamentally new way of thinking.

7.3.2 Phenomenal States in Early Modern Philosophy: Descartes, Spinoza, and Leibniz

A notorious villain often mentioned in discussions of phenomenal states and harm to animals is René Descartes. He is widely cited as providing crucial support for the idea that animals lack feelings (e.g., Fudge, 2006). Descartes' mechanistic conception of animals, it is said, dictates that animals do not have minds and as a result do not have moral status. As Bulliet (2005) states, "by turning nature into a master craftsman, Descartes made the human–animal divide a building block of Enlightenment thought" (p. 45).

The popularity of Cartesianism might thus be taken as an obstacle to an expanding moral circle, one that might explain the apparent lack of expansion over the last 150 years. Nicolas Malebranche, for instance, is reported to have directly inferred, from metaphysical principles about the status of animal minds (or the lack thereof), that animals could therefore be treated however humans wished. The infamous story is that Bernard le Bovier de Fontenelle observed Malebranche kick a pregnant dog and subsequently deny—citing Cartesian principles—that it felt any pain (passages where Malebranche directly addresses the implications of the Cartesian beast-machine doctrine can be found in *The Search for Truth*, 1674–1675; Lennon & Olscamp, 1997, pp. 323–325, 351–353).

However, Descartes' views on animals were not as harsh as many take them to be. Moreover, it is not clear from looking at the views of other prominent Cartesians that their mechanistic metaphysics led directly to any specific moral view concerning animals. To bring this out, let's look at the relationship between the views of Descartes and two other key 17th-century Cartesians, Leibniz and Spinoza, particularly on animals.

Historical scholarship would be much easier if views on animal minds followed straightforwardly from a certain type of metaphysics—say, if Descartes' beast-machine doctrine led directly to brutality. But it appears that this is not the case. The interpretation of Cartesian metaphysics just mentioned has been tempered in recent years by commentators hoping to contextualize Descartes' thought within the relevant 17th-century debates. Thinking about bodies in mechanistic terms, for instance, was in fact a common theme in the 17th century—for understanding both animals and humans (Gaukroger, 2008; Smith, 2011). Mechanistic thinking was not unique to Descartes, nor did it necessarily entail negative moral attitudes.

Moreover, various scholars have argued that Descartes' views on the metaphysics of animal bodies did not involve the claim that animals are unfeeling (Cottingham, 1978; Gaukroger, 1993; Harrison, 1992). John Cottingham's (1978) analysis of Descartes' opinion of animals suggests that Descartes' physiological discussions of animal spirits often attribute what seem to be mental states to animals. He observes that in the *Principles of Philosophy* (IV), Descartes describes the physiological operations within animals as producing *laetitia*, a Latin predicate typically used for describing human mental states. Though animal bodies are described as thoroughly mechanical (consistent with the beast-machine doctrine), Descartes does not directly infer from this that animals cannot be ascribed mental properties. If Descartes thought animals were mere *res extensa* (physical substance), then it is unlikely that he would think they possessed *laetitia*.

There's no reason to get too caught up in scholarly debate about the 17th-century use of *laetitia*, however. Even if Cottingham's analysis is right, it is undeniable that Descartes did not grant much moral significance to animals. He engaged in some degree of vivisection (dissection on live animals) and in his correspondence puts up little resistance when people claim that his ideas are cruel to animals (Miller, M. R., 2013). Perhaps this is a result of understanding *laetitia* as entailing a very thin phenomenal experience. As he says in a letter to Plemius for Fromondus (1637), for instance, even if animals can perceive in some sense, he still claims, "animals do not see as we do when we are aware that we see, but only as we do when our mind is elsewhere" (Cottingham et al., 1991, p. 61). And even if he understood *laetitia* as more thickly phenomenal, he clearly did not think this qualified animals for special moral significance. Whatever mental states animals may possess, Descartes did not think they were sophisticated enough to make animals worthy of moral attention, certainly not for the types of moral or theological debates had about animals at the time.

Nonetheless, it is false that Descartes *endorsed* cruelty toward animals. And he does not seem to have justified poor treatment of animals as a direct result of his metaphysical views. Others may have taken his arguments to justify cruelty to animals, as indicated in the quote from Malebranche, but there is no evidence to suggest that Descartes himself intended such a consequence. It is also questionable whether Cartesian principles are inherently cruel toward animals. As we will see again with Leibniz, mechanistic conceptions of both animals and humans were quite common at the time and were compatible with a range of views on animal minds and moral status. Rosenfield's (1941) study of the effects of Cartesianism, for instance, notes that there were many self-identified Cartesians who claimed that animals could feel pain. In short, the objection that Cartesianism posed a unique obstacle to improving attitudes toward animals does not seem to hold water.

But let's consider some other prominent 17th-century thinkers whose ideas about animals have had some historical impact. Baruch Spinoza is particularly important for this discussion because he adopted much of the Cartesian framework. Though he would extend and critique Cartesian principles, his thoughts on animals diverged only slightly from Descartes.

Laetitia arises in a similar context for Spinoza. In the *Ethics* (3p57s), Spinoza seems to declare that animals can feel but qualifies his assertion by stating that they possess their own type of feeling that is proper to animals. We may know that "the lower animals feel things" but their feelings nevertheless "differ from men's affects as much as their nature differs from human nature" (all citations from Spinoza are from Curley, 1985). This categorical divide persists notwithstanding shared affective states because these states come about only through the type of being something is: "Both the horse and the man are driven by a Lust to procreate; but the one is driven by an equine Lust, the other by a human Lust. So also the Lusts and Appetites of Insects, fish, and birds must vary." Discussing this passage later in the *Ethics* (4p37s), Spinoza furthermore comes to the conclusion on animals that we can "use them at our pleasure, and treat them as is most convenient for us." Although "the lower animals have sensations" they "do not agree in nature with us, and their affects are different in nature from human affects," and so, he concludes, we can treat them according to human needs.

For both Descartes and Spinoza, then, the possession of phenomenal mental states has no bearing on the moral status of animals. Margaret Wilson (1999) asserts that Spinoza's account of animals ultimately fails to provide an adequate account of animals' nature and how that should inform our treatment of them. Spinoza, apparently unlike Descartes, does seem to take moral conclusions about animals directly from his metaphysics. As Wilson says, "explicit attribution of sentience, and affects, to brutes is grounded in his general panpsychism, rather than any particularities of their bodies and behavior" (p. 191). This makes his attribution of mental states to "lower animals" somewhat trivial, according to Wilson, because it is merely a logical consequence of his metaphysics, not a result of inquiry into the mental life of animals (most of his examples deal with apples and stones). Wilson concludes that Spinoza's account, "utterly fails to distinguish beasts from presumably less 'complex' entities—even rocks or tennis balls, let alone plants—with regard to the presence of 'feeling' " (pp. 182–183).

Spinoza's panpsychism, however, was developed in order to provide a critique of Descartes' dualism. So while Spinoza's conclusions about animals may have derived directly from his metaphysics, they do not derive from *Cartesian* metaphysics. Again, then, we see that the adoption of a Cartesian ontology is not required for thinking negatively about animals.

An additional interesting and contrasting view can be found in Gottfried Wilhelm Leibniz. Leibniz also attempted to critique Descartes "from the inside"—embracing certain key tenets of Cartesianism while rejecting others. Leibniz rejected the Cartesian view that denied consciousness to animals as well as the Spinozistic view that endorsed complete subjugation of animals. He also agreed with John Locke that animal species came in natural gradients (a precursor to Darwinian ideas) but still insisted that principled moral distinctions be made between certain types of animals.

Leibniz's views on the metaphysics of animal minds is complicated, but let's look at some highlights (detailed accounts can be found in Kulstad, 1991, and Smith, 2011). Leibniz claims to disagree with the Cartesian ontology, "The Cartesians . . . went wrong in taking away the automatic side of man and the thinking side of animals. I think we should keep both sides for both things. . . . [T]hey are all automata, human as well as animal bodies" (*Comments on Bayle's Note L,* 1705, Woolhouse & Francks, 1998, p. 234). This is the same distinction Cottingham made above, however, with respect to automata that feel. This suggests that in attributing the capacity for feeling to animals, Leibniz continues to see animals mechanistically, and thus may ultimately be more aligned with Descartes than he thought.

Leibniz does say elsewhere that, "[animals] nevertheless have souls and sense, just as mankind thinks they do" (*New Essays,* 1704, Remnant & Bennett, 1997, p. 71) and to "transform or demote animals into mere machines" would be "contrary to the order of things" (*New System of the Nature of Substances and Their Communication,* 1695; Woolhouse & Francks, 1998, p. 144). But this should not be read as contradicting the idea that animals are mechanistic. As Justin Smith says, "For Leibniz, as for Descartes, animals are machines, but they are also, as for Aristotle, machines that are in their own way divine or akin, if only distantly, to the most perfect being" (2011, p. 11). Leibniz objected not to animals as machines but as "mere machines." This is the reason for drawing a comparison to the "perfect being," which of course refers to God, further indicating that Leibniz certainly did not see mechanism as antithetical to mindedness.

Despite Leibniz's belief that animals have souls and the capacity for phenomenal states, he appears to have granted little moral significance to animals. There is an often-retold story, described in Kant's *Lectures on Ethics*, in which Leibniz is said to have shown compassion for a worm by placing it in a tree. No other similar stories about Leibniz have been recounted, however, and this tale is of course second-hand; Kant and Leibniz were not contemporaries. Moreover, as Justin Smith (2011, p. 319) notes, Leibniz had past experience and business interests in rearing silkworms. This particular act may thus have been done out of personal financial interest, not compassion. Even if this story is not a myth and Leibniz had in fact been acting out of compassion, he is also known to have endorsed the dissection of living animals because of the scientific benefits that could be gained (Smith, 2011, p. 49).

Ultimately Leibniz seems to hold what in chapter 4 was described as an agential view of moral status. Rather than phenomenal states, what is important for Leibniz is the ability to "say I," or have a sense of self (see §34 of the *Discourse on Metaphysics*, 1686; Woolhouse & Francks, 1998, p. 86; as well as *On What Is Independent of Sense and Matter*, 1702; Loemker, 1969, p. 549). Though animals "can distinguish good from bad, since they have perception . . . they are certainly not capable of moral good and bad, which presuppose reason and consciousness" (*Remarks on M. Foucher's Objections*, 1695; Woolhouse & Francks, 1998, pp. 185–186). This claim looks more Spinozist: the mental lives of animals possess qualities proper to a domain inferior to that of humans.

There is one final wrinkle to Leibniz's view of animals that is worth mentioning. Toward the end of the *New Essays* (1704), Leibniz attempts to create conceptual space for the *possibility* that animals possess humanlike characteristics. Leibniz pursues two line of reasoning, one epistemological and one metaphysical. His epistemological claim is that we are too far removed from other rational species to be aware of their existence (e.g., certain primate species). He speculates, "[I]n some other world there may be species intermediate between man and beast . . . in all likelihood there are rational animals, somewhere, which surpass us" (Remnant & Bennett, 1997, p. 473). His metaphysical claim is that certain species currently lacking reason could eventually *develop* the capacity for reason: "For there may some day come to be animals which have—in common with all the descendants of men who are alive now—everything we have so far observed in men, but who have had a different origin from us" (p. 400).

This is an interesting departure from Descartes and Spinoza. Humans are still unique for Leibniz, but he allows that other unique—and morally considerable—species could exist. The class of beings capable of reason and having a sense of self remains provisional. Leibniz says, "Reason is as internal to man as anything can be, and ordinarily it declares its presence" (*New Essays*; Remnant & Bennett, 1997, p. 313), yet he continues to emphasize that creatures approximating human abilities should be offered the chance to prove their reasoning abilities. It is in this openness to the possibility that animals can change, with specific proposals for how and why, that distinguishes Leibniz from Descartes and Spinoza. Leibniz not only differs in terms of his positions on general metaphysical issues but also with respect to the nature of animals.

In summary, Descartes, Spinoza, and Leibniz all came to relatively similar conclusions on the moral status of animals, despite holding different metaphysical views on animal minds. Certain areas where their views overlapped did indeed contribute to shared views on animals' moral status (e.g., that animals are of a class inferior to humans). But this is not due to either a mechanistic metaphysics or a denial of minds to animals. It would thus seem unlikely that Cartesianism posed an especially problematic obstacle to changing attitudes toward animals over the last 150 years (for broader historical accounts of animal mental capacities, see Sorabji, 1993, and Steiner, 2005).

7.3.3 *Animals Across Cultures*

One can find favorable attitudes expressed toward animals throughout many cultural traditions (for collections of relevant texts, see Preece, 2002, and Wynne-Tyson, 1985). What matters, however, is not whether people are generally caring toward animals but whether the expanding moral circle captures the way attitudes appear across cultures.

Let's return again to harm. Different cultures prioritize harm differently. This is true for harm to both animals and humans. For illustration, consider Jesse Prinz's summary of why we should not think that human beings are universally opposed to harm-based transgressions:

> Is there a universal prohibition against harm? The evidence is depressingly weak. Torture, war, spousal abuse, corporal punishment, belligerent games, painful initiations, and fighting are all extremely widespread. Tolerated harm is as common as its prohibition. There is also massive cultural variation in whom can be harmed and when. (Prinz, 2008, p. 373)

Variation in who can be harmed, as Prinz alludes to here, is highly relevant to animals. Prinz does not mention it, but harm to animals provides another excellent illustration of the absence of a universal prohibition against harm. If killing an animal for consumption counts as harm, then clearly most human cultures actively promote harm and condone many acts that would be considered cruel if done to other humans (at least those considered part of one's ingroup). Loughnan, Bastian, and Haslam (2014) report that no society has ever consisted of over 10% vegetarians. So even societies that might be considered extraordinarily kind to animals still commit harmful acts that would be considered unconscionable if done to humans.

Diverging moral foundations is a cross-cultural phenomenon. This divergence is arguably responsible for different attitudes toward animals across cultures. For instance, research has shown that Americans tend to choose vegetarianism because they are concerned about animal welfare and harm to animals, while people from India choose vegetarianism for reasons related to self-pollution, not harm (e.g., they are more likely to agree with statements like "Eating meat is spiritually polluting"; Ruby et al., 2013). As we saw earlier, adherence to the binding foundations causes disagreements about animals within the United States. But it may be that Americans are still more likely to draw from the harm/care foundation in their attitudes toward animals than are people from other countries.

To push this hypothesis further, we can look at research on how people think about animal welfare, which is arguably a harm-related concern. Recall the study by Phillips et al. (2012) discussed in chapter 4, which studied people's rankings of animal sentience. The participants in this experiment came from China, the Czech Republic, Great Britain, Iran, Ireland, South Korea, Macedonia, Norway, Serbia, Spain, and Sweden. The results showed that overall there was greater concern for animal welfare (defined as the importance of not causing pain and suffering to animals) in Europe than in Asia. This suggests that drawing from harm/care in one's attitudes to animals might be a Western phenomenon.

If this is right, it provides support for the idea that binding foundations pose an obstacle to increased concern for harm to animals. There is an inherent conservatism in the binding foundations that makes social change difficult. Consider, for instance, Ruby and Heine's (2012) study, also mentioned in chapter 4. They found that thinking about animals' mental states made it more difficult to think of them as consumable. They also found that the thought of eating animals with mental capacities increased the amount of disgust people felt. However, they found that this effect was particularly pronounced among people from Europe, Canada, and the United States. One possible explanation for this is that Anglo-European cultures mainly consider the effects of a practice on the animals themselves, while Asian cultures primarily consider social context and others' attitudes about animals. In support of this explanation, Ruby and Heine also found that level of disgust had less of an impact if a meat item was consumed more frequently with friends and family members, especially among people from Hong Kong and India. That is, the social acceptability of eating commonly consumed animals had more of an influence on people from Hong Kong and India than on Americans and Europeans.

This research might come as a surprise to people who assume that Westerners are particularly cruel to animals. Some have suggested that certain Asian traditions conceive of animals in ways that make cruelty or exploitation difficult (e.g., Chapple, 1993). Hinduism, for instance, treats animals as sacred. Li and Davey (2013) argue that the main tenets of Daoism, Confucianism, and Buddhism are all very favorable to animals. If one looks strictly at the ideas about animals contained in these traditions, we should expect China, among other countries, to be the locus of moral expansion. How do we reconcile these views with the idea that certain Asian countries neglect animals because of underlying moral values?

The answer is that these traditions have less of an impact on actual behavior than one might expect. As Preece (1999) summarizes cross-cultural attitudes to animals, "As with the Aboriginal traditions, so too in India, and, indeed, so too in the West: whatever one's sacred scriptures or myths may say, they are belied, openly, by the reality" (p. 21). Non-Western traditions are not immune to many of the same factors that influence treatment of animals in the West. With respect to China, Li and Davey (2013) argue that economic goals and the ideal of progress have led to strong support for factory farming and other intensive use of animals. They propose that instead of religious traditions, a better explanation for attitudes to animals can be found in "The nature of modern-day politics, especially government and corporate behavior, motivated by the need for economic growth" (p. 44; for numerous similar statements, see Knight, 2004).

This is not to say that non-Western traditions are especially cruel or hypocritical—quite the opposite. They are remarkably similar to Western traditions in being influenced by external forces that dictate their treatment of animals. For example, Wagman and Liebman (2012) review a wide range of legal movements across several world regions that have led to significantly improved legal protections for animals. These movements were partly a result of interconnected social and economic pressures. Their analysis also identifies additional factors, however, that pose obstacles to continued legal protections for animals in certain countries. In some places where economic pressures and binding foundations are particularly influential (e.g., China), it appears that expanding legal protections for animals will be difficult.

So how does the expanding moral circle fit into this? The international legal movement suggests that more and more animals are now receiving better treatment. But beyond that, it is hard to see how the cross-cultural evidence can be explained by the expanding moral circle. The same obstacle that exists within countries, with respect to differing moral foundations, also exists between countries. Suppose, for instance, that American harm-based vegetarianism is the best model for increasing moral concern toward animals. If other countries were expanding their moral concern toward animals, they would similarly need to view harm as of ultimate moral importance. Purity-based vegetarians, for example in India, would need to find a way to become more invested in harm/care-based values pertaining to animals. But given the incompatibilities between purity and harm-based disputes just between Americans, this sort of transition seems unlikely.

7.4 CONCLUSION

The idea of an expanding moral circle does not adequately capture changing attitudes toward animals. Attitudes have changed significantly, and in some sense these changes can be seen as an improvement. But if we aim to be precise in our explanations of these changes, we must look elsewhere besides the expanding moral circle.

One might wonder at this point whether attitudes toward animals *cannot* improve. That would be a misguided conclusion. Certain changes in attitudes toward animals that might seem unlikely could indeed come about. Moral attitudes are flexible, just not in the way suggested by the expanding moral circle. We need to look at a broader range of social, historical, and moral psychological processes to understand changing attitudes toward animals.

We must also consider possible explanations for these changes that are less than flattering. Sensitivity to harm and increased altruism, for instance, do not support an expanding moral circle. Improved treatment for animals could instead have resulted from political movements and legislative goals that do not reflect widespread changes in underlying moral attitudes. This point is instructive for those who wish to improve treatment for animals. If the goal is to expand morally significant protections to animals, then it would be better to rely on an accurate account of how these changes come about.

Chapter 8

Managing Moral Psychology
for Animal Ethics

A wide range of obstacles to moral change are now on the table. But what ought we do about them? Chapter 6 suggested that we must account for human psychology when making ethical prescriptions concerning animals. Some, however, are likely to dig in their heels. They would prefer to retain their prescriptions unaltered. The real problem, one might think, is human psychology; psychology—not ethics—should be the target of change.

In his book *Character as Moral Fiction*, Mark Alfano (2013) takes on a similar task as we have here: presenting an empirically informed account of human psychology and exposing philosophical theories that rely on mistaken psychological assumptions. But he also uses his account in the service of traditional moral goals. His approach "attempts to bridge the gap between moral psychology and normative theory by proposing ways in which we, as moral psychology describes us, can become more as we should be, as normative theory prescribes for us" (p. 9). This chapter adopts Alfano's approach and proposes strategies to alter human moral psychology in order to achieve moral goals.

Of course, changing human moral psychology is quite difficult, and explicit attempts to direct psychology in specific directions are rarely successful. Before jumping into suggestions for changing human thought processes, we must address recent attempts to change human psychology through legal and political regulations, as well as concerns about the moral permissibility of states and nations actively promoting specific moral ideals.

8.1 METHODS FOR MANAGING MORAL PSYCHOLOGY

8.1.1 Preliminary Concerns with Changing Psychology

One primary method for intentionally changing moral psychology is through state-sanctioned laws and policies. As argued in chapter 6, governments possess the resources needed to support the sort of collective action required to enact significant moral changes. This could take many forms, including new laws and regulations, penalties and punishments, and more.

Whatever the method, governments generally work by regulating *behavior*, not underlying psychological dispositions. One reason for this is teleological: the designed function of laws and regulations is to promote certain behaviors instead of others. Regulations can be aimed at underlying causes of behaviors, but these tend to be societal or structural, not psychological. For instance, in order to promote vegetarianism, a government could make meat consumption more costly or provide better information to consumers about the nutritional benefits of a vegetarian diet. These actions would have psychological effects, but the method of transmission would be behavioral change.

Another reason governments regulate behavior and not psychology is normative: it is widely seen as impermissible for liberal societies (like most Western nations) to explicitly endorse specific moral ideals when constructing laws and policies. The reason usually cited for why liberal societies cannot pursue specific moral goals is that liberal societies embrace the doctrine of "exclusion of ideals" (Raz, 1986, pp. 134–136). For instance, not everyone values animals in the same way, and in many cases people's values conflict. Creating laws and policies that promote a specific moral psychological response to animals would thus be seen as impermissible in a liberal society. Regulating behavior, instead of underlying psychology, arguably provides more freedom for people to pursue their own ideals, independent of state restrictions.

However, there has been significant debate over the extent to which liberal societies can in fact promote moral ideals with respect to animals (Donaldson & Kymlicka, 2011; Garner, 2005; Smith, 2012). Governments frequently put in place policies in accordance with *some* conception of the public good, and citizens are not always consulted prior to the implementation of these policies (see Baldwin, Cave, & Lodge, 2012, ch. 7). In practice, the exclusion of ideals may be mostly a myth.

Changing moral psychologies through laws and policies is also an aim of many ethicists and political philosophers, even if the strategies for doing so are not straightforwardly permissible in normal democratic processes. Change is likely inevitable, and laws and policies will steer changes relevant to animals in one direction or another. Insofar as this is true, we must assume that governments and institutions will have some sort of influence on these outcomes and can be evaluated accordingly. The strategies discussed here are presumably within the range of what many current societies could feasibly implement, if only on a small scale.

Another question, though, is how the motivation and societal resources for moral psychological change are supposed to come about if the population at large does not yet support the change (e.g., because they do not have the right moral psychological profile). The proposals that we will explore are aimed at cases in which moral psychological change is instituted by individuals acting relatively independent of the population as a whole (e.g., these policies would not be put through a voting procedure). In the next section, we will look more closely at what Thaler and Sunstein (2008) call "nudges," where people's decision frameworks are modified in order to steer their choices in particular directions. As Sunstein (2013) discusses, many agencies within the U.S. government possess the authority and the resources to initiate nudges, particularly through policy change (the possibility exists in many other countries as well; Sunstein, 2016). These nudges are open to public inspection, but they do not require public support in order to be enacted, thus avoiding the problem of obtaining public support prior to pursuing moral psychological change.

Not all of the proposals we will explore count as nudges, but the nudging framework helps illuminate how moral psychological changes can be enacted through the resources available to states and nations. Nudging proposals—or behavioral interventions, as they are sometimes called—take human psychology as their starting point. More importantly, they take it for granted that much of human decision-making is unconscious and outside of rational control (along the lines of the discussion in chapter 5).

There is a general challenge in getting policy-makers to accept these facts about human psychology (Nosek & Riskin, 2012). People are generally reluctant to accept that they might possess unconscious biases (Pronin, Gilovich, & Ross, 2004); policy-makers are no different. Advocates of nudges acknowledge these facts of human psychology, allowing us to look more directly at other policy implications of the research discussed throughout this book.

8.1.2 The Ethics of Behavioral Intervention

There has been a great deal of recent discussion about the ethics of nudging (Barton & Grüne-Yanoff, 2015; Grille & Scoccia, 2015; Rebonato, 2012; White, 2013). Rather than take an exhaustive look, we will here focus on the most compelling objections, as they would apply to proposals for changing moral attitudes to animals.

Thaler and Sunstein (2008) claim that nudging "tries to influence choices in a way that will make choosers better off, *as judged by themselves*" (p. 5, their emphasis). Perhaps the most common type of nudge frames information in a way to promote certain choices over others. For example, Whole Foods' Animal Welfare Rating System (Whole Foods Market, 2017) provides labels to indicate how an animal was reared. Animal products at steps 4 and 5, which are the most welfare-friendly, are given green labels, while steps 1–3 have orange labels (similar to a traffic light). Assuming that good animal welfare is widely supported among the general public, this labeling system helps consumers make choices in accordance with their values. People who purchase meat products at Whole Foods are likely to be influenced by these labels—consciously or unconsciously— thus increasing the purchase of welfare-friendly meat.

Arguably the most common objection to nudging is that it is paternalistic. Whole Foods' rating system, for example, is making a decision about what is best for consumers—namely, that they should support positive animal welfare. It also assumes that people will not decide to choose welfare-friendly products without some assistance and then provides that assistance without seeking consent. Whole Foods is not forcing people to purchase those products, but it is pushing them in a particular direction.

This objection is also sometimes framed as a problem with the deception involved in nudges; paternalism is particularly problematic when it is difficult to detect. Hausman and Welch (2010) argue that manipulation by nudging is totally different from rational persuasion or appealing to reasons: "To the extent that they are attempts to undermine that individual's control over her own deliberation, as well as her ability to assess for herself her alternatives, they are prima facie as threatening to liberty, broadly understood, as is overt coercion" (p. 130). Instead of simply informing people about welfare-friendly products, for instance, Whole Foods has designed labels in a way that will encourage certain products over others. Though this might seem like a relatively minimal form of manipulation, Hausman and Welch object that "a huge difference in aim and attitude remains" between nudging and influence by rational persuasion.

Within the academic literature, the main line of reply to these objections is that nudging and "choice architecture" are inevitable. As Sunstein (2015a) says, "When choice architects act, they alter the architecture; they do not create an architecture where it did not exist before. A certain degree of nudging, from the public sector, cannot be avoided, and there is no use in wishing it away" (p. 449). The above objection seems to assume that there are certain circumstances in which people are significantly rational and uninfluenced by external forces. But this is unlikely. Consider Whole Foods again. All food products have labels that affect consumers' choices. Whole Foods would not have less of an effect on consumer decisions by getting rid of animal welfare labeling; it would just push them in some other direction besides animal welfare. Whole Foods could engage in an informational campaign to persuade consumers about the importance of animal welfare, thus avoiding a paternalistic approach. But this is unlikely to have as much of an effect as the labels that are already in place, which would continue to push consumers away from animal welfare. Nudging as such then does not seem problematically paternalistic just because it aims to direct people's choices.

Thaler and Sunstein's (2008) "libertarian paternalism" also states that liberty is preserved in nudging because "choice sets" remain unaltered. Customers at Whole Foods still have the option of buying meat that is not labeled welfare-friendly, so the range of options available to them has not changed. But as many have pointed out (including Hausman and Welch), it's not clear whether this helps. *Effective* nudges should routinely lead me to choose the green labeled products, regardless of whether I could conceivably choose something else. The psychology of the nudge is in fact liberty-reducing.

Thaler and Sunstein's reply to the paternalism objection is indeed unconvincing. A better reply is that some degree of external influence—like nudges—is required as part of governance and policy-making (of which food labels is just one example). If the goal is to help people choose according to their values and preferences, then nudges must limit people's choices. If people really do want to choose welfare-friendly products but find it difficult (for whatever reason), then nudges must narrow the options.

Another potential reply to the paternalism objection, though perhaps more controversial, is that nudging is aimed at improving the public good. *Given* that human beings are in fact incapable of making good decisions for themselves, governments should provide some assistance in order to improve overall well-being. Sarah Conly (2013), for instance, argues that anyone who understands human psychology and is concerned about human well-being should embrace some degree of paternalism. Nudges do exploit biases in human reasoning but only because the alternative is allowing people to harm themselves and others. If our goal is to change social and moral norms through policy change, the only option is to operate through these unconscious processes (also see McTernan, 2014).

A related objection to nudging is that it reduces human autonomy. Even if nudging is not problematically paternalistic, repeated directed interventions from external parties could reduce people's ability to live their lives as they want to live them. Hansen and Jespersen (2013) note that the degree of involvement in people's personal lives required by nudging is relatively new in human history. Because nudges are intentionally directed at unconscious processes by government entities, they introduce new ethical problems. They say, "there seems to be a clear and important distinction to be made between a given context that *accidentally* influences behaviour in a predictable way, and someone—a choice architect—*intentionally* trying to alter behaviour by fiddling with such contexts" (p. 10; their emphasis). Even Sunstein (2015a) strongly emphasizes that significant manipulation is indeed a problem for nudging, *regardless* of whether the goals are legitimate or not (e.g., even if pursuing the public good).

Another formulation of this objection is that it produces a "fragmented self" (Bovens, 2008). Nudges are not a one-off event. As nudges become more popular, people will confront multiple competing nudges, which could plausibly undermine autonomy. As Baldwin (2014) puts this concern, "the effects of such accumulations of nudging may be to produce control regimes that are defeatist about the capacities of individuals to become more responsible and deliberative" (p. 851). Even if we accept that human beings make poor decisions, systematic nudging may not provide a good solution.

A plausible response to this objection mirrors the one already mentioned. Governments put into place a framework for decision-making long before individuals begin asserting their autonomy. Nudges are just a way of transforming this framework. As Sunstein (2015b) says, "Any government, even one that is or purports to be firmly committed to active choosing, free markets, and the idea of laissez-faire, will almost inevitably provide a set of prohibitions and permissions, including a number of default entitlements, establishing who has what before bargaining begins" (p. 512). Human agents are already acting within a framework where their decisions are influenced by external factors. There is no neutral position where these influences are absent and full autonomy is preserved (see Mills, 2015, for discussion of this idea).

Nudgers can also reply that in some cases nudging actually increases autonomy and motivates people to take more control over their lives. Returning to the Whole Foods example, suppose some people do not even realize that animal welfare is a potential issue. They might possess the disposition to care for animals but just aren't aware that problematic practices might exist in intensive livestock production. Whole Foods' labeling system would raise awareness of the issue for them and also make it easier to act according to their values (assuming they do in fact value good animal welfare).

A final reply to both of the objections mentioned is that well-intentioned regulators can arguably improve the current level of external influence on decision-making. People are already influenced by those who are less well intentioned (e.g., companies that design attractive food labels for unhealthy products). It's not clear why we should restrict regulators who have the public good in mind because of concerns over reduced autonomy, if the alternative is equally autonomy-reducing and controlled by more nefarious forces.

There is also a question of whether good intentions are sufficient. The basic position outlined thus far is that governments engage in acts like nudging all the time, and indeed some degree of deception and paternalism seems essential to the task of governing society. Government policies are always having effects on us, both intended and unintended. But we can still ask whether nudging does in fact serve the public good. Whether governments are manipulating us (deliberately or not) doesn't seem as important as whether their actions actually help us achieve the things we want to achieve.

What if nudgers lack an adequate understanding of human preferences and, as a result, can't actually help people choose according to their own preferences? Goldin (2015) argues that governments rarely have a precise understanding of the people who are being nudged. Claiming that nudges retain people's preferences is misleading because it's unlikely that any attempt was made to get a thorough understanding of their preferences, and even if an attempt was made, human preferences are notoriously transitory and flexible (see Glod, 2015, for similar criticisms). People might need external assistance to make good decisions but not from those who are no more informed than they are.

Inadequate knowledge of preferences does present a difficult challenge, particularly with respect to animals. We have reviewed a great deal of research on what people think about animals, but it would be a stretch to claim that we've arrived at a thorough understanding of what people prefer regarding their treatment. Nonetheless, what we do know about human psychology provides a sufficient basis for nudges. Experimental research on human psychology aims to identify general tendencies. Nudgers cannot know precisely what people prefer, but they do not need to. It is enough to understand general tendencies from which to make accurate predictions. For instance, it is sufficient for Whole Foods to ask consumers whether they value positive animal welfare. They do not need to know precisely which rearing conditions consumers think would provide good welfare because the labeling system permits disagreements at this more nuanced level. They also do not need exhaustive research on labeling effects to predict that people will make a positive association between green labels and welfare-friendly products.

Goldin (2015) offers a similar solution by suggesting that nudgers should target subgroups of people who are likely to be influenced by particular nudges. Even if we do not know *everyone's* preferences regarding animal welfare, experimental research can give us reliable information about *certain* portions of the population and how they will likely respond to interventions. Experimental research on moral attitudes toward animals is sufficiently fine-grained for assisting with this project.

A final objection claims that nudges are insulting because they treat people as incompetent decision-makers (see Cornell, 2015). This is different from the other objections mentioned already because it fully accepts that people *are* incompetent decision-makers. One potential negative effect of nudging is that it makes people feel as if the government is deciding what is best for them. People might resent the implication that they cannot choose for themselves, even if nudging does in fact help achieve their goals.

Cornell (2015) provides a compelling reply to this objection. He suggests that nudgers appeal to "the idea that we (collectively) wouldn't do what's best for us without government intervention" (p. 1320). Nudges build on the view of human psychology presented in chapter 5 and in essence adopt the social approach discussed in chapter 6. Nudgers embrace human frailty and the fact that external forces already limit what people are capable of. This is not insulting human intelligence but rather acknowledging that efficacious action when acting alone is difficult. Nudgers are also, at least in principle, trying to help people get what they want despite these factors. People might be reluctant to admit that they possess biases in reasoning but presumably accept that occasionally they need help.

In summary, we should embrace external influence like that provided by nudges. Nudges do not, in principle, seem problematically paternalistic or autonomy-reducing. And as we have seen repeatedly, there is reliable research on people's attitudes toward animals. We thus have reasons to think that behavioral interventions are prima facie permissible. Actual nudges for animals, however, require more detail and concreteness.

8.2 ANIMAL BODIES IN MORAL PSYCHOLOGY

One interesting theme of the psychological processes we have investigated is the role of animal bodies. Animal bodies identify animals as outgroup members and potential threats and strongly influence phenomenal mentalizing. We must thus focus on changing our perceptions of animal bodies, which could in turn change moral attitudes toward animals.

An excellent resource for changing attitudes toward any perceived outgroup—including animals—is Lai et al.'s (2014) attempt to identify successful methods for reducing implicit racial bias. They conducted a research contest, in which different research teams attempted to reduce implicit preferences for white people over black people on the Implicit Association Test (an animal version of this test was described in chapter 3, from Viki et al., 2006). They also performed meta-analyses of all studies associated with each attempted intervention. Ultimately they concluded that 8 out of 17 interventions were successful at reducing implicit bias. As we will see, the psychological processes behind these 8 interventions can also be applied to animals.

One cautionary note: a follow-up analysis revealed that all of these successful interventions disappeared within 24 hours (Lai et al., 2016). Their effects had little staying power. A similar possibility exists for proposals to change attitudes to animals. Very little longitudinal research on attitudes toward animals exists, and relevant meta-analyses typically exclude studies measuring attitudes toward non-humans. So any predictions for future psychological change are necessarily somewhat speculative. The suggestions here are meant to enable future empirical inquiry and provide a starting point for changing attitudes toward animals.

8.2.1 The Contact Hypothesis

Gordon Allport's (1954) contact hypothesis predicts that increased physical contact between groups will reduce negative attitudes. Experimental tests of the contact hypothesis have had relative success with changing attitudes between human groups (Gaertner et al., 1994; Kelly, Faucher, & Machery, 2010; Lemmer & Wagner, 2015; Pettigrew & Tropp, 2006). What about animals?

Not just *any* type of contact with another group is sufficient, however; repeated acts of aggression, for instance, will not work. One possibility is that increased physical contact should be combined with information about the other group. In a recent book review, Jessica Pierce (2013) proposes this sort of combination for animals:

> I challenge any skeptic to spend a few weeks immersed in the now extensive literature on animal cognition, emotion, and prosocial behavior—and then spend a couple of weeks in the company of animals—and still come away with a sense that they are less sensitive, less intelligent, less socially attuned than humans. Our skeptic will certainly come away thinking that animals can't do everything we do. . . . But she will also come away with a new appreciation of our own limited capacities and a new respect for other forms of life—including, I would think, a sense that our wanton cruelty and disregard for others' lives and feelings is just plain wrong.

Pierce's suggestions, in effect, provide a transition plan (as discussed in chapter 6) for overcoming many of the psychological limitations outlined in this book. However, we should be skeptical about leaning too heavily toward an "information only" approach since the evidence seems to indicate that merely learning more about animals is ineffective for reducing bias toward them (Hazel, Signal, & Taylor, 2011; Heleski & Zanella, 2006; Jamieson et al., 2012). Physical contact must be the focus, directed at learning more about animals.

For improved efficacy, physical contact with animals must also be directed at aversive responses to animals. Unfortunately, research on contact with animals has not addressed aversion to animals in much detail. Typically researchers study the effects of introducing animals that are already viewed positively, like dogs and rabbits (Daly & Sugg, 2010). "Negative" animals in these studies are usually somewhat familiar to the participants, like fish and frogs. Moreover, researchers usually investigate what people learn about animals from handling them, rather than how aversive responses might be managed. Thus, we do not have a very good idea of how to avoid aversive and avoidant reactions to animals.

There are some exceptions, however. For instance, consider a study by Randler, Hummel, and Prokop (2012). They were able to reduce 11- to 13-year-old children's disgust toward a wood louse, a snail, and a mouse by exposing the children to each animal, combined with basic instruction about proper handling in order to avoid causing harm. They also conducted small experiments that required close observation of the animals (e.g., determining whether the louse preferred dark or light areas).

Another study of 11- to 12-year-old children found that disgust and fear toward toads, frogs, and salamanders were greatly influenced by direct experience with each type of animal, indicating that more experience led to more favorable attitudes (Tomažič, 2011). Lastly, a study of 10- to 15-year-olds found that experience with pets was correlated with positive attitudes toward "negative" animals, including beetles and wolves (Prokop & Tunnicliffe, 2010). Though only suggestive, these studies indicate what sorts of interventions, if pursued on a larger scale, might be able to reduce people's aversive responses to animals.

Increased contact with animals might also have trickle-down effects. For instance, Morris, Knight, and Lesley (2012) found that familiarity with animals, including rodents, increased attributions of mental states, particularly emotions. Given the discussion of phenomenal mentalizing, this would suggest that increased contact with an animal increases the probability of that animal being deemed morally considerable. Depending on the strength of this relationship, increased contact might also help in overcoming our bias toward animals that look and act like human beings. For instance, perhaps people are naturally inclined to deny phenomenal mental states to rats, thereby also denying them moral considerability, but this might be at least partially reversed with certain types of exposure and handling.

8.2.2 Shared Goals

One important aspect of the contact hypothesis is known as the intergroup identity model (Gaertner et al., 1993). The intergroup identity model places a qualifier on the contact hypothesis: in order to produce favorable attitudes toward each other, groups must possess a shared identity or see themselves as working toward a common goal. Physical contact with outgroup members is often inadequate on its own.

For instance, one of the effective interventions in Lai et al.'s (2014) analysis asked white participants to play a game of dodgeball where all of their teammates were black and all of the opposing team was white. There was also a manipulation in which the opposing team cheated. This situation had the effect of reducing implicit bias against black people on the Implicit Association Test. Another successful intervention asked white participants to imagine a post-apocalyptic scenario in which all of their allies were black and their enemies white. This too was effective at reducing implicit bias. These scenarios were effective, according to the intergroup identity model, because the shared goal induced people to recalibrate their group affiliations.

It is difficult to see how human beings could come to view themselves as having a shared goal with animals. Some good candidates, however, are working animals and pets. Trail-riding with a horse, for instance, requires significant cooperation between horse and rider to overcome obstacles and reach the finish. This produces a sense of closeness with the horse that plausibly reduces biases toward horses generally and might also reduce biases toward all animals.

As an intervention, it might be easiest to study the effects of working on tasks with a dog. Animal-assisted therapy, for instance, often asks people to conduct very simple tasks with the animal (usually dogs). I do not know of any research on the effects this has on attitudes to animals in general, but we can predict reduced negative attitudes toward the type of animal and perhaps physically similar animals (e.g., interaction with dogs could affect attitudes toward all mammals).

One challenge identified by intergroup identity theorists is that increased intergroup contact can go very wrong. The circumstances must be right for one group to see the other as friendly rather than hostile. Situational factors that have proven important include "equal status between the groups, cooperative (rather than competitive) intergroup interaction, opportunities for self-revealing personal acquaintance between the members . . . and supportive norms by authorities within and outside of the contact situation" (Gaertner & Dovidio, 2008, p. 116). These are of course difficult to achieve with animals. However, the general lesson is clear: increased contact with animals could *reinforce* negative biases, if not conducted properly. Someone who is fearful of dogs, for example, must interact with dogs in just the right setting. An otherwise harmless eye gaze could be interpreted as aggressive by someone disposed to view dogs negatively.

8.2.3 Imagined Contact

If actual physical contact is too difficult, another possibility is imagined contact (Crisp & Turner, 2009; Turner, Crisp, & Lambert, 2007). Research on imagined contact asks people to think about a hypothetical positive experience with a member of a perceived outgroup (e.g., someone with a different ethnicity or religion). Birtel and Crisp's (2012) method for reducing bias toward outgroups asked people to first imagine an experience that was "negative, tense, and uncomfortable." This allows people to confront their negative attitudes toward the outgroup. Then people are asked to "Imagine that the interaction is positive, relaxed, and comfortable." This has proven effective at reducing bias toward those outgroup members.

Miles & Crisp's (2014) meta-analysis found that imagined contact with a perceived outgroup member was indeed effective for reducing bias, as expressed in both attitudes and behaviors. For example, imagined contact made people more willing to work with outgroup members. However, there have been some failed replications of imagined contact research (including Lai et al., 2014, and McDonald et al., 2014). Nonetheless, the hypothesis is sufficiently interesting that it is worth testing with animals.

Imagined contact is important for people who might be particularly afraid of animals, as well as for animals that are generally non-interactive or difficult to find in contemporary societies. Disgust and fear-inducing animals would be particularly interesting to test, including snakes, rats, lizards, and wolves. Imagined interaction with these animals could potentially be compared to real interactions. It would also be interesting to see whether imagined contact with these animals influences attitudes toward general types of animals, like predators or mammals.

It could also be possible to have *simulated* contact with animals. In 2016, virtual reality video games and devices became more widely available than ever (Gaudiosi, 2016; some currently available games, like the Farm Simulator series, provide a degree of simulated contact). It is perhaps unlikely that animal welfare–oriented video games will be an industry priority, but some researchers are already developing relevant behavioral interventions. Researchers at the Virtual Human Interaction Lab at Stanford University have produced "virtual immersive environments" that allow participants to take the perspectives of animals themselves. In one study, taking the perspective of a cow was found to increase feelings of connectedness with nature (Ahn et al., 2015).

Simulating the perspective of the animal itself is of course interesting, but for reducing negative attitudes it is arguably more effective to view potentially threatening animals from an external perspective. Physical contact with an outgroup perceived as threatening is essential, according to the contact hypothesis. Simulated contact would also help avoid many of the problems mentioned above, including exposure to dangerous or reclusive animals, and provide a context in which shared goals can be pursued more easily.

8.2.4 Shared Animality, Shared Humanity

Martha Nussbaum (2004, 2010) argues that using the emotion of disgust as a moral guide has no role in a society that ascribes to the ideal that all persons are of equal worth. A strategy she outlines in order to eradicate disgust and live up to this ideal is to adopt a "politics of humanity," where we all recognize the humanity we share with groups of people sometimes found disgusting (e.g., immigrants).

A politics of humanity seems to exclude non-humans, but we can imagine extending humanity to certain animals by virtue of shared features (like sentience). We could also imagine a "politics of animality," which emphasizes that these features are not unique to human beings. This might allow us to better control the disgust we feel toward certain animals. For instance, Nussbaum (2003, p. 423; 2004, ch. 2) urges societies to stop appealing to disgust in public policy and portraying entities as disgusting, even if that is in fact the primary emotion they evoke (also see Kelly & Morar, 2014). These practices violate shared animality just as they violate shared humanity.

However, research on terror management theory, as discussed in chapter 2, identifies some problems with relying on shared animality.

Terror management theory predicts that highlighting shared animality will *increase* disgust felt toward animals (indeed a significant amount of evidence supports this prediction; Heflick & Goldenberg, 2014). Though Nussbaum seems to recognize this problem, her solution is inadequate. Drawing from research on terror management theory, she suggests, "if the real issue underlying disgust is the fear and loathing people have for their animal bodies and their own mortality, then a society that wants to counteract its damages must go further, addressing the body itself, and our anxieties about it" (2003, p. 424). Unfortunately, she offers no details on how societies are supposed to face this challenge. And even if she could do so, one wonders whether this would have any impact on human psychology. Mortality salience is deeply rooted in our psychologies. Without significant external support in overcoming the effects of mortality salience, individuals' efforts would be totally insufficient. "Addressing the body itself," as Nussbaum suggests, would only enhance the psychological threat.

Shared humanity, however, has some potential. For instance, there is evidence that emphasizing shared humanity can reduce dehumanization of human outgroups. People attribute more secondary emotions (like hope and regret) to outgroup members if they are prompted to think about their shared humanity (Albarello & Rubini, 2012). Relatedly, Costello and Hodson (2010) found that people expressed more favorable attitudes toward immigrants after reading about animals' capacity to "make choices, create their own destinies, and understand abstract concepts including cause and effect relationships" (p. 12). Thinking about animals as humanlike led people to view another outgroup (immigrants) more positively.

There is also evidence that highlighting the humanness of animals (compared to the animality of humans) can improve attitudes specifically toward animals. Bastian, Costello, Loughnan, and Hodson (2012) asked people to write about human–animal similarities, without specifying whether they should highlight animalistic or humanistic features. Those who emphasized the humanness of animals expressed moral concern for a greater number of animals and were also more likely to attribute phenomenal states to an animal in a separate task. Bastian et al. also asked participants to read essays emphasizing either the humanness of animals or the animalness of humans. Those who read about the humanness of animals expressed moral concern for a greater number of animals than those who read about the animalness of humans. These experiments suggest that the dehumanization phenomenon can be reduced by seeing animals as human-like.

There is still a limitation, however, in that any human–animal comparison poses a symbolic threat. Seeing certain positive human features in an outgroup member can improve attitudes toward that outgroup, but dehumanization research predicts that an upper limit exists. One prediction we can make is that exaggerated descriptions of the human-like features of animals would cause a defensive reaction, leading to negative judgments.

Another potential limitation is that people do not generally seem aware that human–animal comparisons influence outgroup judgments. Costello and Hodson (2014) found that the "human–animal divide" was listed as the least likely, among 15 options, as a possible cause of dehumanization between human groups. Beliefs about human–animal differences are in fact strong predictors of dehumanization attitudes, but apparently this is not sufficiently salient to ordinary human beings. Presumably people similarly lack awareness of how their beliefs about the human–animal divide affect their attitudes toward animals. Without a strong intervention, people are unlikely to revise their human–animal comparisons in a way that would improve attitudes toward animals.

8.2.5 Binding Foundations

This proposal is not about animal bodies as such but rather the moral foundations discussed in chapter 7. Numerous studies have shown that convincing people of moral claims requires an appeal to their underlying moral values. As argued in the last chapter, these moral foundations will differ along political lines when it comes to treatment of animals.

For example, Feinberg and Willer (2015) found that political conservatives were more supportive of the American Affordable Care Act (ObamaCare) if it was described in terms of purity ("uninsured people means more unclean, infected, and diseased Americans") than in terms of fairness ("health coverage is a basic human right"). They were similarly more supportive of same-sex marriage if framed in terms of loyalty ("same-sex couples are proud and patriotic Americans") than fairness ("all citizens should be treated equally").

Something similar could be done to reframe animal welfare concerns. For example, instead of framing duties to animals in terms of harm ("Animals must not be made to suffer") or fairness ("All sentient beings deserve equal treatment"), duties could be framed in terms of loyalty ("Americans show compassion toward animals"). Within specific domains of animal use, improved welfare standards could perhaps be framed in terms of purity (e.g., "Cruel treatment of livestock makes our food unsafe to eat").

Groups like the Humane Society of the United States, the American Society for the Prevention of Cruelty to Animals (ASPCA), and People for the Ethical Treatment of Animals (PETA) could use these messages when creating leaflets as well as when framing policy. Assuming these statements are true, it is not mere rhetoric to frame messages such that they appeal to a wide array of moral values. These are the sorts of nudges that might increase concern for animal welfare while also helping people choose according to their preferences. People who care about the safety of their food, for instance, may not in fact have considered the potential impact of cruelty to livestock animals.

8.2.6 Implicit and Explicit Attitudes

One final proposal is not an intervention but a call for increased empirical research. Like nudges, the goal behind my proposed interventions is to overcome significant, and often unconscious and implicit, psychological biases. But we might think that nudges are not the best way of doing this. One non-nudgey way of reducing the impact of unconscious and implicit biases is by calling attention to their harmful effects. For instance, many have noted that the correlation between implicit biases and explicit discriminatory behaviors against black people seems to be decreasing, plausibly because racism is increasingly seen as morally and socially unacceptable (Oswald et al., 2013). Lai, Hoffman, and Nosek (2013) claim that implicit attitudes can sometimes be influenced by explicit attitudes because of "the social pressures against holding negative attitudes toward some groups and how much people have elaborated on those attitudes" (p. 215). If mistreatment of animals similarly received moral attention and condemnation, perhaps implicit biases against animals would have less of an impact on harmful treatment.

However, as we have seen, people likely lack awareness of how their attitudes toward animals are influenced by the psychology of dehumanization. This makes it unlikely that people will be able to reduce implicit biases against animals without significant assistance. Moral attention needs to be directed at dehumanization as much as forms of potential mistreatment.

Raising such awareness is one primary motivation for writing this book, but much more research is needed to determine the precise relationship between implicit biases against animals and harmful treatment. Nosek (2005) reports that implicit preference for cats and dogs has a moderately strong correlation (.39) with explicit preferences for one over the other. No similar comparison exists, however, for implicit–explicit preferences for human beings over animals. The only related study comes from Viki et al. (2006), discussed in chapter 3. They did not test explicit preferences, however. They only found that British participants were more likely to use animal-related words to characterize Germans and Italians than for fellow Brits. This does not tell us much about explicit treatment of animals, of course.

This research is important because, as argued at the end of chapter 6, we must be wary of false achievability in moral change. This is especially the case when implicit attitudes drive us in a certain direction. For example, Dovidio and Gaertner (2000) found that explicit expressions of prejudice from white people against black people decreased between 1989 and 1999. But the level of discrimination against hiring black people remained steady over the same time period. People become less approving of statements like "I would probably feel somewhat self-conscious dancing with a black person in a public place." But when asked to evaluate job candidates, black applicants were viewed as less qualified than white people to the same degree in 1989 as in 1999 (even though the applications were in fact identical). This was plausibly driven by implicit negative attitudes.

Another illustration of why we need studies of implicit and explicit attitudes toward animals comes from Nosek and Riskind (2012, pp. 123–124). They argue that the psychology of implicit racism does not entail that an implicit racist will be racist all the time. For example, 74% of white Americans voted for Barack Obama, but a greater percentage show an implicit preference for white people in experimental settings. This might seem puzzling, but Nosek and Roskin argue that this is perfectly compatible with the idea that implicit biases significantly impact overt behavior. They note that other studies have shown that implicit race biases did have an influence on voting behavior, even if ultimately they were overshadowed by other factors.

A similar lesson applies to animals. Suppose that 90% of people implicitly associate animals with outgroups or that an even greater percentage have an implicit preference for human beings over animals. This does not mean that these people are incapable of showing moral concern for their pet or even for animals generally. Behavioral dispositions still exist that are influenced by those implicit associations, even if they are not expressed in every situation. Indeed, the psychology of dehumanization indicates that even in the absence of overt denigration of animals, subtle biases will continue to play a strong role.

One final issue that future empirical research should address is that some implicit biases against animals might be quite reasonable. Many interventions for reducing biases against human outgroups aim to correct mistakes. People shouldn't be afraid of interacting with gay men, for instance; they are not actual threats. Many animals, by contrast, could constitute legitimate threats. That's partly the explanation for sustained negative attitudes toward animals (as discussed in chapter 2). It is presumably easier to reduce bias against animals that do not constitute "real" threats.

8.3 IMPLICATIONS FOR ANIMAL ETHICS

Many skeptical remarks have been made throughout this book about the prospects for moral change, and special emphasis has been placed on the often-overlooked influence of negative attitudes toward animals. But we should support creative solutions for improving treatment of animals. The skeptical remarks are aimed not at moral change as such but at the implausible suggestions typically offered for achieving change, as well as the misconceptions about moral psychology that perpetuate these ideas.

So, in the end, what are the main implications for ethicists concerned about changing moral attitudes toward animals? What concrete steps can they take to change moral psychology? Here are a few parting suggestions:

(1) *Give regulation a shot.* The proposals mentioned in this chapter are preliminary. The goal, though, is to create policies and regulations that could alter the way people think about and treat animals. The recent surge in political theorizing about animals has encouraged more practical thinking about social and moral change. This is reflected in the discussion of non-ideal theories in chapter 6. Non-ideal theories push us to focus on regulation just as they require us to contemplate the moral psychological profiles entailed by moral ideals. Ethicists should keep pushing in this direction by engaging with the literature on policy change and how policies can be informed by behavioral economics and cognitive science.

Many nudges are more permanent than my proposals above. For example, altering "choice architectures," or the way decisions are framed, is often intended to replace default choice frameworks. Whole Foods' Animal Welfare Rating System is one such example. Because much more research is still needed on the proposals identified here, it should not be expected that they will become as tightly woven into society as many nudges.

Nonetheless, ethicists and policy-makers should continue to pursue classic nudges for animal welfare. Whole Foods' strategies are an interesting first step, but much more work is needed; and ethicists are well-positioned to take the initiative. Classic nudge domains are good places to start (e.g., tweaking food choices), but ethicists should also aim to expand to new areas. The use of animals in laboratory research, in agriculture, as companions, and in zoos is subject to increased regulation. There may be opportunities in all of these domains to create regulations that alter moral attitudes in important ways.

(2) *Learn more about psychology.* Chapter 6 discussed the importance of outlining strategies for moral change. The impact, transition, and achievability criteria are essential if we aim to create theories that will have a psychological influence on ordinary human beings. Of course, a lot hinges on examination of the empirical details. Outlining a legitimate plan for psychological change requires empirically informed moral thinkers.

This isn't just a matter of reading the literature (although that's an excellent start). Results must be interpreted. This requires a better understanding of philosophy of mind and philosophy of psychology, not to mention the nature of experimental research conducted across the cognitive sciences. Many have been concerned recently about prominent studies that have failed to replicate, particularly in social psychology. Similar concerns might apply to many of the studies discussed in this book. However, skepticism about certain studies does not mean we should dismiss all experimental research (see Doris, 2015, ch. 3, for an excellent discussion). I have tried to bring together multiple compelling streams of research converging on the same conclusions about the psychology of dehumanization. This research cannot be dismissed simply based on the existence of failed replications in the field. I am, of course, open to being shown that the account of dehumanization I have presented here is mistaken. But an adequate refutation would require similar engagement with the empirical literature.

To connect these findings to moral psychology more generally, some knowledge is also required about the history of moral change. Laws and policies also need to match the level of psychological difficulties involved. This of course requires knowledge of how legal regulations operate. Obtaining knowledge in all these domains is of course very difficult, but it would seem to be the only realistic way of pursuing moral change.

(3) *Embrace biases.* Dehumanization is just one of many psychological biases relevant to animals. Research in social psychology has catalogued dozens of psychological processes that are central to our thinking about other human beings. Which others, besides dehumanization, might influence our thinking about animals?

Implicit biases in particular are understudied with respect to animals. As mentioned above, even the Implicit Association Test—which has been used in thousands of studies—has barely been applied to animals. According to the psychology of infrahumanization, where people make subtle devaluations of animals, implicit processes are essential to understanding our attitudes toward animals.

Negative attitudes toward animals are also relatively unstudied. Part of the reason for this, to speculate a bit, is that people do think very positively about certain animals, and these are the examples that come to mind when contemplating one's views about animals. But these are exceptional cases. And as we have seen, even in these cases there are subtle judgments that include negative evaluations, which can enable things like abuse and neglect.

Resistance to negativity may also result from assumptions about an expanding moral circle, or similar ideas. There is a tendency sometimes to think that things cannot improve if we are not part of broader forces sweeping us along. It is of course difficult to act alone, so we imagine that the momentum is in our favor. But not everything has to be part of a movement. If we want to be realistic about moral change, then we must accept that not everyone is an animal advocate, and even those who identify as such are still just human beings with psychological profiles that might run counter to their own self-conceptions. As discussed in chapter 7, many changes in legal regulations concerning animals have been initiated without any consensus on the moral significance of animals. To pursue new policies, it might be less important for everyone to agree about the importance of animals than for policy-makers to understand the relevant moral psychology—including potential biases.

(4) *Counter-revolution.* Some have suggested that animal ethicists should abandon many of their traditional concerns (e.g., Cavell et al., 2008; Weil, 2012; Willett, 2014). For example, debates over sentience and moral status might seem to have been exhausted. Does dehumanization research similarly dictate that animal ethicists should direct their attention elsewhere?

While dehumanization research does alert ethicists to new problems, these problems directly stem from traditional concerns. It is important for animal ethicists to consider moral psychology precisely because it is so important to many long-standing goals. So while breadth is important, managing moral psychology could also be a strategy for achieving more depth in thinking about traditional concerns in animal ethics. For example, chapter 6 provided new tools for thinking about the welfarist/abolitionist debate. People engaged in those debates have made moral psychological claims without looking to the empirical literature. Rather than merely prod ethicists to find new problems, the research discussed in this book can be used to facilitate a more informed discussion. Similarly, the discussion in chapter 4 about mentalizing broaches new ground but mainly by building on ideas that have widespread agreement within the discipline.

There also remain classic concerns within relatively new topics that could benefit from more direct attention. Only recently have zoo animals and companion animals received sustained ethical attention, for instance, despite their immense popularity (e.g., Minteer, Maienschein, & Collins, 2018; Sandøe, Corr, & Palmer, 2015). The moral psychology behind killing healthy animals in zoos or in shelters would be illuminating. These animals are more accessible to most people than are livestock or laboratory animals, which means the research could be more useful for enacting interventions to modify underlying moral attitudes.

8.4 CONCLUSION

We have taken a close look at recent research on the psychology of dehumanization to animals, as well as a range of other psychological processes that interact with dehumanization. What, in the end, can we conclude from this research? Dehumanization entails certain negative evaluations of animals. Sometimes these evaluations can be very subtle and coexist with overtly positive judgments of animals. This is how dehumanization operates even when judging human outgroups. Understanding these psychological processes is particularly important for making psychologically plausible ethical prescriptions, as well as for thinking about moral progress and improving moral treatment of animals. In this final chapter, we have outlined a relatively unexplored method for improving treatment of animals: creating policies aimed at altering moral psychology.

It is continually surprising that no systematic accounts of moral psychology exist within the field of animal ethics. Hopefully this book inspires greater theorizing on the topic. Whether we are interested in animals as academics, advocates, companions, or just as people who live among animals, we need a better understanding of this important aspect of our moral lives.

ACKNOWLEDGMENTS

Research for this book began over a decade ago, when I was working with captive apes and would observe the reactions of guests who seemed oddly ambivalent about creatures that were so much like themselves. Both human and non-human apes provided numerous insights that informed the content of this book. Continued support from friends and colleagues from that time has made the difficult task of writing a book worth the effort.

Much of the book was written while I was a postdoc in the Department of Food and Resource Economics at the University of Copenhagen. I owe a huge debt of gratitude to the department and my colleagues there, as well as my advisor Peter Sandøe, for providing the opportunity to research and write in such a wonderful city.

The book is largely based on a dissertation I wrote at Texas A&M University. I couldn't ask for better tutors in thinking about animals than my advisors Clare Palmer and Gary Varner. They have always been encouraging and generous with their time and advice. All of the more polished ideas in the book are to their credit.

Others at Texas A&M provided invaluable guidance throughout the writing of both the dissertation and the book. Linda Radzik helped me navigate the world of moral philosophy and continually challenged my attempts to think about ethics through the lens of science. José Luis Bermúdez served as a model for how to think and write in philosophy. Working with him vastly improved my approach to interdisciplinary research in cognitive science. Brandon Schmeichel provided helpful advice on issues in social psychology. The reading group in emotions and social psychology run by him and Eddie Harmon-Jones inspired many ideas throughout the book. Teresa Wilcox and the Infant Cognition Lab at Texas A&M also provided crucial training in experimental methods in social and developmental psychology. Lastly, I must thank Michael LeBuffe and Steve Daniel for their training in the history of philosophy, despite my somewhat idiosyncratic interests in the history of attitudes to animals.

The book was greatly improved by feedback I received at various academic venues. Bryce Huebner provided insightful comments on a very early draft of chapter 4, at the 2010 meeting of the Southern Society for Philosophy and Psychology. Chapter 6 received a full dressing down at the 2014 meeting of the American Philosophical Association-Eastern Division. Though the audience was hostile, I learned a great deal about philosophers' wariness of empirical moral psychology. The 2015 workshop on moral psychology hosted by Holly Lawford-Smith was instrumental in developing numerous chapters, especially in rebuilding chapter 6. I can't thank the workshop attendees enough for their instructive suggestions and comments.

Thinking is best done with another person, and I have been fortunate to have many great partners in thought. Megan Kasperbauer has been uniquely capable of inspiring new ideas. In addition to reading and commenting on the entire manuscript, she endured hundreds of alternative versions discussed over meals and on walks from Iowa to Texas to Denmark. This book wouldn't exist without her. Our dog Charlie was also present for these conversations, and although he did not offer much in terms of discussion, he must be thanked for the many examples and counterexamples he provided to claims about the value of animal companions.

Conversations with David Wright, Jake Greenblum, and Collin Rice greatly enriched my thinking about animals, ethics, and moral psychology. David read and commented on nearly every line in the book and has done so for almost everything I have written since we first became office mates at Texas A&M in 2008. I am continuously grateful for his friendship, guidance, and commitment to ideas. I also benefited from valuable discussions and feedback from numerous other people, including Adam Shriver, Katie Wright, Monika Blackwell, Will Kymlicka, Benedicte Spies, Kim Gruetzmacher, James Serpell, Julia Chiabudini, and Brendon Larson.

Thanks are also due to my parents, brothers, and extended family who have patiently accepted my excuses for being absent while writing this book. Their curiosity and support for my work is a constant source of motivation.

Lastly, I must acknowledge publishers that have allowed me to reproduce material here that has previously appeared in other places. Table 2.1 in chapter 2 was reprinted from *Infection, Genetics and Evolution*, Volume 24, Serge Morand, K. Marie McIntyre, Matthew Baylis, "Domesticated animals and human infectious diseases of zoonotic origins: Domestication time matters," pp. 76–81, 2014, with permission from Elsevier. Portions of chapter 3 were originally published in *Biology & Philosophy*, "Animals as disgust elicitors," Volume 30, 2015a, pp. 167–185, T. J. Kasperbauer. These portions are reproduced here with permission of Springer. Portions of chapter 4 were originally published in *Philosophical Studies*, "Mentalizing animals: Implications for moral psychology and animal ethics," Volume 174, 2017, pp. 465–484, T. J. Kasperbauer. These portions are reproduced here with permission of Springer.

REFERENCES

Ahn, S. J., Bostick, J., Ogle, E., & Bailenson, J. N. (2015). Embodying nature's experiences: Taking the perspective of nature with immersive virtual environments to promote connectedness with nature. Paper presented at the Annual Association for Education in Journalism and Mass Communication (AEJMC) Conference, August 6–9, San Francisco, CA.

Albarello, F., & Rubini, M. (2012). Reducing dehumanisation outcomes towards blacks: The role of multiple categorisation and of human identity. *European Journal of Social Psychology, 42,* 875–882.

ALDF (Animal Legal Defense Fund). (2015). 2015 U.S. animal protection laws rankings. Retrieved from http://aldf.org/wp-content/uploads/2015/12/Rankings-Report-2015.pdf.

Alexandratos, N., & Bruinsma, J. (2012). *World agriculture towards 2030/2050: The 2012 revision.* ESA Working paper No. 12-03. Rome: FAO.

Alfano, M. (2013). *Character as moral fiction.* Cambridge: Cambridge University Press.

Allen, M. W., Hunstone, M., Waerstad, J., Foy, E., Hobbins, T., Wikner, B., & Wirrel, J. (2002). Human-to-animal similarity and participant mood influence punishment recommendations for animal abusers. *Society and Animals, 10,* 267–284.

Allport, G. W. (1954). *The nature of prejudice.* Cambridge, MA: Perseus Books.

Amiot, C. E., & Bastian, B. (2015). Toward a psychology of human–animal relations. *Psychological Bulletin, 141,* 6–47.

Angantyr, M., Eklund, J., & Hansen, E. M. (2011). A comparison of empathy for humans and empathy for animals. *Anthrozoos, 24,* 369–377.

Archer, J. (1997). Why do people love their pets? *Evolution and Human Behavior, 18*(4), 237–259.

Ariely, D., & Loewenstein, G. (2006). The heat of the moment: The effect of sexual arousal on sexual decision making. *Journal of Behavioral Decision Making, 19*, 87–98.

Arrindell, W. A., Mulkens, S., Kok, J., & Vollenbroek, J. (1999). Disgust sensitivity and the sex difference in fears to common indigenous animals. *Behaviour Research and Therapy, 37*, 273–280.

Astuti, R., Solomon, G. E. A., & Carey, S. (2004). Constraints on conceptual development. *Monographs in Social Research and Child Development, 69*, 1–135.

Atran, S., Medin, D., Lynch, E., Vapnarsky, V., Ucan Ek', E., & Sousa, P. (2001). Folkbiology doesn't come from folkpsychology: Evidence from Yukatek Maya in cross-cultural perspective. *Journal of Cognition and Culture, 1*, 3–42.

Avramova, Y. R., & Inbar, Y. (2013). Emotion and moral judgment. *WIREs Cognitive Science, 4*, 169–178.

Axelrod, V., Bar, M., & Rees, G. (2015). Exploring the unconscious using faces. *Trends in Cognitive Sciences, 19*, 35–45.

Bain, P. G., Vaes, J., & Leyens, J-P. (eds.) (2014). *Humanness and dehumanization.* New York: Psychology Press.

Balas, B., & Momsen, J. L. (2014). Attention "blinks" differently for plants and animals. *CBE-Life Sciences Education, 13*, 437–443.

Baldwin, R. (2014). From regulation to behaviour change: Giving nudge the third degree. *Modern Law Review, 77*, 831–857.

Baldwin, R., Cave, M., & Lodge, M. (2012). *Understanding regulation,* 2nd ed. Oxford: Oxford University Press.

Barreiro, L. B., & Quintana-Murci, L. (2010). From evolutionary genetics to human immunology: How selection shapes host defence genes. *Nature Reviews Genetics, 11*, 17–30.

Barrett, H. C. (2005). Adaptations to predators and prey. In D. Buss (ed.), *The handbook of evolutionary psychology* (pp. 200–223). Hoboken, NJ: Wiley.

Barrett, H. C., & Broesch, J. (2012). Prepared social learning about animals in children. *Evolution and Human Behavior, 33*, 499–508.

Barton, A., & Grüne-Yanoff, T. (eds.) (2015). Nudge. [Special issue]. *Review of Philosophy and Psychology, 6*, 341–529.

Bastian, B., Costello, K., Loughnan, S., & Hodson, G. (2012). When closing the human–animal divide expands moral concern: The importance of framing. *Social Psychological and Personality Science, 3*, 421–429.

Bastian, B., Laham, S. M., Wilson, S., Haslam, N., & Koval, P. (2011). Blaming, praising, and protecting our humanity: The implications of everyday dehumanization for judgments of moral status. *British Journal of Social Psychology, 50*, 469–483.

Bastian, B., Loughnan, S., Haslam, N., & Radke, H. (2012). Don't mind meat? The denial of mind to animals used for human consumption. *Personality and Social Psychology Bulletin, 38*, 247–256.

Batson, C. D., Thompson, E. R., Seuferling, G., Whitney, H., & Strongman, J. A. (1999). Moral hypocrisy: Appearing moral to oneself without being so. *Journal of Personality and Social Psychology, 77*, 525–537.

Batt, S. (2009). Human attitudes towards animals in relation to species similarity to humans: A multivariate approach. *Bioscience Horizons, 2*, 180–190.

Baumeister, R. F., Vohs, K. D., & Tice, D. M. (2007). The strength model of self-control. *Current Directions in Psychological Science, 16*, 351–355.

Beatson, R. M., & Halloran, M. J. (2007). Humans rule! The effects of creatureliness reminders, mortality salience and self-esteem on attitudes towards animals. *British Journal of Social Psychology, 46*, 619–632.

Beatson, R. M., Loughnan, S., & Halloran, M. J. (2009). Attitudes toward animals: The effect of priming thoughts of human–animal similarities and mortality salience on the evaluation of companion animals. *Society and Animals, 17*, 72–89.

Becker, E. (1973). *The denial of death*. New York: Free Press.

Bekoff, M. (2013). *Ignoring nature no more: The case for compassionate conservation*. Chicago: University of Chicago Press.

Bekoff, M. (2014). *Rewilding our hearts: Building pathways of compassion and coexistence*. Novato, CA: New World Library.

Bell, D. (1992). Racial realism. *Connecticut Law Review, 24*, 363–379.

Bertrams, A., & Schmeichel, B. J. (2014). Improving self-control by practicing logical reasoning. *Self and Identity, 13*, 419–431.

Bilewicz, M., Imhoff, R., & Drogosz, M. (2011). The humanity of what we eat: Conceptions of human uniqueness among vegetarians and omnivores. *European Journal of Social Psychology, 41*, 201–209.

Bird-David, N. (1999). "Animism" revisited: Personhood, environment, and relational epistemology. *Current Anthropology, 40*, S67–S91.

Birtel, M. D., & Crisp, R. J. (2012). "Treating" prejudice: An exposure-therapy approach to reducing negative reactions toward stigmatized groups. *Psychological Science, 23*, 1379–1386.

Boccato, G., Capozza, D., Falvo, R., Durante, F. (2008). The missing link: Ingroup, outgroup, and the human species. *Social Cognition, 26*, 224–234.

Borg, C., & de Jong, P. J. (2012). Feelings of disgust and disgust-induced avoidance weaken following induced sexual arousal in women. *PloS One, 7*, e44111.

Bovens, L. (2008). The ethics of nudge. In T. Grüne-Yanoff & S. O. Hansson (eds.), *Preference change: Approaches from philosophy, economics and psychology* (pp. 207–219). Berlin and New York: Springer.

Boyd, R., & Richerson, P. (2005). *The origin and evolution of cultures*. New York: Oxford University Press.

Brambell, F. W. R. (1965). *Report of the technical committee to inquire into the welfare of animals kept under intensive livestock husbandry systems*. London: H.M.S.O.

Bratanova, B., Loughnan, S., & Bastian, B. (2011). The effect of categorization as food on the perceived moral standing of animals. *Appetite, 57*, 193–196.

Brightman, R. A. (1993). *Grateful prey: Rock Cree human–animal relationships.* Berkeley: University of California Press.

Broesch, J., Barrett, H. C., & Henrich, J. (2014). Adaptive content biases in learning about animals across the life course. *Human Nature, 25*, 181–199.

Brown, C. M., & McLean, J. L. (2015). Anthropomorphizing dogs: Projecting one's own personality and consequences for supporting animal rights. *Anthrozoös, 28*, 73–86.

Brownlee, K. (2010). Reasons and ideals. *Philosophical Studies, 151*, 433–444.

Bulliet, R. W. (2005). *Hunters, herders, and hamburgers: The past and future of human–animal relationships.* New York: Columbia University Press.

Campos, B., Shiota, M. N., Keltner, D., Gonzaga, G. C., & Goetz, J. L. (2013). What is shared, what is different? Core relational themes and expressive displays of eight positive emotions. *Cognition & Emotion, 27*, 37–52.

Cao, Z. J., Zhao, Y., Tan, T., Chen, G., Ning, X., Zhan, L., & Yang, J. (2014). Distinct brain activity in processing negative pictures of animals and objects—The role of human contexts. *Neuroimage, 84*, 901–910.

Carey, S. (1985). *Conceptual change in childhood.* Cambridge, MA: MIT Press.

Carlson, K. A., Tanner, R. J., Meloy, M. G., & Russo, J. E. (2014). Catching nonconscious goals in the act of decision making. *Organizational Behavior and Human Decision Processes, 123*, 65–76.

Carruthers, P. (1992). *The animals issue.* Cambridge: Cambridge University Press.

Carter, E. C., Kofler, L. M., Forster, D. E., & McCullough, M. E. (2015). A series of meta-analytic tests of the depletion effect: Self-control does not seem to rely on a limited resource. *Journal of Experimental Psychology: General, 144*, 796–815.

Castano, E., & Giner-Sorolla, R. (2006). Not quite human: Infrahumanisation in response to collective responsibility for intergroup killing. *Journal of Personality and Social Psychology, 90*, 804–818.

Cavell, S., Diamond, C., McDowell, J., Hacking, I., & Wolfe, C. (2008). *Philosophy & animal life.* New York: Columbia University Press.

Chapman, H. A., & Anderson, A. K. (2012). Understanding disgust. *Annals of the New York Academy of Sciences, 1251*, 62–76.

Chapman, H. A., & Anderson, A. K. (2013). Things rank and gross in nature: A review and synthesis of moral disgust. *Psychological Bulletin, 139*, 300–327.

Chapple, C. K. (1993). *Nonviolence to animals, Earth, and self in Asian traditions.* Albany: State University of New York Press.

Clarkson, J. J., Hirt, E. R., Jia, L., & Alexander, M. B. (2010). When perception is more than reality: The effects of perceived versus actual resource depletion on self-regulatory behavior. *Journal of Personality and Social Psychology, 98*, 29–46.

Clayton, S., Fraser, J., & Burgess, C. (2011). The role of zoos in fostering environmental identity. *Ecopsychology, 3*, 87–96.

Cochrane, A. (2012). *Animal rights without liberation*. New York: Columbia University Press.

Collins, S. (2013). Collectives' duties and collectivization duties. *Journal of Philosophy, 91,* 231–248.

Comas, I., Coscolla, M., Luo, T., Borrell, S., Holt, K. E., Kato-Maeda, M., Parkhill, J., Malla, B., Berg, S., Thwaites, G., Yeboah-Manu, D., Bothamley, G., Mei, J., Wei, L., Bentley, S., Harris, S. R., Niemann, S., Diel, R., Aseffa, A., Gao, Q., Young, D., & Gagneux, S. (2013). Out-of-Africa migration and Neolithic coexpansion of *Mycobacterium tuberculosis* with modern humans. *Nature Genetics, 45,* 1176–1182.

Conly, S. (2013). *Against autonomy: Justifying coercive paternalism.* Cambridge: Cambridge University Press.

Cornell, N. (2015). A third theory of paternalism. *Michigan Law Review, 113,* 1295–1336.

Cosmides, L., & Tooby, J. (2013). Evolutionary psychology: New perspectives on cognition and motivation. *Annual Review of Psychology, 64,* 201–229.

Costello, K., & Hodson, G. (2010). Exploring the roots of dehumanization: The role of animal human similarity in promoting immigrant humanization. *Group Processes & Intergroup Relations, 13,* 3–22.

Costello, K., & Hodson, G. (2014). Lay beliefs about the causes of and solutions to dehumanization and prejudice: Do nonexperts recognize the role of human–animal relations? *Journal of Applied Social Psychology, 44,* 278–288.

Cottingham, J. (1978). "A brute to the brutes?": Descartes' treatment of animals. *Philosophy, 53,* 551–559.

Cottingham, J., Stoothoff, R., Murdoch, D., & Kenny, A. (eds. & trans.) (1991). *The Philosophical Writings of Descartes,* Vol. III. Cambridge: Cambridge University Press.

Cox, C. R., Goldenberg, J. L., Pyszczynski, T., & Weise, D. (2007). Disgust, creatureliness and the accessibility of death-related thoughts. *European Journal of Social Psychology, 37,* 494–507.

Crisp, R. J., & Turner, R. N. (2009). Can imagined interactions produce positive perceptions? Reducing prejudice through simulated social contact. *American Psychologist, 64,* 231–240.

Crouzet, S. M., Joubert, O. R., Thorpe, S. J., & Fabre-Thorpe, M. (2012). Animal detection precedes access to scene category. *PLoS One, 7(12),* e51471.

Cuddy, A. J. C., Rock, M. S., & Norton, M. I. (2007). Aid in the aftermath of Hurricane Katrina: Inferences of secondary emotions and intergroup helping. *Group Processes and Intergroup Relations, 10,* 107–118.

Curley, E. (ed. and trans.) (1985). *The complete works of Spinoza,* vol. 1. Princeton, NJ: Princeton University Press.

Curtis, G. C., Magee, W. J., Eaton, W. W., Wittchen, H. U., & Kessler, R. C. (1998). Specific fears and phobias. Epidemiology and classification. *British Journal of Psychiatry, 173,* 212–217.

Curtis, V. A. (2014). Infection-avoidance behaviour in humans and other animals. *Trends in Immunology, 35,* 457–464.

Curtis, V., & Biran, A. (2001). Dirt, disgust, and disease. *Perspectives in Biology and Medicine, 44,* 17–31.

Daly, B., & Sugg, S. (2010). Teachers' experiences with humane education and animals in the elementary classroom: Implications for empathy development. *Journal of Moral Education, 39,* 101–112.

D'Arms, J. (2005). Two arguments for sentimentalism. *Philosophical Issues, 15,* 1–21.

D'Arms, J. (2013). Value and the regulation of the sentiments. *Philosophical Studies, 163,* 3–13.

D'Arms, J., & Jacobson, D. (2003). The significance of recalcitrant emotions (or Anti-QuasiJudgmentalism). In A. Hatzimoysis (ed.), *Philosophy and the Emotions.* Cambridge: Cambridge University Press.

Davey, G. C. L., Forster, L., & Mayhew, G. (1993). Familial resemblances in disgust sensitivity and animal phobias. *Behavioral Research Therapy, 31,* 41–50.

Davey, G. C. L., & Marzillier, S. (2009). Disgust and animal phobias. In B. O. Olatunji and D. McKay (eds.), *Disgust and its disorders: Theory, assessment, and treatment implications* (pp. 169–190). Washington, DC: American Psychological Association.

De Backer, C. J. S., & Hudders, L. (2015). Meat morals: Relationship between meat consumption consumer attitudes towards human and animal welfare and moral behavior. *Meat Science, 99,* 68–74.

DeGrazia, D. (1996). *Taking animals seriously.* Cambridge: Cambridge University Press.

Des Chene, D. (2006). Animal as category. In J. E. H. Smith (ed.), *The problem of animal generation in early modern philosophy* (pp. 215–231). New York: Cambridge University Press.

Dhont, K., & Hodson, G. (2014). Why do right-wing adherents engage in more animal exploitation and meat consumption? *Personality and Individual Differences, 64,* 12–17.

Dhont, K., Hodson, G., Costello, K., & MacInnis, C. C. (2014). Social dominance orientation connects prejudicial human–human and human–animal relations. *Personality and Individual Differences, 61–62,* 105–108.

Diesendruck, G. (2001). Essentialism in Brazilian children's extensions of animal names. *Developmental Psychology, 37,* 49–60.

Dijksterhuis, A., & Aarts, H. (2010). Goals, attention, and (un)consciousness. *Annual Review of Psychology, 61,* 467–490.

Dimberg, U., Thunberg, M., & Elmehed, K. (2000). Unconscious facial reactions to emotional facial expressions. *Psychological Science, 11,* 86–89.

Donaldson, S., & Kymlicka, W. (2011). *Zoopolis.* Oxford: Oxford University Press.

Doris, J. M. (1998). Persons, situations, and virtue ethics. *Noûs, 32,* 504–530.

Doris, J. M. (2002). *Lack of character: Personality and moral behavior.* New York: Cambridge University Press.

Doris, J. M. (2010). Heated agreement: Lack of character as being for the good. *Philosophical Studies, 148*, 135–146.

Doris, J. M. (2015). *Talking to our selves: Reflection, ignorance, and agency.* New York: Oxford University Press.

Dovidio, J. F., & Gaertner, S. L. (2000). Aversive racism and selection decisions: 1989 and 1999. *Psychological Science, 11*, 315–319.

Eddy, T. J., Gallup, G. G., Jr., & Povinelli, D. J. (1993). Attribution of cognitive states to animals: Anthropomorphism in comparative perspective. *Journal of Social Issues, 49*, 87–101.

Elliot, A. J., Schüler, J., Roskes, M., & De Dreu, C. K. W. (2014). Avoidance motivation is resource depleting. In J. Forgas & E. Harmon-Jones (eds.), *The control within: Motivation and its regulation* (pp. 247–262). New York: Psychology Press.

Elsner, B., Jeschonek, S., & Pauen, S. (2013). Event-related potentials for 7-month-olds' processing of animals and furniture items. *Developmental Cognitive Neuroscience, 3*, 53–60.

Epley, N., Waytz, A., Akalis, S., & Cacioppo, J. T. (2008). When we need a human: Motivational determinants of anthropomorphism. *Social Cognition, 26*, 143–55.

Erikson, P. (2000). The social significance of pet-keeping among Amazonian Indians. In A. L. Podberscek, E. S. Paul, & J. A. Serpell (eds.), *Companion animals and us: Exploring the relationships between people and pets* (pp. 7–26). Cambridge: Cambridge University Press.

European Union. (2014). Seventh report on the statistics on the number of animals used for experimental and other scientific purposes in the member states of the European Union. Retrieved from http://eur-lex.europa.eu/legal-content/EN/TXT/?uri=CELEX:52013DC0859.

Evans, D. R., Boggero, I. A., & Segerstrom, S. C. (2015). The nature of self-regulatory fatigue and ego depletion: Lessons from physical fatigue. *Personality and Social Psychology Review, 20*, 291–310.

Evans, J. St. B. T., & Stanovich, K. E. (2013). Dual-process theories of higher cognition: Advancing the debate. *Perspectives on Psychological Science, 8*, 223–241, 263–271.

Favre, D. S. (2011). *Animal law: Welfare interests and rights,* 2nd ed. New York: Aspen Publishers.

Favre, D., & Tsang, V. (1993). The development of anti-cruelty laws during the 1800's. *Detroit College of Law Review, 1*, 1–35.

Feinberg, M., & Willer, R. (2015). From gulf to bridge: When do moral arguments facilitate political influence? *Personality and Social Psychology Bulletin, 41*, 1665–1681.

Feit, H. A. (1973). The ethno-ecology of the Waswanipi Cree; or how hunters can handle their resources. In B. Cox (ed.), *Cultural Ecology* (pp. 115–125). Toronto: McLelland & Stewart.

Fessler, D., & Navarrete, C. (2003). Meat is good to taboo: Dietary prescriptions as a product of the interaction of psychological mechanisms and social processes. *Journal of Cognition and Culture, 3,* 1–40.

Fessler, D., & Navarrete, C. (2005). The effect of age on death disgust: Challenges to terror management perspectives. *Evolutionary Psychology, 3,* 279–296.

Festinger, L. (1957). *A theory of cognitive dissonance.* Stanford, CA: Stanford University Press.

Festinger, L. (1964). *Conflict, decision, and dissonance.* Stanford, CA: Stanford University Press.

Fine, C. (2006). Is the emotional dog wagging its rational tail, or chasing it? *Philosophical Explorations, 9,* 83–98.

Fiske, S. T., Cuddy, A. J., & Glick, P. (2007). Universal dimensions of social cognition: Warmth and competence. *Trends in Cognitive Science, 11,* 77–83.

Fiske, S. T., Cuddy, A. J., Glick, P., & Xu, J. (2002). A model of (often mixed) stereotype content: Competence and warmth respectively follow from perceived status and competition. *Journal of Personality and Social Psychology, 82,* 878–902.

Flanagan, O. (1991). *Varieties of moral personality: Ethics and psychological realism.* Cambridge, MA: Harvard University Press.

Francione, G. (2000). *Introduction to animal rights: Your child or your dog?* Philadelphia: Temple University Press.

Francione, G., & Garner, R. (2010). *Animal rights debate: Abolition or regulation?* New York: Columbia University Press.

Frankenhuis, W. E., House, B., Barrett, H. C., & Johnson, S. P. (2013). Infants' perception of chasing. *Cognition, 126,* 224–233.

French, R. D. (1975). *Antivivisection and medical science in Victorian England.* Princeton, NJ: Princeton University Press.

Frey, R. G. (1980). *Interests and rights: The case against animals.* Oxford: Clarendon Press.

Frey, R. G. (2014). Moral standing, the value of lives, and speciesism. In H. LaFollette (ed.), *Ethics in practice,* 4th ed. (pp. 321–338). Malden, MA: Wiley.

Frynta, D., Lišková, S., Bültmann, S., & Burda, H. (2010). Being attractive brings advantages: The case of parrot species in captivity. *PLoS One, 5,* e12568.

Frynta, D., Simkova, O., Liskova, S., & Landova, E. (2013). Mammalian collection on Noah's ark: The effects of beauty, brain and body size. *PLoS One, 8,* e63110.

Fudge, E. (2006). *Brutal reasoning: Animals, rationality, and humanity in early modern England.* Ithaca, NY, and London: Cornell University Press.

Gaertner, S., & Dovidio, J. (2008). Addressing contemporary racism: The common ingroup identity model. In C. Willis-Esqueda (ed.), *Motivational aspects of prejudice and racism* (pp. 111–133). New York: Springer.

Gaertner, S. L., Dovidio, J. F., Anastasio, P. A., Bachman, B. A., & Rust, M. C. (1993). The common ingroup identity model: Recategorization and the reduction of intergroup bias. *European Review of Social Psychology, 4,* 1–26.

Gaertner, S., Rust, M., Bachman, B., Dovidio, J., & Anastasio, P. (1994). The contact hypothesis: The role of a common ingroup identity on reducing intergroup bias. *Small Group Research, 25*, 224–249.

Gailliot, M. T., Stillman, T. F., Schmeichel, B. J., Maner, J. K., & Plant, E. A. (2008). Mortality salience increases adherence to salient norms and values. *Personality and Social Psychology Bulletin, 24*, 993.

Gallo, I. S., Keil, A., McCulloch, K. C., Rockstroh, B., & Gollwitzer, P. (2009). Strategic automation of emotion regulation. *Journal of Personality and Social Psychology, 96*, 11–31.

Gantman, A. P., & Van Bavel, J. J. (2015). Moral perception. *Trends in Cognitive Sciences, 19*, 631–633.

Garner, R. (2005). *The political theory of animal rights*. Manchester, UK: Manchester University Press.

Garner, R. (2012). Toward a theory of justice for animals. *Journal of Animal Ethics, 2*, 98–104.

Garner, R. (2013). *A theory of justice for animals*. Oxford: Oxford University Press.

Gaudiosi, J. (2016). Virtual reality video game industry to generate $5.1 billion in 2016. *Fortune*. Retrieved from http://fortune.com/2016/01/05/virtual-reality-game-industry-to-generate-billions/.

Gaukroger, S. (1993). Nature without reason: Cartesian automata and perceptual cognition. *History of Philosophy Yearbook, 1*, 26–40.

Gaukroger, S. (2008). *The emergence of a scientific culture: Science and the shaping of modernity, 1210–1685*. New York: Oxford University Press.

Gawronski, B. (2012). Back to the future of dissonance theory: Cognitive consistency as a core motive. *Social Cognition, 30*, 652–668.

Gelman, S. A., & Gottfried, G. M. (1996). Children's causal explanations for animate and inanimate motion. *Child Development, 67*, 1970–1987.

Gelman, S. A., & Legare, C. H. (2011). Concepts and folk theories. *Annual Review of Anthropology, 40*, 379–398.

Gelman, S., & Wellman, H. (1991). Insides and essences. *Cognition, 38*, 214–244.

Gilabert, P., & Lawford-Smith, H. (2012). Political feasibility: A conceptual exploration. *Political Studies, 60*, 809–825.

Gil-White, F. J. (2001). Are ethnic groups biological "species" to the human brain? Essentialism in our cognition of some social categories. *Current Anthropology, 42*, 515–554.

Gino, F., Schweitzer, M. E., Mead, N. L., & Ariely, D. (2011). Unable to resist temptation: How self-control depletion promotes unethical behavior. *Organizational Behavior and Human Decision Processes, 115*, 191–203.

Glod, W. (2015). How nudges often fail to treat people according to their own preferences. *Social Theory & Practice, 41*, 599–617.

Godfrey-Smith, P. (2001). Three kinds of adaptationism. In S. H. Orzack & E. Sober (eds.), *Adaptationism and optimality* (pp. 335–357). Cambridge: Cambridge University Press.

Goldenberg, J. L., Cox, C. R., Pyszczynski, T., Greenberg, J., & Solomon, S. (2002). Understanding human ambivalence about sex: The effects of stripping sex of meaning. *Journal of Sex Research, 39*, 310–320.

Goldenberg, J. L., Pyszczynski, T., Greenberg, J., Sheldon, S., Kluck, B., & Cornwell, R. (2001). "I am *not* an animal": Mortality salience, disgust, and the denial of human creatureliness. *Journal of Experimental Psychology: General, 130*, 427–435.

Goldenberg, J. L., Pyszczynski, T., McCoy, S. K., Greenberg, J., & Solomon, S. (1999). Death, sex, love, and neuroticism: Why is sex such a problem? *Journal of Personality and Social Psychology, 77*, 1173–1187.

Goldin, J. (2015). Which way to nudge? Uncovering preferences in the behavioral age. *Yale Law Journal, 125*, 226–270.

Goodman, J., Chandna, A., & Roe, K. (2015). Trends in animal use at US research facilities. *Journal of Medical Ethics, 41*, 567–569.

Goodpaster, K. E. (1978). On being morally considerable. *Journal of Philosophy, 75*, 308–325.

Gosling, S. D., Kwan, V. S. Y., & John, O. P. (2003). A dog's got personality: A cross-species comparative approach to personality judgments in dogs and humans. *Journal of Personality and Social Psychology, 85*, 1161–1169.

Graham, J., Haidt, J., Koleva, S., Motyl, M., Iyer, R., Wojcik, S., & Ditto, P. H. (2013). Moral foundations theory: The pragmatic validity of moral pluralism. *Advances in Experimental Social Psychology, 47*, 55–130.

Graham, J., Haidt, J., & Nosek, B. A. (2009). Liberals and conservatives rely on different sets of moral foundations. *Journal of Personality and Social Psychology, 96*, 1029–1046.

Graham, J., Nosek, B. A., Haidt, J., Iyer, R., Koleva, S., & Ditto, P. H. (2011). Mapping the moral domain. *Journal of Personality and Social Psychology, 101*, 366–385.

Gray, H., Gray, K., & Wegner, D. M. (2007). Dimensions of mind perception. *Science, 315*, 619.

Gray, K., Schein, C., & Ward, A. F. (2014). The myth of harmless wrongs in moral cognition: Automatic dyadic completion from sin to suffering. *Journal of Experimental Psychology: General, 143*, 1600–1615.

Gray, K., & Wegner, D. M. (2009). Moral typecasting: Divergent perceptions of moral agents and moral patients. *Journal of Personality and Social Psychology, 96*, 505–520.

Gray, K., & Wegner, D. M. (2012). Morality takes two: Dyadic morality and mind perception. In M. Mikulincer & P. R. Shaver (eds.), *The social psychology of morality* (pp. 109–127). Washington, DC: American Psychological Association.

Gray, K., Young, L., & Waytz, A. (2012). Mind perception is the essence of morality. *Psychological Inquiry, 23*, 101–124.

Greenberg, J., Arndt, J., Simon, L., Pyszczynski, T., & Solomon, S. (2000). Proximal and distal defenses in response to reminders of one's mortality: Evidence of a temporal sequence. *Personality and Social Psychology Bulletin, 26*, 91–99.

Greenberg, J., Pyszczynski, T., & Solomon, S. (1986). The causes and consequences of a need for self-esteem: A terror management theory. In R. F. Baumeister (ed.), *Public self and private self* (pp. 189–212). New York: Springer.

Greenberg, J., Pyszczynski, T., Solomon, S., Simon, L., & Breus, M. (1994). Role of consciousness and accessibility of death-related thoughts in mortality salience effects. *Journal of Personality and Social Psychology, 67*, 627–637.

Greenberg, J., Solomon, S., & Arndt, J. (2008). A basic but uniquely human motivation: Terror management. In J. Y. Shah & W. L. Gardner (eds.), *Handbook of motivation science* (pp. 114–134). New York: Guilford.

Greenberg, J., Vail, K., & Pyszcynski, T. (2014). Terror management theory and research: How the desire for death transcendence drives our strivings for meaning and significance. *Advances in Motivation Science, 1*, 85–134.

Greene, J. D., Sommerville, R. B., Nystrom, L. E., Darley, J. M., & Cohen, J. D. (2001). An fMRI investigation of emotional engagement in moral judgment. *Science, 293*, 2105–2108.

Grille, K., & Scoccia, D. (eds.) (2015). Introduction. [Special issue]. *Social Theory & Practice, 41*, 577–749.

Gruen, L. (2011). *Ethics and animals: An introduction.* Cambridge: Cambridge University Press.

Guerrini, A. (1989). The ethics of animal experimentation in seventeenth-century England. *Journal of the History of Ideas, 50*, 391–407.

Guerrini, A. (2003). *Experimenting with humans and animals: From Galen to animal rights.* Baltimore: Johns Hopkins.

Guiseppe, U., Claus, L., & Singer, T. (2012). The role of emotions for moral judgments depends on the type of emotion and moral scenario. *Emotion, 12*, 579–590.

Hagger, M. S., Wood, C., Stiff, C., & Chatzisarantis, N. L. D. (2010). Ego depletion and the strength model of self-control: A meta-analysis. *Psychological Bulletin, 136*, 495–525.

Haidt, J. (2001). The emotional dog and its rational tail: A social intuitionist approach to moral judgment. *Psychological Review, 108*, 814–834.

Haidt, J., & Graham, J. (2007). When morality opposes justice: Conservatives have moral intuitions that liberals may not recognize. *Social Justice Research, 20*, 98–116.

Haidt, J., Graham, J., & Ditto, P. (2015). A straw man can never beat a shapeshifter: Response to Schein and Gray (2015). Retrieved from http://www.yourmorals.org/blog/2015/10/a-straw-man-can-never-beat-a-shapeshifter/.

Haidt, J., & Kesebir, S. (2010). Morality. In S. Fiske, D. Gilbert, & G. Lindzey (eds.), *Handbook of social psychology*, 5th ed. (pp. 797–832). Hoboken, NJ: Wiley.

Haidt, J., Koller, S., & Dias, M. (1993). Affect, culture, and morality, or is it wrong to eat your dog? *Journal of Personality and Social Psychology, 65,* 613–628.

Hansen, P. G., & Jespersen, A. M. (2013). Nudge and a manipulation of choice. *European Journal of Risk Regulation, 1,* 3–28.

Harman, G. (1999). Moral philosophy meets social psychology: Virtue ethics and the fundamental attribution error. *Proceedings of the Aristotelian Society, 99,* 315–331.

Harman, G. (2009). Skepticism about character traits. *Journal of Ethics, 13,* 235–242.

Harmon-Jones, E., & Mills, J. (1999). An introduction to cognitive dissonance theory and an overview of current perspectives on the theory. In E. Harmon-Jones & J. Mills (eds.), *Cognitive dissonance: Progress on a pivotal theory in social psychology* (pp. 3–21). Washington, DC: American Psychological Association.

Harmon-Jones, E., Simon, L., Greenberg, J., Pyszczynski, T., Solomon, S., & McGregor, H. (1997). Terror management theory and self-esteem: Evidence that increased self-esteem reduces mortality salience effects. *Journal of Personality and Social Psychology, 72,* 24–36.

Harper, K. N., & Armelagos, G. J. (2013). Genomics, the origins of agriculture, and our changing microbe-scape: Time to revisit some old tales and tell some new ones. *American Journal of Physical Anthropology, 152,* 135–152.

Harrison, P. (1992). Descartes on animals. *Philosophical Quarterly, 42,* 219–227.

Harrison, R. (1964). *Animal machines.* London: Vincent Stuart.

Harrod, H. (2000). *The animals came dancing: Native American sacred ecology and animal kinship.* Tucson: University of Arizona Press.

Hart, B. L. (2011). Behavioural defences in animals against pathogens and parasites: Parallels with the pillars of medicine in humans. *Philosophical Transactions of the Royal Society B, 366,* 3406–3417.

Haslam, N. (2006). Dehumanization: An integrative review. *Personality and Social Psychology Review, 10,* 252–264.

Haslam, N., Bastian, B., Laham, S., & Loughnan, S. (2012). Humanness, dehumanization, and moral psychology. In M. Mikulincer & P. R. Shaver (eds.), *The Social Psychology of Morality* (pp. 203–218). Washington, DC: American Psychological Association.

Haslam, N., Kashima, Y., Loughnan, S., Shi, J., & Suitner, C. (2008). Subhuman, inhuman, and superhuman: Contrasting humans with nonhumans in three cultures. *Social Cognition, 26,* 248–258.

Haslam, N., & Loughnan, S. (2014). Dehumanization and infrahumanization. *Annual Review of Psychology, 65,* 399–423.

Haslam, N., Loughnan, S., & Sun, P. (2011). Beastly: What makes animal metaphors offensive? *Journal of Language and Social Psychology, 30,* 311–325.

Hausman, D. M., & Welch, B. (2010). Debate: To nudge or not to nudge? *Journal of Political Philosophy, 18,* 123–136.

Hayden, B. (2013). Hunting on heaven and earth: A comment on Knight. *Current Anthropology, 54,* 495–496.

REFERENCES

Hazel, S. J., Signal, T. D., & Taylor, N. (2011). Can teaching veterinary and animal-science students about animal welfare affect their attitude toward animals and human-related empathy? *Journal of Veterinary Medical Education, 38,* 74–83.

Hecht, J., & Horowitz, A. (2015). Seeing dogs: Human preferences for dog physical attributes. *Anthrozoös, 28,* 153–163.

Hecht, J., Miklosi, A., & Gacsi, M. (2012). Behavioral assessment and owner perceptions of behaviors associated with guilt in dogs. *Applied Animal Behaviour Science, 139,* 134–142.

Heflick, N. A., & Goldenberg, J. L. (2014). Dehumanization: A threat and solution to terror management. In P. G. Bain, J. Vaes, & J.-P. Leyens (eds.), *Humanness and dehumanization* (pp. 86–127). New York: Psychology Press.

Heleski, C. R., & Zanella, A. J. (2006). Animal science student attitudes to farm animal welfare. *Anthrozoös, 19,* 3–16.

Herrmann, P., Medin, D. L., & Waxman, S. R. (2012). When humans become animals: Development of the animal category in early childhood. *Cognition, 122,* 74–79.

Herzog, H. (2010). *Some we love, some we hate, some we eat: Why it's so hard to think straight about animals.* New York: Harper Collins.

Herzog, H., Rowan, A., & Kossow, D. (2001). Social attitudes and animals. In D. J. Salem & A. N. Rowan (eds.), *The state of the animals 2001* (pp. 55–69). Washington, DC: Humane Society Press.

Heuer, U. (2010). Reasons and impossibility. *Philosophical Studies, 147,* 235–246.

Hofmann, W., Vohs, K. D., & Baumeister, R. F. (2012). What people desire, feel conflicted about, and try to resist in everyday life. *Psychological Science, 23,* 582–588.

Hofmann, W., Wisneski, D. C., Brandt, M. J., & Skitka, L. J. (2014). Morality in everyday life. *Science, 345,* 1340–1343.

Holbrook, C., Sousa, P., & Hahn-Holbrook, J. (2011). Unconscious vigilance: Worldview defense without adaptations for terror, coalition, or uncertainty management. *Journal of Personality and Social Psychology, 101,* 451–466.

Horberg, E. J., Oveis, C., & Keltner, D. (2011). Emotions as moral amplifiers: An appraisal tendency approach to the influences of distinct emotions upon moral judgments. *Emotion Review, 3,* 237–244.

Horberg, E. J., Oveis, C., Keltner, D., & Cohen, A. B. (2009). Disgust and the moralization of purity. *Journal of Personality & Social Psychology, 97,* 963–976.

Horowitz, A. (2009). Disambiguating the "guilty look": Salient prompts to a familiar dog behavior. *Behavioural Processes, 81,* 447–452.

Horowitz, A. C., & Bekoff, M. (2007). Naturalizing anthropomorphism: Behavioral prompts to our humanizing of animals. *Anthrozoös, 20,* 23–35.

Howell, S. (1996). Nature in culture or culture in nature? Chewong ideas of 'humans' and other species. In P. Descola & G. Palsson (eds.), *Nature and Society: Anthropological Perspectives* (pp. 127–144). London: Routledge.

HSUS (Humane Society of the United States). (2014). Pets by the numbers. Retrieved from http://www.humanesociety.org/issues/pet_overpopulation/facts/pet_ownership_statistics.html.

Huebner, B. (2013). *Macrocognition: A theory of distributed minds and collective intentionality*. New York: Oxford University Press.

Huebner, B., Dwyer, S., & Hauser, M. (2009). The role of emotion in moral psychology. *Trends in Cognitive Science, 13*, 1–6.

Hutcherson, C. A., & Gross, J. J. (2011). The moral emotions: A social-functionalist account of anger, disgust, and contempt. *Journal of Personality and Social Psychology, 100*, 719–737.

Hyers, L. (2006). Myths used to legitimize the exploitation of animals: An application of social dominance theory. *Anthrozoos, 19*, 194–210.

Ingold, T. (1994). From trust to domination: An alternative history of human–animal relations. In A. Manning & J. Serpell (eds.), *Animals and human society: Changing perspectives* (pp. 1–22). London: Routledge.

Inzlicht, M., & Berkman, E. (2015). Six questions for the resource model of control (and some answers). *Social and Personality Psychology Compass, 9*, 511–524.

Inzlicht, M., Legault, L., & Teper, R. (2014). Exploring the mechanisms of self-control improvement. *Current Directions in Psychological Science, 23*, 302–307.

Inzlicht, M., & Schmeichel, B. J. (2012). What is ego depletion? Toward a mechanistic revision of the resource model of self-control. *Perspectives on Psychological Science, 7*, 450–463.

Inzlicht, M., & Schmeichel, B. J. (2016). Beyond limited resources: Self-control failure as the product of shifting priorities. In K. Vohs & R. Baumeister (eds.), *Handbook of self-regulation*, 3rd ed. (pp. 165–181). New York: Guilford Press.

Inzlicht, M., Schmeichel, B. J., & Macrae, C. N. (2014). Why self-control seems (but may not be) limited. *Trends in Cognitive Sciences, 18*, 127–133.

Jack, A. I., & Robbins, P. (2012). The phenomenal stance revisited. *Review of Philosophy and Psychology, 3*, 383–403.

Jamieson, J., Reiss, M. J., Allen, D., Asher, L., Wathes, C. M., & Abeyesinghe, S. M. (2012). Measuring the success of a farm animal welfare education event. *Animal Welfare, 21*, 65–75.

Jeschonek, S., Marinovic, V., Hoehl, S., Elsner, B., & Pauen, S. (2010). Do animals and furniture items elicit different brain responses in human infants? *Brain and Development, 32*, 863–871.

Job, V., Bernecker, K., Miketta, S., & Friese, M. (2015). Implicit theories about willpower predict the activation of a rest goal following self-control exertion. *Journal of Personality and Social Psychology, 109*, 694–706.

Job, V., Dweck, C. S., & Walton, G. M. (2010). Ego depletion—Is it all in your head? Implicit theories about willpower affect self-regulation. *Psychological Science, 21*, 1686–1693.

Johnson, S. C., & Solomon, G. E. A. (1997). Why dogs have puppies and cats have kittens: The role of birth in young children's understanding of biological origins. *Child Development, 68*, 404–419.

Jonas, E., McGregor, I., Klackl, J., Agroskin, D., Fritsche, I., Holbrook, C., Nash, K., Proulx, T., & Quirin, M. (2014). Threat and defense: From anxiety to approach.

In J. M. Olson & M. P. Zanna (eds.), *Advances in experimental social psychology,* vol. *49* (pp. 219–286). Waltham, MA, and London: Academic Press.

Jones, R. C. (2013). Science, sentience, and animal welfare. *Biology & Philosophy, 28,* 1–30.

Jost, J. T., Rudman, L. A., Blair, I. V., Carney, D. R., Dasgupta, N., Glaser, J., & Hardin, C. D. (2009). The existence of implicit bias is beyond reasonable doubt: A refutation of ideological and methodological objections and executive summary of ten studies that no manager should ignore. *Research in Organizational Behavior, 29,* 39–69.

Kahneman, D. (2011). *Thinking, fast and slow.* New York: Farrar, Straus and Giroux.

Karlsson, E. K., Kwiatkowski, D. P., & Sabeti, P. C. (2014). Natural selection and infectious disease in human populations. *Nature Reviews Genetics, 15,* 279–293.

Kasperbauer, T. J. (2015a). Animals as disgust elicitors. *Biology & Philosophy, 30,* 167–185.

Kasperbauer, T. J. (2015b). Rejecting empathy for animal ethics. *Ethical Theory and Moral Practice, 18,* 817–833.

Kasperbauer, T. J. (2015c). Psychological constraints on egalitarianism: The challenge of just world beliefs. *Res Publica, 21,* 217–234.

Kasperbauer, T. J. (2017). Mentalizing animals: Implications for moral psychology and animal ethics. *Philosophical Studies, 174,* 465–484.

Kasperbauer, T. J., & Sandøe, P. (2016). Killing as a welfare issue. In T. Višak & R. Garner (eds.), *The ethics of killing animals* (pp. 17–31). Oxford: Oxford University Press.

Kayyal, M. H., Pochedly, J., McCarthy, A., & Russell, J. A. (2015). On the limits of the relation of disgust to judgments of immortality. *Frontiers of Psychology, 6,* 951.

Kelley, N. J., Crowell, A. L., Tang, D., Harmon-Jones, E., & Schmeichel, B. J. (2015). Disgust sensitivity predicts defensive responding to mortality salience. *Emotion, 15,* 590–602.

Kelly, D. (2011). *The nature and moral significance of disgust.* Cambridge, MA: MIT Press.

Kelly, D. (2013). Moral disgust and tribal instincts: A byproduct hypothesis. In K. Sterelny, R. Joyce, B. Calcott, & B. Fraser (eds.), *Cooperation and its evolution* (pp. 503–524). Cambridge, MA: MIT Press.

Kelly, D., Faucher, L., & Machery, E. (2010). Getting rid of racism: Assessing three proposals in light of psychological evidence. *Journal of Social Philosophy, 41,* 293–322.

Kelly, D., & Morar, N. (2014). Against the yuck factor: On the ideal role for disgust in society. *Utilitas, 26,* 153–177.

Kelly, R. L. (2013). *The lifeways of hunter–gatherers: The foraging spectrum.* Cambridge: Cambridge University Press.

Kennett, J., & Fine, C. (2009). The implications of social intuitionist models of cognition for meta-ethics and moral psychology. *Ethical Theory & Moral Practice, 12,* 77–96.

Keren, G., & Schul, Y. (2009). Two is not always better than one: A critical evaluation of two-system theories. *Perspectives on Psychological Science, 4*, 533–550.

Kirkpatrick, L. A., & Navarrete, C. D. (2006). Reports of my death anxiety have been greatly exaggerated: A critique of terror management theory from an evolutionary perspective. *Psychological Inquiry, 17*, 288–298.

Knight, J. (2004). *Wildlife in Asia: Cultural perspectives.* London: Taylor & Francis.

Knight, J. (2012). The anonymity of the hunt: A critique of hunting as sharing. *Current Anthropology, 53*, 334–355.

Knobe, J., & Prinz, J. (2008). Intuitions about consciousness: Experimental studies. *Phenomenology and Cognitive Science, 7*, 67–83.

Koleva, S., Graham, J., Iyer, Y., Ditto, P. H., & Haidt, J. (2012). Tracing the threads: How five moral concerns (especially purity) help explain culture war attitudes. *Journal of Research in Personality, 46*, 184–194.

Kollareth, D., & Russell, J. A. (2016). Is it disgusting to be reminded that you are an animal? *Cognition & Emotion.* doi: 10.1080/02699931.2016.1221382. Retrieved from https://www.ncbi.nlm.nih.gov/pubmed/27539816.

Korsgaard, C. M. (1996). *The sources of normativity.* Cambridge: Cambridge University Press.

Kruglanski, A. W., & Gigerenzer, G. (2011). Intuitive and deliberative judgements are based on common principles. *Psychological Review, 118*, 97–109.

Kteily, N., Bruneau, E., Waytz, A., & Cotteril, S. (2015). The ascent of man: A theoretical and empirical case for blatant dehumanization. *Journal of Personality and Social Psychology, 109*, 901–931.

Kugler, M., Jost, J. T., & Noorbaloochi, S. (2014). Another look at moral foundations theory: Do authoritarianism and social dominance orientation explain liberal–conservative differences in "moral" intuitions? *Social Justice Research, 27*, 413–431.

Kulstad, M. (1991). *Leibniz on apperception, consciousness, and reflection.* Munich: Philosophia Verlag.

Kurzban, R., Tooby, J., & Cosmides, L. (2001). Can race be erased? Coalitional computation and social categorization. *Proceedings of the National Academy of Sciences of the United States of America, 98*, 15387–15392.

Kwan, V. S. Y., Gosling, S. D., & John, O. P. (2008). Anthropomorphism as a special case of social perception: A cross-species comparative approach and a new empirical paradigm. *Social Cognition, 26*, 129–142.

Lai, C., Hoffman, K., & Nosek, B. (2013). Reducing implicit prejudice. *Social and Personality Psychology Compass, 7*, 315–330.

Lai, C., Marini, M., Lehr, S., Cerruti, C., Shin, J., Joy-Gaba, J., Ho, A. K., Teachman, B. A., Wojcik, S. P., Koleva, S. P., Frazier, R. S., Heiphetz, L., Chen, E. E., Turner, R. N., Haidt, J., Kessebir, S., Hawkins, C. B., Schaefer, H. S., Rubichi, S., Sartori, G., Dial, C. M., Sriram, N., Banaji, M. R., & Nosek, B. A. (2014). Reducing implicit racial preferences: I. A comparative investigation of 17 interventions. *Journal of Experimental Psychology: General, 143*, 1765–1785.

Lai, C. K., Skinner, A. L., Cooley, E., Murrar, S., Brauer, M., Devos, T., Calanchini, J., Xiao, Y. J., Pedram, C., Marshburn, C. K., Simon, S., Blanchar, J. C., Joy-Gaba, J. A., Conway, J., Redford, L., Klein, R. A., Roussos, G., Schellhaas, F. M., Burns, M., Hu, X., McLean, M. C., Axt, J. R., Asgari, S., Schmidt, K., Rubinstein, R., Marini, M., Rubichi, S., Shin, J. E., & Nosek, B. A. (2016). Reducing implicit racial preferences: II. Intervention effectiveness across time. *Journal of Experimental Psychology: General, 145,* 1001–1016.

Landau, M. J., Solomon, S., Pyszczynski, T., & Greenberg, J. (2007). On the compatibility of terror management theory and perspectives on human evolution. *Evolutionary Psychology, 5,* 476–519.

Landy, J. F., & Goodwin, G. P. (2015). Does incidental disgust amplify moral judgment? A meta-analytic review of experimental evidence. *Perspectives on Psychological Science, 10,* 518–536.

Larson, G., & Fuller, D. Q. (2014). The evolution of animal domestication. *Annual Review of Ecology, Evolution, and Systematics, 45,* 115–136.

Lawford-Smith, H. (2010). Debate: Ideal theory—A reply to Valentini. *Journal of Political Philosophy, 18,* 357–368.

Lawford-Smith, H. (2013a). Understanding political feasibility. *Journal of Political Philosophy, 21,* 243–259.

Lawford-Smith, H. (2013b). Non-ideal accessibility. *Ethical Theory and Moral Practice, 16,* 653–669.

Leach, E. (1964). Anthropological aspects of language: Animal categories and verbal abuse. In E. H. Lenneberg (ed.), *New directions in the study of language* (pp. 23–63). Cambridge, MA: MIT Press.

Lebeau, R. T., Glenn, D., Liao, B., Wittchen, H. U., Beesler-Braum, K., Ollendick, T., & Graske, M. G. (2010). Specific phobia: A review of DSM-IV specific phobia and preliminary recommendations for DSM-V. *Depression and Anxiety, 27,* 148–167.

Leddon, E., Waxman, S. R., Medin, D. L., Bang, M., & Washinawatok, K. (2012). One animal among many? Children's understanding of the relation between humans and nonhuman animals. In G. Hayes & M. Bryant (eds.), *Psychology of culture* (pp. 105–126). Hauppauge, NY: Nova Science Publishers.

Lee, V. K., & Harris, L. T. (2014). Dehumanized perception. In P. G. Bain, J. Vaes, & J.-P. Leyens (eds.), *Humanness and dehumanization* (pp. 66–84). New York: Psychology Press.

Leiter, B. (2013). The boundaries of the moral (and legal) community. *Alabama Law Review, 64,* 511–531.

Lemmer, G., & Wagner, U. (2015). Can we really reduce ethnic prejudice outside the lab? A meta-analysis of direct and indirect contact interventions. *European Journal of Social Psychology, 45,* 152–168.

Lennon, T., & Olscamp, P. (eds. and trans.) (1997). *The search after truth, 1674–1675.* Cambridge: Cambridge University Press.

Lévi-Strauss, C. (1963). *Totemism.* Boston: Beacon Press.

Levy, N. (2006). The wisdom of the pack. *Philosophical Explorations, 9,* 99–103.

Leyens, J.-P. (2009). Retrospective and prospective thoughts about infrahumanisation. *Group Processes & Intergroup Relations, 12*, 807–817.

Leyens, J.-P., Demoulin, S., Vaes, J., Gaunt, R., & Paladino, M. P. (2007). Infrahumanisation: The wall of group differences. *Social Issues and Policy Review, 1*, 139–172.

Leyens, J.-P., Rodriguez-Torres, R., Rodriguez-Perez, A., Gaunt, R., Paladino, M., Vaes, J., & Demoulin, S. (2001). Psychological essentialism and the differential attribution of uniquely human emotions to ingroups and outgroups. *European Journal of Social Psychology, 81*, 395–411.

Li, P. J., & Davey, G. (2013). Culture, reform politics, and future directions: A review of China's animal protection challenge. *Society & Animals, 21*, 34–53.

Liao, M. (2011). Bias and reasoning: Haidt's theory of moral judgment. In T. Brooks (ed.), *New waves in ethics* (pp. 108–127). New York: Palgrave Macmillan.

List, C., & Pettit, P. (2011). *Group agency*. Oxford: Oxford University Press.

LoBue, V., Bloom Pickard, M., Sherman, K., Axford, C., & DeLoache, J. (2013). Young children's interest in live animals. *British Journal of Developmental Psychology, 31*, 57–69.

Loemker, L. (ed. and trans.) (1969). *Gottfried Wilhelm Leibniz: Philosophical papers and letters*. Dordrecht, The Netherlands: Reidel.

Loughnan, S., Bastian, B., & Haslam, N. (2014). The psychology of eating animals. *Current Directions in Psychological Science, 23*, 104–108.

Loughnan, S., Haslam, N., & Bastian, B. (2010). The role of meat consumption in the denial of moral status and mind to meat animals. *Appetite, 55*, 156–159.

Loughnan, S., Haslam, N., Sutton, R. M., & Spencer, B. (2014). Dehumanization and social class: Animality in the stereotypes of "white trash," "chavs," and "bogans." *Social Psychology, 45*, 54–61.

Lovejoy, A. (1936). *The great chain of being: A study of the history of an idea*. Cambridge: Harvard University Press.

Luo, Y. (2011). Three-month-old infants attribute goals to a non-human agent. *Developmental Science, 14*, 453–460.

Macé, M. J.-M., Joubert, O. R., Nespoulous, J.-L., & Fabre-Thorpe, M. (2009). The time-course of visual categorizations: You spot the animal faster than the bird. *PLoS One, 4*, e5927.

Machery, E. (2009). *Doing without concepts*. New York: Oxford University Press.

Mahon, B. Z., Anzellotti, S., Schwarzbach, J., Zampini, M., & Caramazza, A. (2009). Category-specific organization in the human brain does not require visual experience. *Neuron, 63*, 397–405.

Mandler, J. M. (2000). Perceptual and conceptual processes in infancy. *Journal of Cognition and Development, 1*, 3–36.

Mandler, J. M., & McDonough, L. (1993). Concept formation in infancy. *Cognitive Development, 8*, 291–318.

Marinovic, V., Hoehl, S., & Pauen, S. (2014). Neural correlates of human–animal distinction: An ERP-study on early categorical differentiation with 4- and 7-month-old infants and adults. *Neuropsychologia, 60*, 60–76.

Martin, T. E., Lurbiecki, H., Joy, J. B., & Mooers, A. O. (2014). Mammal and bird species held in zoos are less endemic and less threatened than their close relatives not held in zoos. *Animal Conservation, 17*, 89–96.

Martins, Y., & Pliner, P. (2006). "Ugh! That's disgusting!": Identification of the characteristics of foods underlying rejections based on disgust. *Appetite, 46*, 75–85.

Masicampo, E. J., Martin, S. R., & Anderson, R. A. (2014). Understanding and overcoming self- control depletion. *Social and Personality Psychology Compass, 8*, 638–649.

Matchett, G., & Davey, G. C. L. (1991). A test of a disease-avoidance model of animal phobias. *Behaviour Research and Therapy, 29*, 91–94.

May, J. (2014). Does disgust influence moral judgment? *Australasian Journal of Philosophy, 92*, 125–141.

McDonald, M. M., Donnellan, M. B., Lang, R., & Nikolajuk, K. (2014). Treating prejudice with imagery: Easier said than done? *Psychological Science, 25*, 837–839.

McTernan, E. (2014). How to make citizens behave: Social psychology, liberal virtues, and social norms. *Journal of Political Philosophy, 22*, 84–104.

Mead, N. L., Baumeister, R. F., Gino, F., Schweitzer, M. E., & Ariely, D. (2009). Too tired to tell the truth: Self-control resource depletion and dishonesty. *Journal of Experimental Social Psychology, 45*, 594–597.

Medin, D. L., & Atran, S. (eds.) (1999). *Folkbiology*. Cambridge, MA: MIT Press.

Medin, D. L., & Atran, S. (2004). The native mind: Biological categorization and reasoning in development and across cultures. *Psychological Review, 111(4)*, 960–983.

Mench, J. A. (1998). Thirty years after Brambell: Whither animal welfare science? *Journal of Applied Animal Welfare Science, 1*, 91–102.

Midgley, M. (1983). *Animals and why they matter*. Athens: University of Georgia Press.

Miles, E., & Crisp, R. J. (2014). A meta-analytic test of the imagined contact hypothesis. *Group Processes and Intergroup Relations, 17*, 3–26.

Miller, C. (2013). *Moral character: An empirical theory*. Oxford: Oxford University Press.

Miller, C. (2014). *Character and moral psychology*. Oxford: Oxford University Press.

Miller, M. R. (2013). Descartes on animals revisited. *Journal of Philosophical Research, 38*, 89–114.

Mills, C. (2015). The heteronomy of choice architecture. *Review of Philosophy and Psychology, 6*, 495–509.

Miloyan, B., & Suddendorf, T. (2015). Feelings of the future. *Trends in Cognitive Sciences, 19*, 196–200.

Minteer, B., Maienschein, J., & Collins, J. P. (eds.) (2018). *The ark and beyond: The evolution of zoo and aquarium conservation.* Chicago: University of Chicago Press.

Moller, A. C., Deci, E. L., & Ryan, R. M. (2006). Choice and ego-depletion: The moderating role of autonomy. *Personality and Social Psychology Bulletin, 32,* 1024–1036.

Morand, S., McIntyre, K. M., & Baylis, M. (2014). Domesticated animals and human infectious diseases of zoonotic origins: Domestication time matters. *Infection, Genetics and Evolution, 24,* 76–81.

Mormann, F., Dubois, J., Kornblith, S., Milosavljevic, M., Cerf, M., Ison, M., Tsuchiya, N., Kraskov, A., Quiroga, R. Q., Adolphs, R., Fried, I., & Koch, C. (2011). A category-specific response to animals in the right human amygdala. *Nature Neuroscience, 14,* 1247–1249.

Morris, D. (1961). An analysis of animal popularity. *International Zoo Yearbook, 2,* 60–61.

Morris, P., Knight, S., & Lesley, S. (2012). Belief in animal mind: Does familiarity with animals influence beliefs about animal emotions. *Society & Animals, 20,* 211–224.

Moss, A., & Esson, M. (2010). Visitor interest in zoo animals and the implications for collection planning and zoo education programmes. *Zoo Biology, 29,* 715–731.

Motyl, M., Hart, J., & Pyszczynski, T. (2010). When animals attack: The effects of mortality salience, infrahumanization of violence, and authoritarianism on support for war. *Journal of Experimental Social Psychology, 46,* 200–203.

Muraven, M. (2010). Building self-control strength: Practicing self-control leads to improved self-control performance. *Journal of Experimental Social Psychology, 46(2),* 465–468.

Muraven, M., & Baumeister, R. F. (2000). Self-regulation and depletion of limited resources: Does self-control resemble a muscle? *Psychological Bulletin, 126,* 247–259.

Nadasday, P. (2007). The gift in the animal: The ontology of hunting and human–animal sociality. *American Ethnologist, 34,* 25–43.

Nairne, J. S. (2010). Adaptive memory: Evolutionary constraints on remembering. In B. H. Ross (ed.), *The psychology of learning and motivation,* vol. 53 (pp. 1–32). Burlington, MA: Academic Press, 2010.

Nairne, J. S., & Pandeirada, J. N. (2008). Adaptive memory: Remembering with a Stone-Age brain. *Current Directions in Psychological Science, 17(4),* 239–243.

Navarrete, C. D., & Fessler, D. M. T. (2005). Normative bias and adaptive challenges: A relational approach to coalitional psychology and a critique of terror management theory. *Evolutionary Psychology, 3,* 297–325.

New, J., Cosmides, L., & Tooby, J. (2007). Category-specific attention for animals reflects ancestral priorities, not expertise. *Proceedings of the National Academy of Sciences of the United States of America, 104,* 16598–16603.

Newell, B. R., & Shanks, D. R. (2014). Unconscious influences on decision making: A critical review. *Behavioral and Brain Sciences, 37,* 1–19.

Nosek, B. A. (2005). Moderators of the relationship between implicit and explicit evaluation. *Journal of Experimental Psychology: General, 134,* 565–584.

Nosek, B. A., & Riskind, R. G. (2012). Policy implications of implicit social cognition. *Social Issues and Policy Review, 6,* 113–147.

Nussbaum, M. (2003). *Upheavals of thought: The intelligence of the emotions.* Cambridge: Cambridge University Press.

Nussbaum, M. (2004). *Hiding from humanity: Disgust, shame, and the law.* Princeton, NJ: Princeton University Press.

Nussbaum, M. (2006). *Frontiers of justice: Disability, nationality, species membership.* Cambridge, MA: Belknap Press.

Nussbaum, M. (2010). *From disgust to humanity: Sexual orientation and constitutional law.* Oxford: Oxford University Press.

Oaten, M., Stevenson, R. J., & Case, T. I. (2009). Disgust as a disease-avoidance mechanism. *Psychological Bulletin, 135,* 303–321.

Oaten, M., Stevenson, R. J., & Case, T. I. (2011). Disease avoidance as a functional basis for stigmatization. *Philosophical Transactions of the Royal Society of London Series B: Biological Sciences, 366,* 3433–3452.

Öhman, A., & Mineka, S. (2001). Fears, phobias, and preparedness: Toward an evolved module of fear and fear learning. *Psychological Review, 108,* 483–522.

Olatunji, B. O., Haidt, J., McKay, D., & David, B. (2008). Core, animal-reminder, and contamination disgust: Three kinds of disgust with distinct personality, behavioral, physiological, and clinical correlates. *Journal of Research in Personality, 42,* 1243–1259.

Opfer, J. E. (2002). Identifying living and sentient kinds from dynamic information: The case of goal-directed versus aimless autonomous movement in conceptual change. *Cognition, 86,* 97–122.

Oswald, F. L., Mitchell, G., Blanton, H., Jaccard, J., & Tetlock, P. E. (2013). Predicting ethnic and racial discrimination: A meta-analysis of IAT criterion studies. *Journal of Personality and Social Psychology, 105,* 171–192.

Palmer, C. (2010). *Animal ethics in context.* New York: Columbia University Press.

Passmore, J. (1975). The treatment of animals. *Journal of the History of Ideas, 36,* 195–218.

Pauen, S., & Träuble, B. (2009). How 7-month-olds interpret ambiguous motion events: Category-specific reasoning in infancy. *Cognitive Psychology, 59,* 275–295.

Pettigrew, T. F., & Tropp, L. R. (2006). A meta-analytic test of intergroup contact theory. *Journal of Personality and Social Psychology, 90,* 751–783.

Phillips, C. J. C., Izmirli, S., Aldavood, S. J., Alonso, M., Choe, B. L., Hanlon, A., Handziska, A., Illmannova, G., Keeling, L. J., Kennedy, M., Lee, G. H., Lund,

V., Mejdell, C. M., Pelagic, V., & Rehn, T. (2012). Students' attitudes to animal welfare and rights in Europe and Asia. *Animal Welfare, 21*, 87–100.

Phillips, C. J. C., & McCulloch, S. (2005). Student attitudes on animal sentience and use of animals in society. *Journal of Biological Education, 40*, 17–24.

Piazza, J., Landy, J. F., & Goodwin, G. P. (2014). Cruel nature: Harmfulness as an important, overlooked dimension in judgments of moral standing. *Cognition, 131*, 108–124.

Piazza, J., Ruby, M. B., Lougnan, S., Luong, M., & Kulik, J. (2015). Rationalizing meat consumption: The 4ns. *Appetite, 91*, 114–128.

Pierce, J. (2013, December 28). [Review of the book *Can animals be moral?*, by M. Rowlands]. *Notre Dame Philosophical Reviews*. Retrieved from http://ndpr.nd.edu/news/45240-can-animals-be-moral/

Pinker, S. (2011). *The better angels of our nature: Why violence has declined*. New York: Viking Penguin.

Pizarro, D. A., & Bloom, P. (2003). The intelligence of moral intuitions: Comment on Haidt (2001). *Psychological Review, 110*, 193–196.

Pizarro, D. A., Detweiler-Bedell, B., & Bloom, P. (2006). The creativity of everyday moral reasoning: Empathy, disgust and moral persuasion. In J. C. Kaufman & J. Baer (eds.), *Creativity and reason in cognitive development* (pp. 81–98). Cambridge: Cambridge University Press.

Plous, S. (1993). Psychological mechanisms in the human use of animals. *Journal of Social Issues, 49*, 11–52.

Plous, S. (2003). Is there such a thing as prejudice toward animals? In S. Plous (ed.), *Understanding prejudice and discrimination* (pp. 509–528). New York: McGraw-Hill.

Poncet, M., & Fabre-Thorpe, M. (2014). Stimulus duration and diversity do not reverse the advantage for superordinate-level representations: The animal is seen before the bird. *European Journal of Neuroscience, 39*, 1508–1516.

Poulin-Dubois, D., Crivello, C., & Wright, K. (2015). Biological motion primes the animate–inanimate distinction in infancy. *PLoS One, 10*, e0116910.

Preece, R. (1999). *Animals and nature: Cultural myths, cultural realities*. Vancouver, Canada: UBC Press.

Preece, R. (2002). *Awe for the tiger, love for the lamb: A chronicle of sensibility to animals*. Vancouver and Toronto, Canada: UBC Press.

Prickett, R. W., Norwood, F. B., & Lusk, J. L. (2010). Consumer preferences for farm animal welfare: Results from a telephone survey of US households. *Animal Welfare, 19*, 335–347.

Prinz, J. (2002). *Furnishing the mind*. Cambridge, MA: MIT Press.

Prinz, J. (2006). The emotional basis of moral judgments. *Philosophical Explorations, 9*, 29–43.

Prinz, J. (2007). *The emotional construction of morals*. Oxford: Oxford University Press.

Prinz, J. J. (2008). Is morality innate? In W. Sinnott-Armstrong (ed.), *Moral psychology* (pp. 267–406). Cambridge, MA: MIT Press.

Prokop, P., & Fancovicová, J. (2013). Self-protection versus disease avoidance. *Journal of Individual Differences, 34*, 15–23.

Prokop, P., Fančovičová, J., & Fedor, P. (2010). Health is associated with antiparasite behavior and fear of disease-relevant animals in humans. *Ecological Psychology, 22*, 222–237.

Prokop, P., & Tunnicliffe, S. (2010). Effects of having pets at home on children's attitudes toward popular and unpopular animals. *Anthrozoös, 23*, 21–35.

Pronin, E., Gilovich, T., & Ross, L. (2004). Objectivity in the eye of the beholder: Divergent perceptions of bias in self versus others. *Psychological Review, 111*, 781–799.

Protopopova, A., Gilmour, A. J., Weiss, R. H., Shen, J. Y., & Wynne, C. D. (2012). The effects of social training and other factors on adoption success of shelter dogs. *Applied Animal Behaviour Science, 142*, 61–68.

Railton, P. (2014). The affective dog and its rational tail: Intuition and attunement. *Ethics, 124*, 813–859.

Randler, C., Hummel, E., & Prokop, P. (2012). Practical work at school reduces disgust and fear of unpopular animals. *Society & Animals, 20*, 61–74.

Rawls, J. (1971). *A theory of justice*. Cambridge, MA: Harvard University Press.

Raz, J. (1986). *The morality of freedom*. Oxford: Clarendon Press.

Rebonato, R. (2012). *Taking liberties: A critical examination of libertarian paternalism*. New York: Palgrave Macmillan.

Regan, T. (1983). *The case for animal rights*. Berkeley: University of California Press.

Regan, T. (1991). *The thee generation*. Philadelphia: Temple University Press.

Remnant, P., & Bennett, J. (trans.) (1997). *New essays concerning human understanding*. Cambridge: Cambridge University Press.

Rhodes, M., & Gelman, S. A. (2009). A developmental examination of the conceptual structure of animal, artifact, and human social categories across two cultural contexts. *Cognitive Psychology, 59*, 244–274.

Riffkin, R. (2015). In U.S., more say animals should have same rights as people. May 18. Retrieved from http://www.gallup.com/poll/183275/say-animals-rights-people.aspx.

Robbins, P., & Jack, A. (2006). The phenomenal stance. *Philosophical Studies, 127*, 59–85.

Rollin, B. E. (2006). *Animal rights and human morality*. New York: Prometheus Books.

Rosenblatt, A., Greenberg, J., Solomon, S., Pyszczynski, T., & Lyon, D. (1989). Evidence for terror management theory: I. The effects of mortality salience on reactions to those who violate or uphold cultural values. *Journal of Personality and Social Psychology, 57*, 681–690.

Rosenfield, L. C. (1941). *From beast-machine to man-machine*. New York: Oxford University Press.

Rothgerber, H. (2014). Efforts to overcome vegetarian-induced dissonance among meat eaters. *Appetite, 79*, 32–41.

Rowan, A. N., & Loew, F. M. (2001). Animal research: A review of developments, 1950–2000. In D. J. Salem & A. N. Rowan (eds.), *The state of the animals 2001* (pp. 111–120). Washington, DC: Humane Society Press.

Rowan, A. N., & Rosen, B. (2005). Progress in animal legislation: Measurement and assessment. In D. J. Salem & A. N. Rowan (eds.), *The state of the animals III: 2005* (pp. 79–94). Washington, DC: Humane Society Press.

Rozin, P., & Fallon, A. E. (1987). A perspective on disgust. *Psychological Review, 94*, 23–41.

Rozin, P., Haidt, J., & McCauley, C. R. (1993). Disgust. In M. Lewis & J. M. Haviland (eds.), *Handbook of emotions*, 1st ed. (pp. 575–594). New York: Guilford Press.

Rozin, P., Haidt, J., & McCauley, C. R. (2008). Disgust. In M. Lewis, J. Haviland, & L. F. Barrett (eds.). *Handbook of emotions*, 3rd ed. (pp. 757–776). New York: Guilford Press.

Rozin, P., Lowery, L., Imada, S., & Haidt, J. (1999). The CAD triad hypothesis: A mapping between three moral emotions (contempt, anger, disgust) and three moral codes (community, autonomy, divinity). *Journal of Personality and Social Psychology, 76*, 574–586.

Ruby, M., & Heine, S. (2012). Too close to home. Factors predicting meat avoidance. *Appetite, 59*, 47–52.

Ruby, M. B., Heine, S. J., Kamble, S., Cheng, T. K., & Waddar, M. (2013). Compassion and contamination. Cultural differences in vegetarianism. *Appetite, 71*, 340–348.

Rudman, L. A., Ashmore, R. D., & Gary, M. L. (2001). "Unlearning" automatic biases: The mal- leability of implicit prejudice and stereotypes. *Journal of Personality and Social Psychology, 81*, 856–868.

Russell, D. (2009). *Practical intelligence and the virtues.* Oxford: Oxford University Press.

Russell, N. (2011). *Social zooarcheology.* Cambridge: Cambridge University Press.

Russell, P. S., & Giner-Sorolla, R. (2011). Moral anger is more flexible than moral disgust. *Social Psychological and Personality Science, 2*, 360–364.

Russell, P. S., & Giner-Sorolla, R. (2013). Bodily-moral disgust: What it is, how it is different from anger and why it is an unreasoned emotion. *Psychological Bulletin, 139*, 328–351.

Ryder, R. D. (1989). *Animal revolution.* Oxford: Basil Blackwell.

Saminaden, A., Loughnan, S., & Haslam, N. (2010). Afterimages of savages: Implicit associations between "primitive" peoples, animals, and children. *British Journal of Social Psychology, 49*, 91–105.

Sandøe, P., Corr, S., & Palmer, C. (2015). *Companion animal ethics.* New York: Wiley Blackwell.

Sauer, H. (2011). Social intuitionism and the psychology of moral reasoning. *Philosophy Compass, 6*, 708–721.

Sauer, H. (2012a). Education intuitions: Automaticity and rationality in moral judgment. *Philosophical Explorations, 15*, 255–275.

Sauer, H. (2012b). Psychopaths and filthy desks: Are emotions necessary and sufficient for moral judgment? *Ethical Theory & Moral Practice, 15*, 95–115.

Sauer, H. (2014). The wrong kind of mistake: A problem for robust sentimentalism about moral judgment. *Journal of Value Inquiry, 48*, 247–269.

Schaller, M. (2011). The behavioural immune system and the psychology of human sociality. *Philosophical Transactions B, 366*, 3418–3426.

Schein, C., & Gray, K. (2015). The unifying moral dyad: Liberals and conservatives share the same harm-based moral template. *Personality and Social Psychology Bulletin, 41*, 1147–1163.

Schmeichel, B., Gaillot, M. T., Filardo, E., McGregor, I., Gitter, S., & Baumeister, R. (2009). Terror management theory & self-esteem revisited: The roles of implicit self-esteem in mortality salience effects. *Journal of Personality & Social Psychology, 96*, 1077–1087.

Schmeichel, B. J., & Martens, A. (2005). Self-affirmation and mortality salience: Affirming values reduces worldview defense and death-thought accessibility. *Personality and Social Psychology Bulletin, 31*, 658.

Schussler, E. E., & Olzak, L. A. (2014). It's not easy being green: Student recall of plant and animal images. *Journal of Biological Education, 42*, 112–118.

Seligman, M. E. P. (1970). On the generality of the laws of learning. *Psychological Review, 77*, 406–418.

Serpell, J. A. (2003). Anthropomorphism and anthropomorphic selection—Beyond the "cute response." *Society & Animals, 11*, 83–100.

Serpell, J. (1996). *In the company of animals*, 2nd ed. Cambridge, UK: Cambridge University Press.

Serpell, J., & Paul, E. S. (2011). Pets in the family: An evolutionary perspective. In C. A. Salmon & T. K. Shackelford (eds.), *The Oxford handbook of evolutionary family psychology* (pp. 297–309). Oxford: Oxford University Press.

Setoh, P., Baillargeon, R., & Gelman, R. (2013). Young infants have biological expectations about animals. *Proceedings of the National Academy of Sciences of the United States of America, 110*, 15937–15942.

Sevillano, V. S., & Fiske, S. T. (2016). Warmth and competence in animals. *Journal of Applied and Social Psychology, 46*, 276–293.

Sheldon, O. J., & Fishbach, A. (2015). Anticipating and resisting the temptation to behave unethically. *Personality and Social Psychology Bulletin, 41*, 962–975.

Sheridan, C. L., & King, R. G. (1972). Obedience to authority with an authentic victim. *Proceedings of the Annual Convention of the American Psychological Association, 80*, 165–166.

Sherman, G. D., & Haidt, J. (2011). Cuteness and disgust: The humanizing and dehumanizing effects of emotion. *Emotion Review, 3*, 245–251.

Sherman, G. D., Haidt, J., & Coan, J. A. (2009). Viewing cute images increases behavioral carefulness. *Emotion, 9*, 282–286.

Shriver, A. (2009). Knocking out pain in livestock: Can technology succeed where morality has stalled? *Neuroethics, 2,* 115–124.

Shweder, R. A., Much, N. C., Mahapatra, M., & Park, L. (1997). The "big three" of morality (autonomy, community, and divinity), and the "big three" explanations of suffering. In A. Brandt & P. Rozin (eds.), *Morality and health* (pp. 119–169). New York: Routledge.

Siegrist, M., & Sütterlin, B. (2014). Human and nature-caused hazards: The affect heuristic causes biased decisions. *Risk Analysis, 34,* 1482–1494.

Silverstein, H. (1996). *Unleashing rights: Law, meaning, and the animal rights movement.* Ann Arbor: University of Michigan Press.

Simion, F., Regolin, L., & Bulf, H. (2008). A predisposition for biological motion in the newborn baby. *Proceedings of the National Academy of Sciences of the United States of America, 105,* 809–813.

Simmons, A. J. (2010). Ideal and nonideal theory. *Philosophy & Public Affairs, 38,* 5–36.

Singer, P. (1981). *The expanding circle: Ethics and sociobiology.* New York: Farrar, Straus and Giroux.

Singer, P. (1990). *Animal liberation.* London: Thorsons.

Singer, P. (2015). *The most good you can do.* New Haven, CT, and London: Yale University Press.

Sinnott-Armstrong, W. (1984). "Ought" conversationally implies "can." *Philosophical Review, 93,* 249–261.

Sloman, S. (1996). The empirical case for two systems of reasoning. *Psychological Bulletin, 119,* 3–22.

Slovic, P., & Peters, E. (2006). Risk perception and affect. *Current Directions in Psychological Science, 15,* 322–325.

Smith, J. E. H. (2011). *Divine machines.* Princeton, NJ: Princeton University Press.

Smith, K. (2012). *Governing animals.* Oxford: Oxford University Press.

Snow, N. (2010). *Virtue as social intelligence: An empirically grounded theory.* New York: Routledge.

Solomon, G. E. A., & Zaitchik, D. (2012). Folkbiology. *WIREs Cognitive Science, 3,* 105–115.

Solomon, R. C. (1999). Peter Singer's *Expanding Circle*: Compassion and the liberation of ethics. In D. Jamieson (ed.), *Singer and his critics* (pp. 64–84). Oxford and Malden, MA: Blackwell.

Solomon, S., Greenberg, J., & Pyszczynski, T. (1991). A terror management theory of social behavior: The psychological functions of self-esteem and cultural worldviews. In M. P. Zanna (ed.), *Advances in experimental social psychology,* vol. 24 (pp. 91–159). San Diego, CA: Academic Press.

Sorabji, R. (1993). *Animal minds and human morals: The origins of the Western debate.* Ithaca, NY: Cornell University Press.

Sousa, P., Atran, S., & Medin, D. (2002). Essentialism and folkbiology: Evidence from Brazil. *Journal of Cognition and Culture, 2,* 195–223.

Springer, K., & Keil, F. (1991). Early differentiation of causal mechanisms appropriate to biological and nonbiological kinds. *Child Development, 62,* 767–781.

Staggenborg, S. (2012). *Social movements,* 2nd ed. New York: Oxford University Press.

Stanovich, K. (2010). *Rationality and the reflective mind.* New York: Oxford University Press.

Steiner, G. (2005). *Anthropocentrism and its discontents.* Pittsburgh, PA: University of Pittsburgh Press.

Steiner, G. (2008). *Animals and the moral community: Mental life, moral status, and kinship.* New York: Columbia University Press.

Steiner, G. (2013). *Animals and the limits of postmodernism.* New York: Columbia University Press.

Stemplowska, Z., & Swift, A. (2012). Ideal and nonideal theory. In D. Estlund (ed.), *The Oxford handbook of political philosophy* (pp. 373–389). Oxford: Oxford University Press.

Stiner, M. C. (2002). Carnivory, coevolution, and the geographic spread of the genus *Homo. Journal of Archaeological Research, 10,* 1–63.

Stocker, M. (1971). "Ought" and "can." *Australasian Journal of Philosophy, 49,* 303–316.

Streumer, B. (2007). Reasons and impossibility. *Philosophical Studies, 136,* 351–384.

Strohminger, N. (2014). Disgust talked about. *Philosophy Compass, 9,* 478–493.

Sunstein, C. (2013). *Simpler: The future of government.* New York: Simon & Schuster.

Sunstein, C. (2014). *Wiser: Getting beyond groupthink to make groups smarter.* Boston: Harvard Business Review Press.

Sunstein, C. R. (2005). Moral heuristics. *Behavioral and Brain Sciences, 28,* 531–573.

Sunstein, C. R. (2015a). Nudging and choice architecture: Ethical considerations. *Yale Journal of Regulation, 32,* 413–450.

Sunstein, C. R. (2015b). Nudges, agency, and abstraction: A reply to critics. *Review of Philosophy and Psychology, 6,* 511–529.

Sunstein, C. R. (2016). The council of psychological advisors. *Annual Review of Psychology, 67,* 713–737.

Surinova, M. (1971). An analysis of the popularity of animals. *International Zoo Yearbook, 11,* 165–167.

Sytsma, J., & Machery, E. (2012). The two sources of moral standing. *Review of Philosophy and Psychology, 3,* 303–324.

Tan, T., Li, H., Wang, Y., & Yang, J. (2013). Are we afraid of different categories of stimuli in identical ways? Evidence from skin conductance responses. *PLoS One, 8,* e73165.

Tauber, S. C. (2015). *Navigating the jungle: Law, politics, and the animal advocacy movement.* New York and Abingdon, UK: Routledge.

Taylor, K., Gordon, N., Langley, G., & Higgings, W. (2008). Estimates for worldwide laboratory animal use in 2005. *Alternatives for Laboratory Animals, 36,* 327–342.

Teper, R., Tullett, A. M., Page-Gould, E., & Inzlicht, M. (2015). Errors in moral forecasting: Perceptions of affect shape the gap between moral behaviors and moral forecasts. *Personality and Social Psychology Bulletin, 41*, 887–900.

Thaler, R. H., & Sunstein, C. R. (2008). *Nudge: Improving decisions about health, wealth, and happiness*. London: Penguin.

Thomas, K. (1984). *Man and the natural world*. New York: Oxford University Press.

Tomažič, I. (2011). Seventh graders' direct experience with, and feelings toward, amphibians and some other nonhuman animals. *Society & Animals, 19*, 225–247.

Träuble, B., & Pauen, S. (2011). Infants' reasoning about ambiguous motion events: The role of spatiotemporal and dispositional status information. *Cognitive Development, 26*, 1–15.

Tritt, S. M., Inzlicht, M., & Harmon-Jones, E. (2012). Toward a biological understanding of mortality salience (and other threat compensation processes). *Social Cognition, 30*, 715–733.

Turner, J. (1980). *Reckoning with the beast*. Baltimore: Thorsons.

Turner, R. N., Crisp, R. J., & Lambert, E. (2007). Imagining intergroup contact can improve intergroup attitudes. *Group Processes Intergroup Relations, 10*, 427–441.

Tybur, J. M., Griskevicius, V., & Lieberman, D. (2009). Microbes, mating, and morality: Individual differences in three functional domains of disgust. *Personality Processes and Individual Differences, 97*, 103–122.

Tybur, J. M., Lieberman, D., Kurzban, R., & DeScioli, P. (2013). Disgust: Evolved function and structure. *Psychological Review, 120*, 65–84.

U.S. Department of Agriculture. (2015). Annual report animal usage by fiscal year. Retrieved from https://www.aphis.usda.gov/animal_welfare/downloads/7023/Animals%20Used%20In%20Research%202014.pdf.

Vaes, J., Bain, P. G., & Bastian, B. (2014). Embracing humanity in the face of death: Why do existential concerns moderate ingroup humanization? *Journal of Social Psychology, 154*, 537–545.

Vaes, J., Leyens, J.-P., Paladino, M. P., & Miranda, M. P. (2012). We are human, they are not: Driving forces behind outgroup dehumanisation and the humanisation of the ingroup. *European Review of Social Psychology, 23*, 64–106.

Valentini, L. (2012). Ideal vs. non-ideal theory: A conceptual map. *Philosophy Compass, 7*, 654–664.

Van Dellen, M. R., Shea, C. T., Davisson, E. K., Koval, C. Z., & Fitzsimons, G. M. (2014). Motivated misperception: Self-regulatory resources affect goal appraisals. *Journal of Experimental Social Psychology, 53*, 118–124.

Van Leeuwen, F., & Park, J. H. (2009). Perceptions of social dangers, moral foundations, and political orientation. *Personality and Individual Differences, 47*, 169–173.

Varner, G. (2012). *Personhood, ethics, and animal cognition: Situating animals in the two-level utilitarianism of R. M. Hare*. Oxford: Oxford University Press.

Viki, G., Winchester, L., Titshall, L., Chisango, T., Pina, A., & Russell, R. (2006). Beyond secondary emotions: The infra-humanization of groups using human-related and animal-related words. *Social Cognition, 24*, 753–775.

Vohs, K. D., Baumeister, R. F., & Schmeichel, B. J. (2012). Motivation, personal beliefs, and limited resources all contribute to self-control. *Journal of Experimental Social Psychology, 48*, 943–947.

Wagman, B., & Liebman, M. (2012). *A worldview of animal law.* Durham, NC: Carolina Academic Press.

Ware, J., Jain, K., Burgess, I., & Davey, G. C. L. (1994). Disease-avoidance model: Factor analysis of common animals fears. *Behaviour Research and Therapy, 32*, 57–63.

Waxman, S. R., Medin, D. L., & Ross, N. (2007). Folkbiological reasoning from a cross-cultural developmental perspective: Early essentialist notions are shaped by cultural beliefs. *Developmental Psychology, 43*, 294–308.

Waytz, A., Morewedge, C. K., Epley, N., Monteleone, G., Gao, J.-H., & Cacioppo, J. T. (2010). Making sense by making sentient: Unpredictability increases anthropomorphism. *Journal of Personality and Social Psychology, 99*, 410–435.

Webb, K., & Davey, G. C. L. (1992). Disgust sensitivity and fear of animals: Effect of exposure to violent or revulsive material. *Anxiety, Stress & Coping, 5*, 329–335.

Webber, D., Schimel, J., Faucher, E. H., Hayes, J., Zhang, R., & Martens, A. (2015). Emotion as a necessary component of threat-induced death thought accessibility and defensive compensation. *Motivation & Emotion, 39*, 142–155.

Weil, K. (2012). *Thinking animals.* New York: Columbia University Press.

Weiss, A. (2017). Personality traits: A view from the animal kingdom. *Journal of Personality*. doi: 10.1111/jopy.12310. Retrieved from http://onlinelibrary.wiley.com/doi/10.1111/jopy.12310/full

Weiss, R. A. (2001). Animal origins of human infectious disease. The Leeuwenhoek Lecture. *Philosophical Transactions of the Royal Society of London B, 356*, 957–977.

Westbury, H. R., & Neumann, D. L. (2008). Empathy-related responses to moving film stimuli depicting human and non-human animal targets in negative circumstances. *Biological Psychology, 78*, 66–74.

Whalen, P. J., Rauch, S. L., Etcoff, N. L., McInterney, S. C., Lee, M. B., & Jenike, M. A. (1998). Masked presentations of emotional facial expressions modulate amygdala activity without explicit knowledge. *Journal of Neuroscience, 18*, 411–418.

White, M. D. (2013). *The manipulation of choice: Ethics and libertarian paternalism.* New York: Palgrave Macmillan.

Whole Foods Market (2017). 5-Step Animal Welfare Rating. Retrieved from http://www.wholefoodsmarket.com/mission-values/animal-welfare/5-step-animal-welfare-rating.

Wiens, D. (2012). Prescribing institutions without ideal theory. *Journal of Political Philosophy, 20*, 45–70.

Wiens, D. (2013). Demands of justice, feasible alternatives, and the need for causal analysis. *Ethical Theory & Moral Practice, 16,* 325–338.

Willerslev, R. (2007). *Soul hunters: Hunting, animism, and personhood among the Siberian Yukaghirs.* Berkeley: University of California Press.

Willett, C. (2014). *Interspecies ethics.* New York: Columbia University Press.

Wilson, M. D. (1999). "For they do not agree in nature with us": Spinoza on the lower animals. In *Ideas and mechanism: Essays on early modern philosophy* (pp. 178–195). Princeton, NJ: Princeton University Press.

Wilson, T. D., & Gilbert, D. T. (2005). Affective forecasting—Knowing what to want. *Current Directions in Psychological Science, 14,* 131–134.

Winkielman, P., & Berridge, K. C. (2004). Unconscious emotion. *Current Directions in Psychological Science, 13,* 120–123.

Wolfe, N. D., Dunavan, C. P., & Diamond, J. (2007). Origins of major human infectious diseases. *Nature, 447,* 279–283.

Woodzicka, J. A., & LaFrance, M. (2001). Real versus imagined gender harassment. *Journal of Social Issues, 57,* 15–30.

Woolhouse, M. E. J., & Gowtage-Sequeria, S. (2005). Host range and emerging and reemerging pathogens. *Emerging Infectious Diseases, 11,* 1842–1847.

Woolhouse, R. S., & Francks, R. (eds. and trans.) (1998). *G. W. Leibniz: Philosophical texts.* New York: Oxford University Press.

Wright, E. O. (2010). *Envisioning real utopias.* London: Verso.

Wynne-Tyson, J. (1985). *The extended circle: A dictionary of humane thought.* Fontwell, UK: Centaur Press.

Xu, H., Bégue, L., & Bushman, B. J. (2012). Too fatigued to care: Ego depletion, guilt, and prosocial behavior. *Journal of Experimental Social Psychology, 48,* 1183–1186.

Yang, J., Bellgowan, P. S. F., & Martin, A. (2012). Threat, domain-specificity and the human amygdala. *Neuropsychologia, 50,* 2566–2572.

York, R., & Mancus, P. (2013). The invisible animal: Anthrozoology and macrosociology. *Sociological Theory, 31,* 75–91.

Zajonc, R. B. (1980). Feeling and thinking: Preferences need no inferences. *American Psychologist, 35,* 151–175.

Zaki, J., & Cikara, M. (2015). Addressing empathic failures. *Current Directions in Psychological Science, 24,* 471–476.

INDEX